UNWRITTEN HISTORY OF SLAVERY

Autobiographical Accounts of Negro Ex-Slaves

Fisk University, Nashville.
Social Science Institute

NCR MICROCARD EDITIONS
901 TWENTY-SIXTH STREET, N.W., WASHINGTON, D. C. 20037, 202/333-6393

INDUSTRIAL PRODUCTS DIVISION, THE NATIONAL CASH REGISTER COMPANY

1968

Unwritten History of Slavery was originally issued in 1945 as a 322 page, softbound, processed volume, by the Social Science Institute, Fisk University, Nashville, Tennessee, and was designated as Social Science Source Document No. 1.

TABLE OF CONTENTS

INTRODUCTION

Much has been written about the slavery system as an aspect of the economic order. Little as yet has been written about the system as a moral order; that is, the system in which the individual attitudes, sentiments, habits, and conduct are fashioned and channeled as one lives within that framework. It was with the idea of throwing some light on this neglected aspect of American history and social research that these documents are made available.

Slavery was first and foremost an adjustment of divergent and dissimilar individuals to an impersonal competitive process. It was, essentially, an exploitative system, in which a relatively small number of individuals, equipped with superior technology and capital, directed and controlled the energies of a numerically superior, but culturally inferior population. In the historical situation, the system took the form of white dominance over colored peoples, specifically, transplanted African Negroes, within the plantation economy. It was inevitable under the circumstances that, in the end, there would be developed a form of racial symbiosis within a single society.

The institution of slavery as it existed and functioned in the American South had within it its own political and moral super-structures. Thus, within the system, the conduct of both the slave and the master was channeled and circumscribed: that of the slave by the authority of the master; and that of the master by conventional duties and obligations toward the slave. The authority of the master was kept well within the bounds of custom and convention, and likewise within the limitations set by a body of institutional paraphernalia and functionaries. It was this framework of the slavery system *in toto* that kept the master-slave relationship on an impersonal level, and molded the kind of attitudes and sentiments, habits and conduct, which aided the perpetuation of the institution once it had evolved in the society.

The slave developed within the system a set of attitudes and sentiments, habits and conduct which were complementary to those of the master. Both sought to attain maximum satisfaction of their wants and needs; each had his status; each discovered the goal he expected to pursue, and each sought the means to achieve these goals. In short, the institutional framework provided the norm of conduct which made mutual survival possible and tolerable. It is, thus, within this broad context that the mentality of the slave and the master has long needed to be studied and defined.

The accommodation of person and institution is never a complete process. At each stage in the process of adjustment or readjustment, there is a kind of equilibrium of opposing forces. Since competition is universal and ever present, the slavery system was always an object of attack from without and an object of defense from within. It was out of this conflict situation that the institution evolved a body of ideologies with which it defended itself against the destructive forces from within and without. By means of this body of ideologies, the system weathered, for a long period, the political attacks from without and, at the same time, circumscribed the competitive process within. Within this bulwark of ideologies, the institution survived long after its usefulness had disappeared. Indeed, it continued to define these human relationships long after the shells of the system had collapsed.

These documents herein made available, reveal some of the personal experiences of the slaves in the declining days of the institution. They tell what the slaves saw and remembered; how they, themselves, or others whom they knew lived through the drudgery of menial work and the fear of the impending precarious world; how the slaves met their basic needs of sex, hunger and rest, within the very narrow confines of the system. They represent essentially the memories of child-hood experiences, and provide, in a measure, a personal history of the social world as recreated and dramatized by these slaves in course of the telling. Taken as a whole, these autobiographies constitute a fabric of individual memories, which sheds interesting light on the mentality of the slave.

The merit of these documents lies not so much in the accurate recording of the historical events, as in the realistic fabrication of the experiential world of the persons themselves. This reporting is accepted as presenting not the objective validity of the social events and the in-stitutional structure primarily, but the individual's subjective evaluation of them. Thus, the documents suggest how one's subjective experience functions as a determinant in carving out a series of events lying outside of oneself and makes these events a part of one's own experience. They suggest the way in which a person acquires a personal perspective of the social world of which he is a part. For in the final analysis, it is personal perspective that provides one with a conception of himself and thus determines one's status within one's group.

There is another aspect of these documents: The very fact that the personal stories, as told by these ex-slaves, are not always accurate and not always true to the objective facts, but are told well and are adequately dramatized, throws light on the kind of materials out of which the folk tale is made, and out of which legendary characters emerge in the course of social transmission. They reveal, further, the way in which family traditions have their beginning.

These documents are regarded as valuable as source material because they help us to under-stand the manner in which personality enters into social change. There are, for example, illus-trations of how certain individuals, unable to fit themselves into the rigid requirements of the slavery system, revolt and are punished; how other individuals—"witty and smart"—break through the impersonal relationship of the conventional definitions, and establish personal relationships with the master. One is impressed by the fact that the slavery system as a socially defined human relationship is one thing, but as the system existed in the moral order of personal relationship of expectations and obligations, it is quite another. One is struck by the wide range of variation, from impersonal to personal relations, that existed within the American slavery system. On the whole, the smaller the slave group, the more intimate the relationship between the slaves and the master. Thus is revealed throughout, the telling effects of human nature upon impersonal forces, and likewise, the importance of the well nigh impenetrable bulwark of ideol-ogies which forever fought to maintain impersonal relationship between the slave and the master classes.

The interviews with these ex-slaves were conducted during 1929 and 1930 by Mrs. Ophelia Settle Egypt, then a member of the Research Staff of the Social Science Institute at Fisk Uni-versity. The subjects resided, for the most part, in Tennessee and Kentucky. Although more than a hundred ex-slaves were interviewed at that time, all but a very few are now dead. It is re-garded as fortunate that these rare fragments of history, and these glimpses into the mentality of a group so rigidly regimented by an unique economic structure and its supporting ideology, could be recorded before the last of these ex-slaves had passed irrevocably into history.

Ophelia Settle Egypt
J. Masuoka
Charles S. Johnson

One of Dr. Gale's "Free Niggers"

Just the other day we were talking about white people when they had slaves. You know when a man would marry, his father would give him a woman for a cook and she would have children right in the house by him, and his wife would have children,too. Sometimes the cook's children favored him so much that the wife would be mean to them and make him sell them. If they had nice long hair she would cut it off and wouldn't let them wear it long like the white children.

They would buy a fine girl and then a fine man and just put them together like cattle; they would not stop to marry them. If she was a good breeder, they was proud of her. I was stout and they were saving me for a breeding woman but by the time I was big enough I was free. I had an aunt in Mississippi and she had about twenty children by her marster. On Sunday they would get us ready to go to church. They would dress us up after we ask them if we could go and they would have me walk off from them and they would look at me, and I'd hear them saying, "She's got a fine shape; she'll make a good breeder," but I didn't know what they were talking about.

There was another man in Nashville, on the Granny White Pike, and he had a regular farm of slaves—he'd just raise them to sell. He had a sugar plantation in Louisiana and he would sell some and send some down there and then he would hire some out around here. He would let all that was near enough come home for Christmas, but on New Year's day you would see a string of them as long as from here to Fisk (about three or four miles) going south. They would have two covered wagons to carry the children and some of the women in, but the others would be walking. One of the wagons would be in front and the other behind the walkers. We children didn't know the grief of it then, but they would sell them apart. Of course some of the buyers would have pity on them and buy them all that was in one family if possible. Old Gale (her master) was mighty nice about that. He had a woman once and he caught her crying several times, and asked her to tell him what the trouble was; so finally she told him that they sold her away from her children and didn't give her a chance to tell them goodbye. She said she didn't mind being sold but they took her to town and she didn't know they were going to sell her and she didn't get to tell her children she was gone. Old Gale saw the man and got him to let the children come to see her one Christmas, and he would let her go to see them the next.

Then there was old Sam Watkins, —he would ship their husbands (slaves) out of bed and get in with their wives. One man said he stood it as long as he could and one morning he just stood outside, and when he got with his wife he just choked him to death. He said he knew it was death, but it was death anyhow; so he just killed him. They hanged him. There has always been a law in Tennessee that if a Negro kill a white man it means death.

Now, mind you, all of the colored women didn't have to have white men, some did it because they wanted to and some were forced. They had a horror of going to Mississippi and they would do anything to

1

keep from it. A white woman would have a maid sometimes who was nice looking, and she would keep her and her son would have children by her. Of course the mixed blood, you couldn't expect much from them.

The meanest thing they did was selling babies from the mother's breast, but all of them didn't do that. The man across the street and our folks seemed a little more enlightened. It just seemed that some of them would buy a woman with children just to sell her away. They would tell her to take the market wagon to town and when she got there they would sell her, and she wouldn't know what he was taking her for 'til he started selling her.

There was an old man lived on the Shelby place, Dr. Shelby, and somebody was always suing him for beating people almost to death and then selling them; they would die two or three days afterwards. His people (slaves) never saw their house in the day time. They would go to work at night and come back at night.

Dr. Gale (her master) had about 25 up here in Tennessee, but I reckon he had thousands in Mississippi, and lots of them was his children. They had (his children) to work just like we did and they had to call him marster too; and the overseer would take them down and whip them just like the others. The mother would have a better time, but the children didn't. The only advantage they had was that Marster Gale wouldn't sell them. My grandfather was an Irishman and he was a foreman, but he had to whip his children and grandchildren just like the others.

I reckon I was eight or nine years old (when the War came). I might have been older than that because I can remember too much to have been so young. I remember when the white people were getting up a regiment and drilling round and they would give them farewell parties. I remember the Civil War better than I remember the World War. We were right between the two armies when Hood's raid was, and when all the fighting was, we was right between the two battlefields. They started fighting on Wednesday . . . . (told approximately how they fought each day) and they fought until Friday and then the Rebels throwed down their arms and give up. The women just throwed up their hands and hollered: "Nasty stinking cows! Just running! Why don't they fight?"

We were called Dr. Gale's free niggers. He never did allow the padderollers on our place. My old marster had some relatives here named McNairy and he always looked after it if they bothered us. We had to get a pass to go off the place but McNairy's place was right joining ours and right across the road was Mrs. Cantrell's place and we could go to their places without a pass. Some of the others (owners) would shut down on them (slaves). Many a time they'd have church there and there was a thicket near and the padderollers would get in there and wait and whip them as they were leaving church. Old Alfred Williams was the preacher, and he would send somebody after his marster Andrew and he would sit there with his gun on his lap to keep them from whipping him 'til his marster would come and take him home. Yes, he was colored and a slave, too, but they used to have good meetings there 'til old Mr. Cantrell said they would have to stop that. He was a Presbyterian minister, and he said they had God troubled on the throne, and they didn't 'low no two or three men to be standing about talking either. They feared they was talking about being free. They didn't bother the women that way, but no man better not try it; they would search the slave houses for books, too.

During the War, the colored men that had wives at other places, they wouldn't let them go to visit them at all; they said they'd get to talking, and they threatened to shoot any who tried to go.

I remember when they nominated Abe Lincoln and Jeff Davis just as well as I remember when they nominated Hoover and Roosevelt. We children heard the old folks talking about it. Yes, I'll tell you: they would go round to the windows and listen to what the white folks would say when they was reading their papers and talking after supper. Sometimes they would be laughing and talking in their marster's house while the argument was going on between the two sides, and they marsters would say, "You needn't be laughing and talking, you ain't gonna be free." Now the slaves wouldn't be talking about being free at all, but they might just feel a little jolly and the marsters would say that to them.

You notice most white people in the South say "daddy" and "mother." In slavery time colored couldn't say papa; they had to say "daddy" and "mammy" and when they got free they started saying "papa" and then the white people started saying "daddy." Now the colored are right back at "daddy" again; they will copy after them.

My mother was born in Mississippi and brought here. My father was born in Maryland. He was an old man when he come here, but they just bought them and put them together. My mother was young—just fifteen or sixteen years old. She had fourteen chillen and you know that meant a lots of wealth. Yes, it was a large family of us, but there's just two of us living now. I have a half-sister in Washington. I had just two children to live, a boy and a girl, and they both died after they got grown.

In the fall the white folks went and bought you what you need. They would buy just what we called cotton ginghams for a chemise, and two lengths of underskirts and a dress and a pair of old brogan shoes. Colored children didn't wear drawers, and you'd knit your own stockings. They would shear the sheep and sell the best wool and then the second wool you would take and knit your stockings and hang them up for Christmas. I tell you we would be just as anxious for Christmas to come so Santa Claus could come down the chimney and put something in our stockings. The old folks told us there was a Santa Claus and we didn't think about not believing it. We'd get ginger cakes and stick candy and we thought we had something. We went barefooted 'til Christmas and we would put on our new stockings and shoes and we would be so proud. Before we put on our shoes we would go out and catch everybody's Christmas gift so they couldn't hear us coming.

In the spring, they would buy brown domestic and make underclothes out of that and you would have two dresses. Some of the mean ones just had white gingham dresses and they would be so narrow that they would split them sometimes.

Old Mr. _____ never would give them enough to eat. They would slip off and come to our house at night and our people would feed them. Old Mrs. _____ lived out on Granny White Pike, and she was so mean her husband couldn't stay with her. She had one old woman and a boy and a girl; they come to her by her mother, and that was all the slaves he left her when he went off. She used to whip that old woman 'till she would run away, and they put a big iron bell on her and fixed it so she couldn't get to the clapper and put it on her neck with an iron collar. Then when she would run away they could hear the bell and you could see her and her half-crazy sister riding horseback through the woods and listening to hear that bell. Just before the war they sent her to the greenhouse to make the fire—you see they had a sort of florist place, but they didn't sell flowers. People would just come there to look at them, but nobody ever visited her at all. Well, she stayed so long in the greenhouse that the old lady got the cowhide and went out to see what the trouble was, and there was the old lady bending down just like she was making the fire and old lady _____ cut her a lick with the cowhide, and lo and behold she was dead. She come running over to our house to get someone to lay her out, and she was just crying like she had lost her best friend. Huh, crying because she didn't have nobody to whip no more.

When the War broke out her daughter was in Columbia in school and she rode right through the lines with just a boy driving her—the boy was one of my brothers. We let him go with her to drive for her usually, and she got that girl and come on back. Governor Johnson would send guards there to guard her house and she said she didn't want them. She said, "Just send me some ammunition and I'll take care of myself. The Yankees walking 'round here with all that blue on gets on my nerves." She had a nice house. We would go there to see the girl. It was just her and the girl and her crazy sister there, and it was my idea of a beautiful house, but it got burnt down one night. They think somebody set it on fire, but they don't know who. It was way in the middle of the night and they had to run out in their night clothes. They didn't save a thing. She had a watch and she told the man where it was and said if he got it he could have it. Her husband had given it to her when they were engaged, and she didn't want it to burn up. He tried to get it, but the house started falling in before he could get to it and he had to give it up. She had some more little houses in the yard, and she moved in one of them, and somebody set that on fire; and she just moved into another one. That was just past Belmont College on the Granny White Pike. A house is still there on the place, but it doesn't look like nobody lives in it. I know she can't be living, but somebody might still live there. She was just so mean the white folks and nobody could stand her.

Mrs. Bradford lived up above us on the Granny White Pike. That was Mrs. Henry Allen Boyd's people. They were called Bradford's "free niggers" because they was nice to them, too. Old man Johnson—the man that carried so many to sell—had a nice time there, too, but he'd just sell them, some one day and some another. But I can say one thing for him, there was never no half-white children among his group. All of them was colored. He would let them come home Christmas, and they would have candy pullings, and he'd just give them anything he could to make them have a good time, but they would be crying all the time because they knowed what they would get New Year's morning. That was their money, and after the War when their slaves were taken away, the whites were poor, some of them poorer than their slaves because if they had any money it was counterfeit.

When I was quite a girl I went to a colored person's wedding. She was as black as that thing there (card table top) but she was her young marster's woman and he let her marry because he could get her anyhow if he wanted her. He dressed her up all in red—red dress, red band and rosette around her head, and a red sash with a big red bow. She was so black that when we saw a person who was real black and we wanted to say how black he was, we would say "black as aunt Mary Jane," and you can imagine all that black and all that red; but they had a little ceremony and all the young white folks were there looking at them get married. It was the funniest looking sight I ever did see, black and all that red, and she married a yellow man and had two yellow girls to wait on her! After the ceremony, there was a dance. She and her husband belonged to the church and they didn't dance, but the rest of them did, and the white men and women were standing 'round looking at them dance all night.

We had dances often in the summer, down in the woods. They would have lanterns hanging out in the trees all around. In the winter they would have candy pullings, but some of them (slaves) didn't have any pleasure at all. They just had to work and go to bed. We could get a pass to go to any of them (parties). Jimmie Baxter's was a place that we could go and have a good time. There, the white folks would have a party and when they finished eating, they would set the things out on the table for the colored to eat. Some of them were right good to colored—no responsibility, and some of them had a better time than they do now. Of course they whipped them but some of them need it, and when I look around and see them doing some of the things they do now, I think it would be a good thing if some of them could be whipped now.

They taught us to be against one another and no matter where you would go you would always find one that would be tattling and would have the white folks pecking on you. They would be trying to make it soft for themselves. I had an aunt by marriage who would peep around and tell the women things. She wouldn't tell marster because he always said he wouldn't have a tattler on his place, and if he found one he would sell her just as far as wind would carry.

It is just natural for Negroes to steal. Our folks would do it, and they had plenty. They would kill a hog and put it under the bed and cook it at night, and they would eat what they wanted then put a top over the skillet and set it back under the table and nobody would never know nothing about it. Course the children wouldn't know; they'd be in bed, and if you come up and the old folks was talking you didn't no more dare come in there than you would stick your head in the fire. Old lady McFerrin worked in the house and she told on one once and almost got him sold. Marster said that was the only thing he would separate his folks for, stealing. Later when I had grown and could hire out for myself, I would never hire out where there were two or more servants, for they would keep up a disturbance all the time. If you are doing well they'll tell the white folks something to make them mad. You see they trained them that way in slavery time when they came from Africa and it has just come down from generation to generation. You know the Bible says that it will come down from generation to generation, to your children and your children's children.

Sho' nough rich white people, if they had a girl on the place and she had a baby, they would say, "Just do it again, and I'll sell you as far as water and wind will carry you. I'll sell you to Mississippi."

Yes, we had log rollings and house raisings. They would give a big dinner and put up the frame of a house in one day. It was just logs and they would daub it with dirt and when that dirt would fall off you could look out and see the snow falling. Sometimes you would get up out of your warm bed and the side towards the wall would be full of snow. They had great big grates with a big back log and a little log in front, and we would put chips in between. That fire would might nigh run you out.

No, they didn't tell you a thing. I was a great big girl twelve or thirteen years old, I reckon, and a girl two or three years older than that and we'd be going 'round to the parsley bed looking for babies; and looking in hollow logs. It's a wonder a snake hadn't bitten us. The woman that would wait on my mother would come back and tell us here's her baby; and that was all we knew. We thought she brought it because it was hers. I was twenty years old when my first baby came, and I didn't know nothing then. I didn't know how long I had to carry my baby. We never saw nothing when we were children.

In summer time we had all kinds of vegetables and bacon, but in the winter we had potatoes and sweet potatoes and turnips. We'd just eat the things in season. In the spring when turnip salad come in every body was just wild. Rice and light bread and things like that you never saw unless somebody was sick; and tea was another thing. They would kill a chicken and make a little soup for the sick and put a little rice in it, and you'd have some toast maybe, but that was all it was good for, and I think that's all it is good for now. We had three hot meals, breakfast at six, dinner at one and supper at six in the evening. For breakfast we'd have mush and gravy and meat. The children would just have mush, but the grown folks would have meat. On Saturday evening, they would take their pans and go to the big house to get the things to cook for Sunday. We'd get brown sugar, meat, flour, syrup, and on Sunday we'd get coffee with milk in it; the white folks had the cream. We'd have good things to eat, too, out of that on Sunday.

On my place, each family had a chicken house and they had to raise chickens. They'd (the white people) buy them from you. They'd do that to keep you from stealing, and they would give you a load of corn and a load of hay; you could pull it and sell it. I remember just as well when I got big enough to pull a load of hay and sell it; and when you got big enough they would give you a hen house. They'd give you a load of fodder and a truck patch, too; but you would have to pull your fodder at night. They said they done that to keep you from stealing, but we would steal anyhow—that is, the grown folks would. They would have sweet potatoes and steal the white folks' sweet potatoes.

When they would kill hogs, the chillen would have to pick up chips to smoke the meat. The colored had the heads and scraps like that, and then they would have the fat part of the middling, but they would save the lean parts and the shoulders for the white folks. Some wouldn't give their slaves enough to eat, but we had plenty, and my folks would steal meat and give it to them. I've seen them many a time giving meat to those half starved slaves who would slip over for something to eat; but we were not supposed to see anything so we couldn't say nothing. They were afraid we would say something that would give them away.

If anybody would die, there was an old man on the place who would make a box. They had a graveyard for the colored and they would call in some people and have a short funeral service over the grave, then later on they would have a real funeral at the church. The first real coffin I saw was after the War. My mother had a little baby to die soon after the War and a friend of hers had a spring wagon, and he went to town and got a coffin. A lady made a winding sheet for the child, and it had lace on it.

No, we didn't have to turn the pot down on our place, but an old man lived up in the country named Mr. Compton and his folks would have prayer meeting and the people would slip there, and they would have the pot down to drown the sound. They would be scared to death that the white folks would hear them. We had wooden shutters and they would just pull those shutters to and do the door some way, and pray and sing in the room together.

There was an old man who belonged to Dr. Shelby, and he said if he ever got free he wasn't ever going to get up any more, and after he got free he really stayed there 'til he starved to death and died. He was an old man, too. He was just so happy to know that he could lay in bed and nobody could make him get up, he just wouldn't even get up to eat. You sho' couldn't do that (lie in bed) on old man Shelby's place. He'd whip niggers to death and then sell them before they died. The white folks got down on him for it and he was always in a lawsuit with somebody about selling a slave he had beat so bad that he died soon after the other man got him.

(Runaways). Many a one has come in our house and we'd hide 'em in the closets—men, women and children, too. They wouldn't let us chillen see it, but we'd see it anyhow. They wouldn't tell us a thing. I remember once there was a comet and we was standing there looking at it and we didn't know what it was.

We'd sing "Steal Away to Jesus," "This World Is Not My Home." At corn shuckings they would sing, "Walk Jawbone, Come Jine the Re." I don't know what the "Re" was.

Our cabin was just a little weatherboard cabin with two rooms. My mother had so many chillen she had to have two rooms. It had old fashioned windows that you would just shut, no glass at all. There was a fireplace in each room that would come out on the inside. We called that the hob, and we chillen would climb up on it sometimes. For women that worked in the house, the cabin was whitewashed; it was closer to the house, you see, so the white folks could get to them easy if they wanted them; and they had to have it that way to keep from spoiling the looks of the big house.

Chillen couldn't sit in chairs; we had to sit on little blocks; you couldn't think you were grown and they said if you sit in chairs it would make you think you were grown. When I was a child I was so long getting grown, I didn't know it. I used to say, Lord, if I ever had any chillen, I wouldn't treat them like I was treated. They would never ask you what you liked, they would just fix it and give it to you, and you had to eat it 'cause you were chillen. You'd see grown folks eating the best things! And you dasen't to look at it. In some places they had troughs for the chillen, and they had to get down and eat just like hogs; but we didn't have that at our place.

My mother hired me out during the War, and I learned how to use a knife and fork by looking at the folks there. My folks were away during most of the War. In September they would always go South because it was warmer, and they went like this fall and in the spring the Battle of Ft. Donelson came off and the Yankees took Nashville, so they were cut off. Our young mistress was sick and they left her here. The day they took Ft. Donelson, the soldiers had a dress parade and a newsboy was running 'round with papers, hollering, "Extra! Extra! Fort Donelson has fallen and the enemy will be here tomorrow!" I remember young mistress took some table linen and started South to her folks. We could hear the Rebels singing as they retreated, "I Wish I was in Dixie," and right now at the reunions when those old soldiers start singing that, they just jump around and shout. And the Yankees were singing as they advanced, "It must be now the kingdom coming, in the year of jubilee; old marster run away and the darkies stay at home."

Yes, the slaves stayed and took care of the place 'til the white folks came back, and some of them stayed there 'til they died. Colonel McNairy—the relative of his that I told you lived joining places—he took charge of the place when our folks were away, but he had to go to war. He had been in West Point, and he said that before he'd let his mother bake bread and his sister wash and iron, he would wade in blood up to his stirrups, and he went off to war and he got blown to pieces in one of the first battles he fought in. They wasn't sure it was him but you know they had special kinds of clothes and they found pieces of his clothes and they thought he was blown to pieces from that. When he left, his brother looked after us. He would get the provisions and things like that. You see there wasn't many of us on the farm up here, so we never had a white overseer, we just had a foreman, you know, and he was colored.

We used to play a game we called "smut," but we would play it with corn spots instead of cards. We played it just like you would with cards only we would have grains of corn and call them hearts and spades, and so forth, and go by the spots on the corn. We would play marbles, too, and this time of year our biggest amusement was running through the woods, climbing trees, hunting grapes and berries and so forth. We would play peeping squirrel too. We would say, "Peep, squirrel, peep dibble, dibble, dibble; walk, squirrel, walk, dibble, dibble, dibble; then run, squirrel, run, dibble, dibble, dibble," and we would run after the squirrel (child).

Children never knew anything went on at night; all of their play was in the day. We played "Goosey, goosey, gander," too. We had a lots better time then than children have now, in our playing.

The white people in the summer time would sit out on the porch in the front of the house and the colored folks would sit on the kitchen porch. We didn't have porches to our cabins and we'd sing to the white folks. You know white folks always did like to hear niggers sing, "I'll court Miss Millie Simmons on a long summer's day."

We used to play Sugar and Tea, too, and Frog in the middle and can't get out, and we would play songs like "The Americans are gaining the day:"

> The British government beating,
> War's all over and we'll turn back;
> I'll make my way back home
> If the British guns don't kill me.

We would play them plays for games when we'd go to parties and get tired of dancing, then we would play with songs like that . . . . I can't get all of that, but anyway, I know it was "Americans Are Gaining the Day." That was the play and we didn't know what "Americans" were.

We chillen would get in the woods and have meetings and sing them (spirituals), but we wouldn't sing them to the white folks. I remember another one we used to sing to the white folks:

> Bullfrog dies with the whooping cough
> Sparrow died with the colic
> Young ladies, ain't you sorry?

That was a Rebel song, and another one was, "I'll make my way back home again, if the Lincolnites don't kill me."

Oh, they tried to scare us; said they had horns (Yankees) but when we saw them with their blue clothes, brass spurs on their feet and their guns just shining, they just looked pretty to us.

None of our slaves went to war. They were all either too old or too young on our plantation. Some might have went from the Mississippi plantation.

"White Folks" Pet

I was a slave a good many years before the Civil War. When the War broke out I was in Bowersville, Texas. My master was a good man. I had a young mistress and she was from Hampton, Virginia. Her father give me to her for a wedding present when she married, you know. I was supposed to be a kinda maid and companion for her. I was a very delicate child, and of course wasn't much use on a big plantation, so he was kinda glad to git rid of me, he, he. In that way, you see, I got to do a lot of traveling.

My old master was named Mr. Gillum. I never called him "marster" or nothing. When the War broke out I was sent to Key West, Florida, me and my old missus. You see her husband was the property of the United States, standing army, you know, and of course they moved from place to place. Then after we went to Key West we went to New York, then back to Louisville, and after that time our headquarters was Philadelphia. About two weeks after he come from Key West he was ordered here to Nashville, to take charge and be quartermaster. Now, during the Battle of Nashville he was in Knoxville. Yes'm, I did get to travel 'round right smart, for a nigger, in them days. My mistress and master was nice to me, too.

Well, it was a long time before I knew that I was a slave, you know, and then one day ole Miss Gillum say to me, "Lucy, I am going to set you free." Well, I began to understand things then; and now I know that the Lord just opened the way for the po' nigger. Don't you believe that? You see, the reason I didn't hardly know that I was supposed to be a slave, was 'cause I was really ole Mis' housekeeper; kept house, took care of her money and everything; she was one o' these kinda women that couldn't keep up with nothing, kinda helpless, you know, and I just handled her money like it was mine almost.

Now, in dem days we had to travel in boats. I remember once when we was traveling on the boats we met a boat full of slaves going down South to be sold. I jest thought it was terrible then, although I was a little tike. Yes, we was traveling, and we come to a farm one Sunday, and decided to rest and wash up for the rest of our journey. Now, I and ole Miss Gillum, too, far as that goes, had been raised in a Christian home and, chile, when we saw them slaves working out in the fields and around on the plantation just like it was Monday, or any other week day, well, me and Ole Missus was just shocked; and we thought it was something scandalous. You see, I was young and I didn't know and understand conditions as they was then, like I can see things now. I remember I says to Old Missy, "Lawd, they wouldn't work me like that, just like it was Monday morning, no sirree." Oh, chile, I was one sassy chile! She said, "But, Lucy, they have to work if they wants them to," and me, I was just young and smart, you know, I says, "Well, I sho' wouldn't work on Sunday for nobody." Now wasn't that silly? he, he, he. You see, I didn't know, that was all. Well, then we was on our way to Texas. We stayed at Galveston all night, I remember, and we was coming on toward San Antonio that next morning, and we saw a large white house, and we stopped there, and chile, there sho' was a mean ole woman stayed there. Why she just worked her poor ole nigger slaves something awful. She worked 'em until way in the night. I don't believe they got any sleep.

Well, we had to stay in that house that night and you know, just like I tole you, my ole missy was funny, you know; she had done been used to things. Well, the sheets there at that house I was talking about was made out of some kinda blue stuff, and my ole missy didn't want to sleep on it, and me, miss smart aleck, of course, I up and tell Ole Missy to take her petticoat and spread it out on the bed to sleep on—you know in them days the skirts was terrible wide, —wide enough for two or three of the kind you girls wear now, he, he, he.

Honey, that sho' was a mean ole woman there. I remember when I went to bed that night the ole woman slave, the cook you know, was piddling 'round in the kitchen, and that ole woman was just actually driving her. I know that po' thing never went to sleep that night. Well, that ole woman had a parrot, one of these ole talking kind, and he was smart and talkative like me. The next morning the po' ole slave come out and say breakfast was ready; it was before six o'clock then. Then the crazy ole parrot say right loud, "Listen at that damn nigger talking about breakfast ready, and the coffee ain't even made." Well, I turned 'round and spoke that parrot out. I say, "Shut yo' mouth, drat you," and I said a whole lots more, too; and that ole white woman heard me, and she went in and tole Mrs. Gillum.

Well, you know, course Ole Missy didn't git after me or nothin', but she tole me after a while, "Lucy, don't you say nothin' to that woman; you will make her whip that poor old slave; she is terrible mean." I was awful airish and smart, you know, and I laughs and says, "Huh, if she tried to whip me, I would hit her back." Ole Missy she just smile and say, "Oh, Lucy, you really just don't know." So you see now that I really didn't know. Ole Missy tole Mr. Gillum 'bout what I said to that ole parrot, when she thought I wasn't listening, and he just laughed fit to kill hisself, he, he, he. I was one sassy chile when I was little, I tell you.

Well, it went on like that while we was there; that woman was sho' mean to the po' ole cook, and all the rest of dem slaves, too, I reckon; and 'fore we left Ole Missy says to me that she wanted to give that po' ole soul something but she didn't want the mean ole woman to know it. Ole Missy was sorry for her, too, you know. Well, she gimme a dollar and tole me not to let the ole white woman see me give it to her, 'cause she wouldn't have let her keep it, you know, and wouldda beat her besides.

I went out in the kitchen with the dollar, and I asked her, "Will you please give me some warm water?" Po' thing, she was so humble; she hustled 'round and fetched it to me, and when she handed me the kettle I just slipped the money in her hand. Po' thing, she was so thankful that her eyes just filled with tears, and she just nodded her head and never said a word.

Yes, honey, sometimes I git to thinking about it now. I remember my Ole Missy used to have a little red flannel bag, had paint on it like they have nowadays, —rouge, you know, and she used to rub with that little flannel and make her cheeks real nice and rosy; and 'course me, smart, would go right behind her and rub my cheeks, too; and 'course I wasn't the right color. I would say, "My cheeks don't git red as your'n," and she would say, "Lucy, you have to rub 'em harder," he, he, he. I didn't know, I was so silly and young, but smart. Chile, I was sharp as a tack.

Yes, I give that po' woman the dollar; the po' thing couldn't even say thank you. I went back and tole Ole Missy, "I sho' would kill that ole white woman if she come foolin' with me like that." That's the only kinda revenge I ever thought about then. I was always gonna kill somebody for something they did; didn't know no better, that's all. I really don't see how that po' ole slave had time to rest though, honest; 'cause she was at it when I went to bed and still at it when I would git up of mornings.

Well, we went on to San Antonio, and there we heard about a worse one than that one. There was a woman there what beat her ole slave so that the poor woman died. Yessiree, just beat her to death. They say when the woman was beating her, up till the time she died, she just say in a po', moanful voice, "Oh, pray, Miss Mary." Now wasn't that awful? I asked some of the folks what tole me 'bout it, "Why'n that woman hit her back," and they looked at me right funny, he, he, he. Well, honey, in a way I was glad that po' ole woman was dead, 'cause if she was treated bad as that ole slave we knowed, it was better to have death, I tell you. You think of beating people to death, it's terrible.

My ole master owned over one hundred head of slaves, and he didn't 'low nobody, I mean nobody, to hit one of his niggers. He didn't even 'low us to let white chillen hit us without hitting 'em back. We was always called "Jones' free niggers." Yes, but I was born in Virginia.

Well, they had so many slaves on the farm working, and then a good many in the house, too, and then sometimes in the rush season, you know, they hired some of them out to other farms. I remember once they had a overseer, and he struck one of my ole master's niggers, and do you know, Ole Master made him leave the farm right on off. Then he got another overseer, and he was real nice, and we all called him

"Cousin Jimmy." They didn't 'low us to even look at the po' white chillen. I 'member we used to slip and play with 'em anyway.

About a mile from the house there was a lane, and we would git all the chillen together and play with them down in that lane, where our white folks couldn't see us; then we would make 'em skit home! We say, "Ya'll gwan now, here come the white folks," he, he, he. We would drive 'em home and tell 'em Ole Master would whip them if they saw us with 'em. We'd say, "Come on, git out of here, here come the ole master," he, he. Next morning we would go and get 'em and play with 'em again. We would tell 'em we was better'n they was, he, he, he.

Yes, mam, right now I think I'm better'n a certain class of white folks; and I don't mind tell'em so, neither. I knows 'em, I knows white folks from their birth; only difference is I ain't birthed one, that's the only difference. The sight of 'em don't excite me one bit, I tell you, 'cause I know white folks from the cradle up.

Why one time I had seven chillen in school; three of 'em lives right here in Nashville; the other one is married and lives in Hot Springs; but the rest is dead. I am a mother of fourteen chillen. No'm, you sho' would never believe it by looking at me, would you? Two of 'em went to Fisk.

Yes, I always had a hand for "killing" everybody what bothers me, but 'course I never did nothing of the kind. You know that's what I always said. I remember once, real early in the morning, the last time I was at home before the War, I got up and went to the toilet. Now, you know in them days the houses like that was outside the big house, of course. We had a big turkey gobbler, and that old thing got up and run at me when I come out in the yard; and you know I was so little, why he come near knocking me down. I reached down and picked up a little bitta stick, and just kinda pecked at him with it, and lo and behold, that big old gobbler just fell over dead. Well, I just looked at him and went on down to the toilet and come back and went to sleep. Long up in the day I heard Ole Master say, "I know Lucy killed that turkey," and I never said a word. Everybody 'round the farm believed I done it, but Ole Missy and she didn't, but I never said nothin'. Well, a long time after that I up and tole her about it, and she said, "Why, Lucy, and I was the only one what said you didn't kill him."

Her maiden name, her first name you know, was Margaret Ann, and all of us 'round the big house called her that—behind her back, he, he. One of the boys, Alvin C. Gillum, is still in the army. When he come to town he always comes out here to see me. They was a fine family, I tell you.

Well, on the farm they worked half-day on Saturday, but sometimes it was according to the crop; you see they worked all day and long in the night.

You know, our folks just won't hang together; they won't be in no union or nothin'. It's a shame. Yet, 'course, I'm proud of my race, all of 'em, 'cause it tis my race, I guess. I remember Ole Missy used to quite often tell me this, and I know it's so now. She say, "Lucy, your race is against each other; you'll see it a long time from now; you don't understand now," she used to say. Well, I would git so mad, and I would bawl her out, too, and just sass her something awful; and she would just cry; then Mr. Gillum never would take her part, and that made her feel worse, he, he. Ole Mr. Gillum was a wonderful man; and he was a East Tennessean, too. He sho' lost a lot of money when the War broke out; but he said he didn't mind losing all he had in such a worthy cause; funny to hear a southern man talk for the Union, ain't it?

Well, yes, they used to have lots of nice parties. We would have quilting parties, and we'd put three or four quilts in the frame on top of one another; and then they would put the frame way up high; then while they were quilting each quilt they would sing and have lots of fun. I remember they used to have a little song, but I can't remember but one line of it to save my life, —went something like this—les see, "Jim crack corn and I don't care . . ."

They was a good hand for singing in them days, you know, but I don't remember many of the songs. It been so long, and I never stayed on the farm after I was eight years old, you know. I remember there used to be a lady come to stay with us, a white woman, and she would sit out on the porch after the darkies quit work and write down all the songs they would sing. 'Course, I guess she's dead long ago. The niggers used to sing—"Jesus have gone to Galilee." I used to like that song, but I can't remember it now. They'd sing:

> "Jesus have gone to Galilee.
> And how do you know that Jesus is gone?
> I tracked him by his drops of blood,
> And every drop he dropped in love."

I was real young when I learned that song; there's lots more verses; yes, wasn't more'n 15 years old, I know.

They used to have prayer meetings. In some places that they have prayer meetings they would turn pots down in the middle of the floor to keep the white folks from hearing them sing and pray and testify, you know. Well, I don't know where they learned to do that. I kinda think the Lord put them things in their minds to do for themselves, just like he helps us Christians in other ways. Don't you think so?

In them days the people professed religion just like they do now, but they was more ignorant, and yet I sometimes think they was more honest and sincere than they are now. I begin to think about religion right early; but I never professed till I come here and had chillen, too. I wanted to join St. Paul, and I begin to think about it a lot. I prayed and thought, and thought and prayed; I went to church and prayed, and come home and I got on my knees and I asked the Lord to tell me what church to join. Well, seem like he showed me the way. Seem like something kept telling me over my shoulder, "Go down yonder on Pearl Street and join Murray's church." The Lord sho' tole me that. I hadn't never been in that church then. It sounded like a natural man talking to me. I kept thinking about it. I said, "Lord, that's the Baptists what's always having a lot of fusses and rows in the church," but something just answered like a natural man, "Don't make no difference; you go down on Pearl Street and join Murray's church." Well, for a while I didn't know what to do.

I was a wild thing when I was young. Why I was more on dancing than my Ole Missy, and she taught me to dance, too. Well, after I joined the church, I didn't have no desire to dance no more. You know, I really object to Christians dancing. Now dancing don't bother me one bit, and it never did after I married. I see sin in dancing. I prayed to the Lord to take that off of me, and he sho' did. For a long time, you know, I could not git religion 'cause I wanted to dance, yessiree, I know what my religion done for me; it cleared my soul for all eternity. Dancing was an injury to me, I see it now.

We had a man named William—I can't think of that man's name to save my life. Anyway, he baptized my sister. I don't see how I forgot his name. Brother William—I don't see why I can't think of it; but my sister was baptized on the very same ground she was buried on. I went back there about twenty years ago; and all the folks what lived 'round there and knowed my sister and me was sho' nice to me. I stayed almost six weeks. All the white folks was so nice to me. 'Course, all my own old white people was dead 'cept just one family. He is a lawyer. His name was Howard. Me and him used to fuss and fight something awful when we was kids. When I went back there he said, "Lucy, I remember grandpa give me a good beating about you, didn't he?" I hadn't forgot it either, and we laughed about it a lot.

Well, they used to say when your right eye jump you was going to have good luck, and when your left eye jump, you going to cry. Then when the raincrow holler, it sho' going to rain. Why it hollered right out here in the front of the house yesterday, and it sho' rained before the day was over, didn't it? It used to be 'round here that it would be so dry; be six months before we have rain sometimes. Another thing, just as sho' as you born, when a bird comes in the house, it sho' going to be death right there in the family. Why a bird come in this here house, and flew right on my daughter's shoulder before she died. She was sixteen years old. I was so nervous from it. The bird had been eating polk berries and he left some on her dress. Well, she went on to church, and coming back she fell down, and she come on home to me, just about half crying, you know. She always in poor health. She come on home and went to school Monday, Tuesday and Wednesday; and I had just went to see a lady about giving her fancy work lessons. Well, she went to school on Wednesday morning; and in a little while Martha come in. Martha was the youngest. I said, "Where is Lucy?" and then somebody come and told me my child had done got sick at school, and I said, "Lord, don't let my child die in school, please." I told Mr. King to go get a horse and buggy and go get her; and he was so nervous he couldn't hardly go; and so I sent for Dr. Hadley and Reverend Taylor, and they had done sent her home in a carriage. They didn't tell me for a long time that she done had a real heavy hemorrhage at school. She lived just three weeks, right to a day, poor child. And she was the only one named for me; her pa named her for me, and everybody said she looked like me, too. She had the prettiest hair; when she died she had a sick spell, and was gone just that quick.

No, I don't do much dreaming now. I'm too old; if I live to see the 27th day of next month I will be seventy-nine years old. I professed religion in 1866, and the Lord have taken good care of me, I think. The only real sin I committed, I was a dancer, that's all.

Yes, I was here in Nashville when they killed Grizzard. I remember those white people. They brought him and hung him over the bridge. The white people oughta been stoned to death for a trick like that. They brought that poor nigger up here from down in Tennessee. Well, after it happened the people said the girl's father give that old white girl to that man hisself. I remember there was a girl working at the hotel soon after that by the same name, and them old white folks and the steward asked her if she was any relation to them, and she said yes she was a sister; and they fired her at the hotel. Yessiree, they got rid of her right away; and that was the most disgraceful thing what ever happened in Nashville; and I tell you the real sho' nuff white folks was sick of it.

You know up there where Jubilee Hall is built; well, it's built right on Colonel Gillum's fort. There's a plate on that concrete wall right in the middle with his name on it.

Yes, I run with a bunch of children what lived on the neighboring big plantations like our'n; and one thing we used to do. I always did have a lot of nerve, and 'course I was the leader in the gang. We had to be always nice and clean and everything, and sometime we would be out playing, and would take a notion that we wanted something to eat. I was the pet of the farm, you see, and they always had me to go and ask Ole Missy for something. Well, I'd go in and tell Ole Missy we was hungry, and she would say, "Well, Lucy, you go and tell Carrie to give you something." Carrie knew she better give it to us, too. Then we would all go in and sit 'round the Ole Missy and eat. Then, sometime the bunch would tell me, "Lucy, you go ask Ole Missy kin we have something good to eat," and I would go in and say, "Good morning, Miss Margaret Ann, how are you this morning?" then I would say we was hungry, and she would call, "Carrie, give me the store room keys," and she would give us anything we asked for in the cellar. 'Course, that was 'fore I left with young Miss Margaret, you see. One thing, my old master sho' hated to see niggers goin' 'round with their heads down.

When I was kinda small I used to put sand stuff in my dinner, to keep from eating it, and then sit up and laugh. White folks never done nothin' to me neither. Ole Missy used to tell me, "Lucy, if I hadn't loved your mother so, I sho' would whip you," but she never did. I was forever into something or other.

Why, if it was in this day and time, and I acted like I done then, folks would kill me, and I know. Why, many morning, I've gone down in the kitchen and got my coffee and cream before the white folks got theirs. Used to make the old cook so mad, and she would tell Ole Missy, too. I didn't want to wait for breakfast, and I just didn't. Ole Mr. Gillum just say, "Sure, let Lucy have her coffee; she wants it, don't she?"

I sho' nuff was sassy. I didn't pick nobody to sass neither. I sassed everybody. Mr. Gillum was offered $1000 for me when I was 14 years old, 'cause I sassed a nigger trader. Yes, I sho' sassed him. He shook his fist in my face, and I just sassed him something awful. Then he started after me, and I kept looking back and kinda running, and I yelled, "Mr. Gillum will kill you if you tech me." He come up to me and asked where I lived, and he told me to git there quick. I sho' told him where I lived and just flew home.

Well, that old nigger trader come on down to the house and I went to the door and let him and went and told Mr. Gillum there was a man to see him—I didn't say Gentleman, I just said man. Then they went to talking, and I peeked through the keyhole and listened, too, and Mr. Gillum say, "Why, her weight in gold can't buy her, that's all."

Yes, my white folks was good to me.

When It's Right
to Steal From Your Master

Mr. Huddleston: I was born a slave myself. I remember they used to whip us; what you all needs now.

Mrs. Sutton: This race coming up now don't know nothing 'bout hard work. Over there, see a road all turned up like this one and you would see men and women both throwing up dirt and rocks; the men would haul it off and the women would take picks and things and get it up. You would get hungry, but you never could stop till that whistle blow or an old gong sounded 'bout 1:00 o'clock or after; but you'd never get nothing to eat before. Then we didn't have nothing to eat but sour milk what was so sour you could hear it biling 'fore you got there. The women would work hard all day and in the evening when they came home they would have to help spin. One would hold the cord and the other would get the thread to spin the cloth for the ole white woman. Then we would get a little sour milk and go to bed; and had to git up and go to work next morning when the ole man blowed the bugle, long 'fore mistiss got up. You could any day see a woman, a whole lot of 'em making on a road.

Mr. Huddleston: Do you know what a slide was? It was a kinda wagon what men pulled.

Mrs. Sutton: I could cut wood. I have done anything any man ever done 'cept cut wheat; but then after they cut it I would gather it up. I am way up in 80 now; before the War I worked plenty, just like men. Could look up any day and see ten women up over dar on the hill plowing; and look over the other way and see ten more. I have done ever thing on a farm what a man done 'cept cut wheat. You would have to do everything, and some of them very same devils what made you do it are in hell burning now.

Mr. Huddleston: Maybe they ain't in hell, maybe they is at the other place.

Mrs. Sutton: Niggers would run away and go from city to city, in the woods. I know my boss bought two sold off in the woods. Whenever they'd get overstocked with niggers, like cattle now-a-days, they would gather up all the niggers and have a big block and stan' them up there, and there was a man to cry them off. He would put up a girl and say, "How much am I offered for her?" Some one would say "Five hundred dollars;" then maybe some one else would say "Five hundred and fifty," till they disposed of all of them.

Mr. Huddleston: They would advertise that they would have a nigger sale, and they would set the day, too, when they were going to carry them South. They would buy and sell them off every year, and carry them South. Maybe a woman would sell, a woman and her baby would be put up. Maybe someone wouldn't want the baby, but they would want the mother; then the baby would be sold to someone else. That's the reason niggers are so scattered out, 'cause they never would sell them as a family, but as individuals. I was only six years old when the War come along. I can remember only what I heard the folks talk about.

Mrs. Sutton: I don't know how many they had. Some worked at the iron works and others on the farm, and lots in the woods. The white folks would tote him vittles and knew he was in the woods. He knew he was out there all the time. Then when the slave was sold in the woods, he'd buy him in. Some white families may not have had but two or three families, but lots had gangs of slaves. If they had a lots of slaves, they would call where the niggers lived "nigger's quarters," with lots of houses.

Mr. Huddleston: They had what we call foremen; they used to call them overseers. They had what they called padderollers, too, whose business it was to see that niggers would not rove around at night without the master's knowing about it. If something was going on and you would leave, without your mass'r knowing it, to go to some other nigger's house, they took you and whipped you. They would hit you 49 lashes; that all the law allowed them to hit you. If your mass'r thought you could go when you asked him, you would ask for a "pass" and they would write you out one, and when the padderollers would catch you, you would show them this pass.

Mrs. Sutton: The War started up good fashion. A man's hoss got cripple, and he wanted to say Gilbert done it. Gilbert sweared to the last that he didn't, but this ole po' white man had so much agin him till he wouldn't listen. The other man had on all his regaliar to hang him with, and another man spoke up and say he knew Gilbert didn't do it. And the man what was gonna hang him said, "I can't hang this man," and another man stepped up and said, "I'll put the rope around that God damn nigger's neck," and then more hosses got their legs broke. The man what hang him broke his leg jumping off the scaffold. (This reference is to a man who was hanged in Nashville on a charge of rape. It was before Eph Grizzard's time.)

Mr. Huddleston: When you and the young man want to marry, he would have to go and ask your mas'r if he would let you marry or not, and he would have to ask his mass'r if he could marry Mr. John's gal, Sal. You would have to git consent from both mass'rs. They wouldn't have no license. They would have a preacher that would just say some kind of ceremony.

Mrs. Sutton: You married the same way on my place.

Mr. Huddleston: You could not go to see your wife only when ole mass'r gave his consent for him to go. Some could go once and some twice a week. The children would b'long to the wife's master. Maybe if a scrubby looking nigger like me would ask the girl's mass'r, he wouldn't let her marry; but take a sturdy stock of niggers, he would be glad to have him.

Mrs. Sutton: Some of the children would sleep on pallets in the white folk's house. I was in Maury County, Tennessee, and they was some mean out there. They had some of the highest blooded niggers; they just kept hiding out to keep an old white man from whipping 'em.

Mr. Huddleston: Have you ever heard about trunnel beds? It was a little bed you pushed under the big bed. You would pull it out at night, and the children would sleep in it, and in the morning you would push it back under the big bed. They had one room, and had everything in the one room, and they did that to save space. They did their cooking in this one room. 'Course it would be as big as two of these rooms put together.

Mrs. Sutton: One family would have to have a house of two or three rooms to it; they had so many children.

Mr. Huddleston: Whenever the children growed up, and they would not sell them off, they would build another room to the house.

Mrs. Sutton: No'm, (no half-white). There was enough out on the outside, but none on my place. Where I lived the man was the same as a nigger. He would teach us how to steal. This was the son of the man who owned the farm. He would say, "Now you can do this if you don't tell the ole boss." Darkies are agin one 'nother now more than they were then. They would stick together.

There was two classes of white folks, some who wouldn't bother with nigger women and others who would; but the ones who wouldn't wouldn't mix with those who would. They would make women do that. Some of them would treat these children better, and some of them wouldn't.

No'm (Mulattoes wouldn't run away any more than the other kind). All of them wouldn't let the white man whip them less they would slip up on them and git him. When he would come up to a nigger, the nigger would say, "Isn't this cotton chopped like the hoe chopped it. I know you'll tell mass'r, but if you hit me, I'll sho' beat you." They was some high blooded niggers there now if there ever was.

Sometimes the niggers would turn the white man up—when the white man would say, "Take this sack of flour or sugar and hide it behind the bush, and I'll get it after dark," and the nigger would go and tell the mass'r that he tole him to git him a sack of sumpin and hide it for him. The mass'r would say, "All right, Sam, I'll see after it. You just git it and put it there." And that night he would come 'cross the ole white man carrying a sack and say, "What is you got in that sack, a pig, or a sack of corn?" Niggers wouldn't stand to be whipped, and some time they would be in the woods two years, and be sold to the highest bidder.

You are going to have a preaching this evening—preaching to the niggers. And the preacher would start off:

No more, no more we'll never turn back no more.
You'll have to obey your mass'rs and mistiss.

Mr. Huddleston: Sometime the preachers would try to make the niggers steal from the mass'rs. While he was preaching he would have a nigger trying to steal him a goose. The nigger would go back of the shed and make the goose holler, and then the white man would see him, and would just turn the damn son-of-a-bitch off. He said he couldn't have no preacher what was teaching his niggers to steal. They let the niggers go to church. 'Course they would have to get a pass, but they could go to church.

Mrs. Sutton: The way they was brought up, on hard licks and things, you'd think they would stick together more than they do. Lot of 'em wouldn't take it either. Lot of them would want to have meetings in the week, but the white people wouldn't let them have meetings, but they would get a big ole wash kettle and put it right outside the door, and turn it bottom upwards to get the sound, then they would go in the house and sing and pray, and the kettle would catch the sound. I s'pose they would kinda have it propped up so the sound would get under it.

Mr. Huddleston: I don't know about that, but I heard my mother and grandmother talk about it.

Mrs. Sutton: If there ever was a nation of people what stood together, it ought to be the colored race.

Mr. Huddleston: They had no conception of unity at that time. They never got together that much.

Mrs. Sutton: Yes'm, I remember all that (concerning prayer), after all that hard time they used to have. They had some good singers at that time. No'm, the colored people didn't have no books to sing about like you do now. They sang a lots of songs that you sing now.

Mr. Huddleston: Yes, I hear them sing them now. One is "Swing Low Sweet Chariot." I hear'd them sing that at the school. Some others the cullud people used to sing before the War. Yes'm, they used to sing that, too ("Nobody Knows the Trouble I see").

Mrs. Sutton: I never did 'spec to see this time—that was way back. And such hard times. Yes, Lawd, we had good times at times, and sometimes we would hit a devil of a time when the overseer got the devil in him. They would have nice suppers and nice quiltings, and play the fiddles, and have a good time. You would have to git permission from the old mass'r to have a good time like that. He would say, "I don't want no fussing or no shooting."

Mr. Huddleston: Cullud folks been had guns all their life. They kept them hid.

Mrs. Moore: The other niggers off other places would steal from the masters and sell to po' white folks, and they would give them things for it. That's how they did on my place. I stayed in the house with the white folks, and I don't know nothing about having hard times.

Mr. Huddleston: They always had money; they would get it some way or 'nother. Most of the white folks would let the niggers clean up a little place of ground. He could go out wherever he wanted to and clean up just as much as he could after work time. He planted that ground, and after he is through his task working for his mass'r, he could plant his patch. He would grow corn, 'backer, and he would take this and sell it; and sometimes he could sell it to his master and get money. Some of them would cook ginger cake and take it where they were having dances, and make money. And they used to bootleg; yes, sell whiskey, just like they do now.

They used to have some mighty good ones, though. The camp meetings they would have them in the fall of the year, after they had laid the crops by. The white folks would have a camp meeting like the niggers would. Maybe they would gather round for ten and twelve miles. They would sing and pray and shout and preach all day, and at night they would all stay, and the next morning they would wake up and start again. Those close round would go home, and come back early next morning. If they lived far away, they would bring their beds, quilts and straw, and sleep on them.

Mrs. Sutton: We had some good times then, and some good music. No'm, I danced all night long. The white folks drove us so, and we would not know when Sunday came we was so glad when we could get together. You'd hear the darkies say, "Promenade on," and that was the time to promenade all over the place. Of course, I know what I felt and seen, too. It appeared as a voice from heaven; there wasn't nothing what I didn't hear.

They would have the nicest kind of songs, with books in front of them, and a preacher to preach. No, they didn't burry them the same place the white folks were.

Mr. Huddleston: They would wear clothes just like her—hat and dress.

Mrs. Sutton: (About to leave). I can go when I please and come back when I please. I'll come to see you, I must go home now. I am a free rooster. I got nobody to tell me nothing. I live right over there, you can throw a rock over there. Come on, I'll show you. (Mrs. Sutton left.)

Mr. Huddleston: The clothes resembled them Sister Sutton had on. You would never see a grown woman with a dress on shorter than hers, and sometimes they would be longer. When they dressed up on Sunday, their dresses would drag on the ground.

No, I never heard 'em tell anything about that: I don't think they knew anything about that; maybe they knew it in Virginia. (Slaves from Africa) I know a colored slave from North Carolina, he used to talk about the slaves that just came over, but I don't remember anything.

They had remedies for nearly everything at that time. If they got sick they would never have a doctor. The older people would doctor on them, and sometimes they died, but it was a rare thing to hear of a doctor on a nigger.

Mrs. Moore: They used blackberry root.

Mr. Huddleston: Yes, and hickory bark, red pepper tea to gargle your throat. Sometimes they would kill a cat and make soup out of it. I remember my uncle killed one once, and made a soup for one of us in the family who had the whooping cough. For babies, they made different kinda teas. One they called sheep's apple, made out of sheep's balls. They would make teas out of that. I don't remember all about remedies; but they had remedies for that, too (fevers).

Both Mr. Huddleston and Mrs. Moore: Oh yes, if you are going 'long and a rabbit crossed the road in front of you, sometimes you would just stop and go back home, and some would stop and make a cross and spit in that cross, and then go on, and some would go backwards. They were 'fraid of a rabbit more than anything else. If a screech owl get to hollerin' they would take a poker and stick it in the fire, and stop him from hollerin'.

Mrs. Moore: I don't know about a poker, but if you take your left foot shoe, and turn it over under the bed, it would stop. They said there would be death around the neighborhood. I don't know whether that stopped him or not, but they would stop. I know lots of signs, but I can't think of them now. If you sneeze when you are at the table you would have to get up and not eat anything; that was bad luck, and the old folks would make you get up. If you swept dirt out of the door after sundown, that was bad luck.

In confinement, you couldn't pick up ashes until the baby was four weeks. When you was confined you couldn't sweep under the bed. I hear about the younger generation, speaking about sweeping under your foot. People get up in a hurry and go and put on some of your clothes and not be looking and put it on wrong side outwards, it was good luck; and don't turn it until up in the day.

Christmas time, they done just like you do now. They had amusements and things. What is that about the finger nails; there was some sign about that. You would have to burn them up, not throw them out, 'cause on judgment day you would have to hunt around and find them. And you can't throw your hair out, if you did the birds got it and put it in their nest, and you would have headaches. If a hen crowed you would have to kill her—bad luck. If a rooster crowed before your door, a stranger would come.

Mr. Huddleston: Eph Grizzard? Oh, yes.

Mrs. Moore: I don't know, but my husband worked right across from the bridge. He was working there where Phillip and Burdock's, and people were standing up all on the houses.

Mr. Huddleston: Yes, I remember, and people were all over the streets, and I asked what it was and somebody tole me there was a mob in town and they were hanging a nigger.

Mrs. Moore: My mother was cook, and her children stayed right with her; and her house was right in the yard. They built her two rooms. All her children was just nachul pets around the house. I stayed in the house most of the time. I stayed in so much that they said I was carrying the white folks news; but I weren't. We stayed there till my mother left to go to a large ranch what the Yankees got. They made lots of the mean mass'rs give up their plantations and leave, and they got a plantation, and my mother and her husband went there. There was thousands of acres and lots of Negroes came there from Georgia and Alabama and all around, and brought their children. When my mother left that she took her children with her. When I lived with the white folks, I stayed in the house most of the time, and they fed me right there in the room, on the floor. My brother would come in rattling his spoon in his cup, and ask for coffee, and ask the white woman to give him some. Of course we went with my mother. The white woman cried, 'cause we were the same as her children. All her children was grown, and she had one son to go to the War. I don't know nothing about the slashing and whipping.

Mr. Huddleston: I don't know nothing either, but I have heard, 'cause some of them would whip their niggers, and a lot of white people in the neighborhood would not whip their niggers. I heard the old people say that some of them would take the niggers and strip their clothes down and lash them till they put blisters on their backs, and then mix salt and pepper and put it on their backs to make them more miserable.

Mrs. Moore: My father, well he worked on the farm. He was hired to the Yankees. They had refugees on this farm from all around. What they paid them on this farm, I don't know, but I know they sho' fed them a heap. I don't know how long we stayed there, but right when peace was declared, that is when we left. War went on four years. It started in 1861, and after the surrender my parents moved to another place and worked on the farm, and I picked cotton and chopped cotton, and cut cotton stalks in the spring of the year, getting ready for farming. I went to school early in the summer and in late of fall, while others went all the year, and went all the way through; but I didn't have that chance. When I was 13 years old I married; that was in 1867. I wasn't quite 13. I married in March and was 13 in June. I married, and before I was 18 I was the mother of four children. No'm (in answer to question as to whether or not she had any letters or old papers).

Speaking of Eph Grizzard, did you ever hear about that Martin Knox and Kelly? They wasn't mobbed, they were legally hanged. That has been about 50 years ago. Kelly was accused of an old white woman. Knox was killed about an ole man and his wife and a grandchild. Don't know how ole the chile was.

(Slave carpenters) No, no doctors, but carpenters. They had some of the finest carpenters they was.

Mr. Huddleston: My wife had an uncle who was the finest carpenter around. Yes, there was lots of free Negroes; the only difference, they couldn't sell 'em, and they wouldn't have to work for a white man. He didn't have any social privileges, but he could hire out and work for who he pleased. There were lots of Negroes who had trades. They could make brooms and chair bottoms, and lots of them made a lots of money that way. They would take care of it, and sometimes they would take money and buy their wife and children, and then buy himself. If he was able to pay the price, he could buy his freedom.

The average price of a slave was from $1,500 to $3,000. It was a common thing to sell a well developed colored man for $2,000. Women sold from $1,000 to $1,500. A woman who bore children fast, they would sell her for as much as a man. A woman who was barren, they wouldn't sell her for so much.

(Illegitimate children) Yes, there was right smart of that. (Did they look down on the mothers of them?) No, they wouldn't do that.

Slaves Have No Souls

For what intent have you come here? I don't know how many slaves my old marster had, but I know he had a yard full of niggers. I was a boy in slavery. Now you talk about hard times, I have had hard times. I started plowing at eight years old. I called my old marster "Marster." Called old lady "Mistress." Called Jim "Mr. Jim" and Ella "Miss Ella." That is what we learned to do. I cannot tell you all about slavery but I can give you an outline of it. I served my old marster until freedom taken place—my mother, my father, and five or six children was there.

I was raised on pot-likker. I love it till today. I would take it and crumble a little bread in it. We never did get meat at night—mostly buttermilk.

Them times peoples children was lousy as a pet pig. Mothers would stay home on Sundays and look at their heads and kill them. I worked at herding of the cows. Every morning I would go into the woods and drive them up. I was bare-footed as a duck. Sometimes I would drive the hogs out of their warm place to warm my feet. I used to work in the tobacco patch catching worms off the leaves. Some of them worms was as big as my finger. Marster would come behind me and if he would find a worm I would have to bite his head off. That was done in order to make me more particular and not leave worms again.

You as teachers used to whip the children with a paddle or something, but my whip was a raw cowhide. I didn't see it but I used to hear my mother tell it at the time how they would whip them with a cowhide and then put salt and pepper in your skin until it burn. The most barbarous thing I saw with these eyes—I lay on my bed and study about it now—I had a sister, my oldest sister, she was fooling with the clock and broke it, and my old marster taken her and tied a rope around her neck—just enough to keep it from choking her—and tied her up in the back yard and whipped her I don't know how long. There stood mother, there stood father, and there stood all the children and none could come to her rescue.

Now it is a remarkable thing to tell you, some people can't see into it, but I am going to tell you, you can believe it if you want to—some colored people at that wouldn't be whipped by their marster. They would run away and hide in the woods, come home at night and get something to eat and out he would go again. Them times they called them "run-away-niggers." Some of them stayed away until after the War was over. Some of them would run to the Yankees and would bring the Yankees back and take all the corn and meat they had.

Now I had a young marster named Colonel Hale. All of them is dead but me. I seen the clod put on Mars Jim. After freedom taken place we still called them Marster and Old Miss, but they used to tell us not to call them that. Jim Hale before he died told me not to call him Mars, but Mr. Hale.

Time has been that they wouldn't let them have a meeting, but God Almighty let them have it, for they would take an old kettle and turn it up before the door with the mouth of it facing the folks, and that

19

would hold the voices inside. All the noise would go into that kettle. They could shout and sing all they wanted to and the noise wouldn't go outside.

Now they had what they used to call "nigger traders," and they would call a man a "nigger buck" and a woman a "nigger wench." They would buy them and carry them down to Mississippi and put them on the cotton farms. The overseer would ride up and down the field with a gun over his shoulder to see that they kept working. When they would carry them to Mississippi they didn't go by train, neither by automobile—there wasn't any then. They would go by foot. Someone would drive the wagon behind them and if any of them would give out they would put them in the wagon. Many children have been taken away, suckling babies sometimes away from their mothers and carried to Mississippi. Now let's treasure these things up and look at them in another way. Every nationality ever before has had a better time than the Negro. Sometimes when I am on my wagon I look at the children coming from school, and I say, "If I had had that opportunity when I was coming up I would be 'sons of thunder'." Then, a Negro wasn't allowed a book in his hand. What little they got they would steal it. The white children would come out and teach them sometimes when the old folks wasn't looking.

The first Sunday school I went to was after the War. The house was an old oak tree. We used to carry our dinner and stay there from eight o'clock until four. In slavery they used to teach the Negro that they had no soul. They said all they needed to do was to obey their mistress. One old sister was shouting in the back of the church and her mistress was up in the front and she looked back and said, "Shout on old 'nig' there is a kitchen in heaven for you to shout in, too." The people used to say "dis," "dat," and "tother," now they say "this," "that" and "the other." In all the books that you have studied you never have studied Negro history, have you? You studied about the Indians and white folks, what did they tell you about the Negro? If you want Negro history you will have to get it from somebody who wore the shoe, and by and by from one to the other you will get a book.

I am going to tell you another thing. A Negro has got no name. My father was a Ransom and he had a uncle named Hankin. If you belong to Mr. Jones and he sell you to Mr. Johnson, consequently you go by the name of your owner. Now, whar you got a name? We are wearing the name of our marster. I was first a Hale then my father was sold and then I was named Reed. He was brought from old Virginia some place. I have seen my grandma and grandfather, too. My grandfather was a preacher and didn't know *A* from *B*. He could preach. I had a uncle and he was a preacher and didn't know *A* from *B*. I had a cousin who was a preacher. I am no mathematician, no biologist, neither grammarian, but when it comes to handling the Bible I knocks down verbs, break up prepositions and jumps over adjectives. Now I tell you something—I am a God sent man. But sometimes Jim calls and John answers. The children of Israel was four hundred years under bondage and God looked down and seen the suffering of the striving Israelites and brought them out of bondage. Young folks think old folks are fools, but old folks know young folks are fools. How many old folks do you find in prison?

To get salt to go in your bread in slavery, well they would dig up the dirt where the fresh meat hung over and had been dripping salt, and would boil this to get the salt. They would get and parch sweet potato peelings to make coffee. You all are blessed children, you are living on flowery beds of ease. I would to God sometimes that I was able to express myself.

A child seven or eight years old back there was sold for $1800 and $2000—that is, if it was a healthy child. I remember seeing my old mother spinning with tears running down her cheeks, crying about her brother who was sold and carried to Arkansas. She would sing,

> Oh, my good Lord, go low in the valley to pray,
> To ease my troubling mind.

Oh, where else can we go but to the Lord? The young people don't live close to God now as they did in them times. God lived close to them, too. Some of them old slaves composed the songs we sing now. God revealed it to them. We were brought from Africa and made slaves of. Did you ever hear of Blind Tom? He could tell you how many months was in the year, how many days was in the year, and could even tell how many minutes was in a year. He told of how Blind Tom was challenged once for incorrectness in his calculations, but Tom called attention to the fact that he was figuring in a leap year. Now what do Solomon say about wisdom? "The beginning of wisdom is to fear God and keep His commandments." What nationality was Solomon? He was a black man. "Forsake me not because I am black." Who was it that bore the cross when Christ was wagging the cross up Calvary hill? He was a black man, Simon of Cyrean.

(Some of the Songs Sung in Slavery) "I am bound for the promised land," "No more, no more, I'll never turn back no more." "Come on moaner, come on moaner, come on before the judgment day," "Run away to the snow field, run away to the snow field, my time is not long," "Moses smote the water and the children they crossed over, Moses smote the water and the children they crossed over, Moses smote the water and the sea gave away," "Quit this sinful army and your sins are washed away."

Young people don't pay enough respect to old gray-headed folks. I have been a Christian every since I was 17 years old. I have been a minister every since I was 22. In 1885 I carried on a week's meeting in White County—had 24 converts and 20 additions to the church—Cumberland Presbyterian Church. I was coming down the road one night and met a boy who was just drunk enough to have devilment in him. He came up to me and said, "Who are you?" I said, "Reed is my name and I'm from Hartsville, Tennessee." He said, "What in the hell and damnation, by God, are you doing here?" I told him to go on about his business and that I was a preacher on my way to church. He said, "Well, by God, you got to pray for me." I didn't know what to do, but I stood up and looked him straight in the eye and prayed to God to deliver him. You know you're supposed to close your eyes when you pray, but that was one time I kept mine open. I heard later that he professed religion and was a deacon in the church.

I don't believe that I will be held up on my wagon. I have got faith in God. Everybody owes me, everybody knows me, and nobody pays me.

I bought this house in 1919. When I first bought it everybody told me that I wouldn't pay for it, but by the grace of God I did. Buried my wife, daughter and grandchild. I have been in Nashville over forty years, been a hard working man, working and preaching. I have never been arrested in my life, never was drunk, never cussed but once; got scared and quit. Never give my parents any sass. I am out in all kinds of weather and never sick. I live close to the Lord. He will not forsake them that walk upright. In Genesis 6 and 7 it says, "Be not deceived, God is not mocked, whatsoever a man soweth that shall he also reap."

I didn't go to school until I was a man. I would go out and plow and take my book with me. We used to have spelling matches. If one would beat the other spelling he would turn him down.

Preachers used to get up and preach and call moaners up to the moaner's bench. They would all kneel down and sometimes they would lay down on the floor, and the Christians would sing:

Rassal Jacob, rassal as you did in the days of old,
Gonna rassal all night till broad day light
And ask God to bless my soul.

They would call for moaners first night, and moaners would come up for two or three nights waiting to feel something, or to hear something. Sometimes they would walk way out in the woods after getting religion. They would get to rolling and shouting and tell everybody that they had found Jesus and they would shout and shout, and sometimes they would knock the preacher and deacon down shouting. But about a week after that they would go to a dance, and when the music would start they would get out there and dance and forget all about the religion.

Note: While waiting for Mr. Reed, his nephew told the investigator some things concerning the value of slaves that his father had told him. Some of the things were: That the value of slaves was determined by the amount of his intelligence and of the usefulness to his master, whether he was a coachman, maid, cook, butler. They would have slave markets and sometimes the more intelligent ones would bring as high as $5,000. Some of them would be promptors for a dance—call off the numbers for the quadrille. Some of the slaves could not talk one bit of English, they would not sell for very much because they couldn't. They would be taught to do things at the slave market before being sold. Sometimes the white children would teach them to speak English. A man's wealth was measured by the number of slaves he owned. After the War it was mighty hard for him to do something that had always been done by slaves.

(Mr. Reed again) Now I want to tell you all something about the Civil War. I believe the breaking up of slavery was started some by the churches. There was some churches that wouldn't suffer for a member to be a slave owner. The North and South rebelled on account of slavery. The great War went on four long years. There was a vast number of Negroes in that war. Many of them joined the Yankees and fought for freedom.

All the money was Confederate money then. After the War was over it was worth about as much as this handkerchief is. After that come the paper dimes and paper fifty cents, then the large paper dollars. They had silver nickels. You don't see them today. I have seen changes made in money three and four times.

After we was set free my father took charge of me. He told me I was free but as long as I was under the roof of his house he was boss. That was when I went out to find me a job. I went two miles from home and got a job and worked all day for fifty cents. I was paid off that night and I thought I was putting it in my pocket, but when I got home I found that I had lost the money that I had worked all day for. It was a paper fifty cents. I worried all night about losing it, but the next morning I got up early and went back and thar on the ground lay the money covered with dew, just where I had dropped it. I been losing and finding money every since.

I remember just as well as if it was yesterday—my father give us three boys a patch to make us a tobacco patch. We would take the money and buy us clothes. I remember the first shirt I bought was a pleated bosom shirt. I bought me some shoes and a hat. I tell you I been a traveling man. Been getting up and falling down every since.

One blessed thing, I got good religion and live close to the Lord. Now ladies, I can't think of everything, but if you want to ask me any questions I will answer them for you.

When people 'fess religion in these days all you have to do is answer a few questions. Do you believe that Jesus Christ is the Son of God, and if so give me your hand. I don't believe in all that what the people say about having to see a little white man. That is all fogieism. What was it for them to see? Always a little *white* man. This is a progressive age, children, an intelligent age. Don't believe nothing like that. The Lord said, "Follow me," now what else was for you to do but do that? A vast number of our preachers still preach that kind of stuff. Now I just felt that there was something for me to do—some work for the Lord. I felt that I was condemned in the sight of God.

I never went to school until I was a man. I went to a denominational school at Bowling Green, Kentucky. I worked for my board at the college. Children was running all over me with education. The teacher would tell the children if you all had the mother-wit that Mr. Reed had you would be "sons of thunder." I remember trying to diagram a sentence. That sentence was, "Mary, sister Julia, has lost her diamond ring." Can you diagram it? What is the subject? Mary, ain't it?

My mother would spin. She would make our clothes. She would take the cotton and card it, then she would weave that, and after that it would come to cloth; then she would take that and put it in the loom and weave it. My mother done all the washing and ironing and cooking and work in the field, too. She would do the house work before going out to the field. When time come to go back to the house to cook, she would quit and go back. She would tend the crop. We had meat and bread and mighty little of that. In them days parents could just look at children and out their eyes at them and they would know what that meant. And if you said anything they would give you a back-hand lick without even looking at you. Young people today don't know how to treat old folks.

I know plenty of slaves (women) who went with the old marster. They had to do it or get a killing. They couldn't help it. Some of them would raise large families by their owner. I know an old banker in Lebanon who gave one of his children a home after they come free.

I remember the time when Eph Grizzard was hung over the bridge. That time they had what they called a "dummy" running from here to East Nashville. Run right down by the jail. Eph was in the jail. They had a black mother-hubbard on him to tell him from the rest of the prisoners. They took him out of jail and went running up First Avenue to the bridge, and tied the rope around his neck and threw him over. It was about three o'clock. He hung there from three until about six o'clock. They would take a-hold of that rope every once in a while and give it a yank. The sheriff of Goodletsville got up on the bridge and made a speech and said, "If anybody, rich or poor, black or white, grizzly or gray, get up and say anything in this nigger's behalf we will take them and do them the same way." Five or six men was killed trying to get to the jail to get Eph out. I was working down on the wharf at Broad this side of the Tennessee Central station. My heart ached within me. I looked to see that bridge fall in there was so many people on it that day. I heard that woman had a child afterwards, but I don't know. They killed him and burned him up.

Since you ladies been talking to me so much you got my brain stirred up to the top of my head. And if I could tell you more I would. I can't think of everything at one time.

I Was a Boy Slave

I was small in the time of slavery. I remember when the slaves was being used as slaves, and I remember that in the time of slavery colored people didn't have no churches of their own; they had to go to the white people's church when they were through, and usually they had to use the white folks' preachers.

I remember when they were drilling for war. Every Friday they would march down to Flat Rock, and they would wear grey suits and tall plumes in their caps. I remember when the padderollers would come at night and would go around the country to other houses to see if they could find slaves away from home; and if they did find them, without a pass, they'd whip them. I remember, too, that some of the masters would chastize their servants till they would run away and hide around till they'd catch them. I've known my mother to help them the best she could; they would stay in the thick woods and come in at night, and mother would give them something to eat. When the slaves would die, they would make a square box, usually plain poplar wood, and sometimes they would stain it, but mostly not; they would put them in that and place it on an ox cart and bury them. That's the way we rode to church, too, when we did ride to church. We had an old ox cart and oxen, and we would pile up in it and drive the oxen. But we wasn't allowed to go to church or anywhere else without a pass. They'd have prayer meetings at times at home, but they had to get permission, and if they didn't I've known them to have to turn down a pot to keep the sound in. No'm, I have never known them to get caught while the pot was turned down at my home; but I have heard of them getting caught. They would run them out and whip them, and send them home and then report to the master what they had done. Of course the master approved of that. There was one family near us, though, named Wright, and he would let them go without a pass, so his servants was called "free Negroes." He wouldn't give them a pass and didn't 'low 'em to be whipped at all. If they got caught out, and there was any whipping done, it would be to the colored where they went, because the padderollers wouldn't bother them.

The white ministers would baptize them when they 'fessed religion; the colored ministers wasn't allowed to do so. They didn't know enough to carry out the service. The first colored minister I knowed was Jack Maney; and Cal Overall was one of the first colored ministers, too. They were both Methodists. Jack Maney lived here; he belonged to Newt Maney's grandfather. The first church I was ever in was Overall's church. It was an old shed, and the seats was made out of rails. We would get old slabs and rails and things, and have seats of them. I remember seeing my master when he whipped one of the women and tied her down across a log till she fainted away. Something she didn't do; that's what he claimed; seems to me she resisted like, and pouted. I remember his son lived on the place and got married into another family and murdered one of the servants. It was not his servant, because it came by his wife. His name was Brown, and he had a wife at my place, and he came there every night to see her; so he came that night and didn't

23

get back as early as he thought he ought to. Brown was a strong man and this white man that was the son of my master attempted to whip him; so Brown threw him and ran to the woods. He pursued him, and found him sleep on a sand bar out in the river; so he killed him in his sleep and threw him in the river. I know he did it because he told my master, and he sent them to the river to fish for him. They brought him from the river home on a handbar. No, it wasn't a wheelbarrow. They didn't have them, it was a handbar (described it, but investigator didn't get it very well.) They never did anything about it except burry him. I did hear that his wife's father taken that out of her part that was coming to her.

I was born out at a place about eight miles from here. My father belonged to the Maney's here, and my mother belonged to Jones out there, and I stayed with my mother. He'd (his father) come home every Saturday night and be back here early Monday morning. He worked on the farm; just a regular farm hand. This man, he had about ten slaves, I reckon; about five men and five or six women. He had a blacksmith on his place, and a wood workman, and a leading hand—I guess it was about ten grown people and their families, but sometimes the men and women would be married but their husbands and wives didn't live on my place, just like my father and mother, but of course there was children growing up.

My boss had one free woman on his place. She bought herself and she was free. No, I don't know how she bought herself, but I think she got someone to buy her. Her name was Millie, and she was free, but the old boss owned her son, and he was set free, too; but she died before freedom. I think some white person paid for her. She had a little lot on the place, and she had a spring that was called "Aunt Millie's spring," and it goes by that name yet. Yes, Aunt Millie's son was said to be his son (master). She never married that I know of. I know she lived alone and she was what we called a widow woman, because she lived alone. She had just that one child, and he was real bright. I have heard the old folks say that he favored him (master) and that his actions was just like his. She had a home off from the house, and she (Aunt Millie) lived alone. The other servants lived in the yard in little cabins stuck round in the yard. Some had wives on other places, but they had a shed to sleep in. Sometimes they could go on Wednesday nights to see their wives, but it was understood on Saturday night that he could stay till Monday morning, and they would feed them while they was there. If they went on Wednesday they had to come back the next morning.

My mother worked in the field. All of the women worked in the field except two; that was the cook and the house woman. The women had to work in the field and spin four cuts before they went to bed. That was a yank (he explained in detail just how a yank was made; defined broach, spindle, etc., but details recorded by investigator are not accurate enough to record). They made a cut then they could go to bed. They had a loomist that would weave. She'd work the broaches off and make a shuttle, then the broach would lay down in there so as not to ruin the thread and scotch it. There was little fine places like broomstraws, and they would run the shuttle through them. Then they'd use—I can't think of the name of it, but it was something that they'd run up there to beat the thread through, and that would make the actual cloth. They would cut out that cloth into garments, and we wore them. Boys until they got up large enough to work wore little slips. We called them shirts; they'd sew it up like a sack and cut a hole in the neck for your head to go through, and you wore that till you were ten or twelve years old. There was not much difference in the dress of girls and boys. The women wore theirs straight, too, and they called them sacks. It was just cloth sewed up wide enough to step, and they would gather it up at the waist, and put a kind of body to it and fasten the body on, and the sleeves in. Sometimes it would fit and sometimes it wouldn't.

He had ten or twelve slaves to my knowledge. He wasn't as hard on us as some that owned slaves generally. He did his own whipping, and he didn't have no overseers at all. He would get up early in the morning and get on his horse. A man had to be in front of him to let the fence down and put it up again, or to open the gate and close it when he had to go through. He just tended to the horse and followed him around all day, and he would fix up the fences and things like that when they needed it. He had a regular man for that so that when he left home on his horse, he wouldn't get down till he got back home.

No, we had what we called good times, but they were not *real* good times. He allowed his hands to go to church, but they had to get a pass from him. It was not often we had church; the church was on some man's farm, and the colored could go some afternoon. They didn't have services like we do now. They had circuits, and they just had meetings once in a while. Sometimes some minister would preach to the white in the morning and in the afternoon to the colored. They was mostly Methodists around here. The Baptists were not much known then. The Methodists always had the lead. The colored was not much on Denomination. They just preached the Bible as well as they knew. Bob Barnes was one of them. His master's living

right here now, running a store not far from the ice plant. He talked to us about his servant, Bob, who was a great minister. He would read it to him, and he would preach it to the slaves. Andrew Jett was a kind of old-timer, too. The War come up when he was aspiring to the ministry. They didn't have no light to read by. they had to slip old planks and things in the house in the summer, and they would light that and sit down and read from the light of the fire—those that learned to read a little. I remember when the women would have lamps made at the shops. They was made out of iron; they would beat it and shape it into a lamp, and get some grease and put in it. It would come to a point and they would have a rag extending from that point, and that would make a blaze. They had another piece of iron that would extend up into a ring, and they would stick it into the lamp and sit and sew by that. The white folks had candles; they would fill the tins full of hot tallow and when it would get cool they would catch hold of a stick they had in it and pull them out. It was soft beef tallow they used then. They had something they put in the tallow to make it kind of firmer. I think it was alum.

I remember when they began to fight. I had two young masters that went to the War. I remember when they packed up and said goodbye. The old Whigs was opposers to freedom, and you know the leader of them was Jeff Davis. They broke the Union; that's why they had the War.

The hands usually stayed on the place (during the War) and after freedom was declared they had to pay them. I never saw a battle, but they fought all around here in Murfreesboro. My people left home and came to the army camp. We came next morning and the pickets stopped us till marster come up. We left home at night, and we were all packed up, and whoever was willing could go back to the farm, and the others went on in and lived around in the camps till freedom was declared. In the camps they was teaching them about their citizenship. I remember well when the people had to marry over. They all come together, and the magistrate would meet them and marry them. I remember my mother and father went and got married, but some slaves wouldn't do it.

I don't know (age), my old boss said they lost the Bible in the time of War. They had one for the colored and one for the white, and it was the colored one that got lost, so our ages was guessed at by the white chillen's ages. I guess I was ten or twelve years old when the War come up. I was a boy around the house. I remember they had brushes to keep the flies off with, and the real wealthy people had theirs made out of peafowl feathers, and it was a mighty pretty sight to see them stuck on a stick and waving back and forth. I had to use that to keep the flies off the table, and my old marster would take a nap after dinner every day, and I'd have to keep the flies off of him. Sometimes I would go to sleep myself and drop the brush on him, and he would take it and hit me on the head with the other end. I had to run the stock and hogs and do things like that. I know after the men went to the War we little ones of my size had to go to the field and work and chop. Some of the men was carried off to war, and all during the War they couldn't buy or sell any slaves, but they could hold them they had till freedom. Yes, slaves knew (freedom was coming) but the slaveholders said it would never be—they told us that so much that it was a joy to the slaves when it come—they hardly expected it.

She (mother) had four children at that time. None of them was sold on our place, but some places they did; they would take them to the slave block, and sometimes they would sell the woman and keep the child.

Sold From Block
at Four Years Old

Yes, the South is a beautiful place; it's so pretty. Well, you see, Honey, picking cotton wasn't so much fun to me because I was compelled. Yes, I was compelled to do it. Yes, I look around at the girls these days, and I think they ought to be mighty good and kind. They oughta be much more polite than they are; we have gone through a lot for them.

Well, I'll tell you all I can, dear. I was four years old when I was put on the block and sold; and I had to set by the cradle and rock my old mistress' baby, and keep the flies off her before I was five years old. Then, of course, you know from time to time I had to learn how to cook and do most everything about a house. I had my five cuts a day to make, just like the old folks, you know. Well, that is a roll of five threads, and when it turns over five times, well it cracks, and you wind it in a hook like this, and make a loop of several threads; now five of them is five cuts, you see. You see, I had to pull the thread like this, and pull it over the loom like this, and then cord it. It was real work, I tell you, dear. You had that to do until you got that roll spun up; then you started on another one. Then to put it on, you would thread it like this and sorta turn the wheel 'til it made a twist, then you was ready to start back and forth, back and forth, just like this. Then you took that thread, and you had to run it on a broach and wet a shuck and run it on a spindle, holding that old shuck all the time. Yes, it really was work.

Well, dear, it was nobody but me and my brother, and we had all that to do. My mother died when I was young, way before the War. We was both together until way after the War, too.

Well, it's just like this, I will give the devil his dues. I was reared up jest like all the colored people in dem days was—you know, dear. My ole mistress was good in a way and mean in a way, too. She had to be strict, because I had no mother, you see, dearie, and now I realize that she was just strict as any other mother should be with their children.

Well, it was just like this, when her children got done eating at the table, me and my brother went to that same table and ate. Yes, she was good to me in a way. She just made an effort to keep me from messing and mixing with everybody; and I'm still that way, do you know it? I don't mix with everybody right to this day. I just speak to 'em and pass 'em by.

My father belonged to another set of white people. When my mother was living, he come most every week to see her. Then after she died he come every two weeks to see me and my brother. Yes'm, they both been gone on for a long time, dear; and I am surely thankful to the Lord for preserving me. I really have been well-blessed, yes, indeedy, dear.

Well, dearie, I'll tell you—my father didn't take him away from me, 'cause I wouldn't let him. And my father didn't take me to him, neither. I just went to him, he, he, he. Yes, I remember when they took him away from us. They said the niggers was gitting ready for an uprising, and they took me and my brother way down in Cheatham County. No, I was born in Wilshire County; then my home was in Franklin, you see, but we went to Cheatham County and stayed about six months with the white folks.

'Course we wasn't far away from Pappy, but you know, far enough so he couldn't come to us, and we cried and cried, and when any of the white people went down that way they would see Pappy, and he would send messages to us by them. Yes, dear, they would tell us exactly what Pappy said.

Then we came back. I don't know how long that was before the War broke out, but we stayed with the same white people until the War ceasted. Now you know what happened then. They told us we were free, but of course we didn't know where to go nor nothing. The ole mistress asked me if I was glad we was free, and I, of course, child like, say yes I sure was; and my ole mistress sure did get mad at me; and she got mad at my brother, and said she was going to send him South, just like he wasn't free and equal. Well, dear, I didn't know nothin' about what they meant, but I just knew that he was going away from me. I didn't have sense enough to know much, but I knew that much. Well, he was going on a Monday morning—that was on a Saturday. So, on Saturday night I says to my brother, "In the morning you take them clothes you got on now on your arm, as you come through the house, when you go to do your work." You see, I had to get breakfast, and there wasn't nobody up that time in the morning but me and my brother. I told him, "I will be in the kitchen and you go down in the field and change your clothes, and go to the courthouse and get yourself a pass." And then I told him which way to go to get to Pappy's farm. I didn't know the names nor the directions, but I just said, "You get such-and-such a road and walk till you get to the white fence," and like that, you know. I knew right where Pappy lived. I told him after he got to a certain place anybody would tell him where Pappy lived.

Well, on Monday morning my old master got up and found my brother's work wasn't finished, and I was out there cooking breakfast and he come up and asked me, "Ain't Dave come to the house yet?" I said, "Naw, I ain't seen him," he, he. I told that story and I was scared, too. Well, he looked around a while and went on down in the yard, and then about an hour the men come through the back going to the field across the way to do the plowing, and he asked them about Dave. None of them had seen him. Well, I was so tickled that I couldn't hardly get breakfast, and then while they was talking a man—he was a friend of me and my brother—from the next farm, and he come up in the yard and I said, "Uncle Bob, Dave's gone." He said, "Damn good thing," and went on through the yard. Don't nobody know about my brother but me and Uncle Bob.

Well, that was on Monday; on Tuesday the old boss went to town and was asking around about Dave. Well, the ole boss' sister lived right on the edge of town and she told the ole marster that she saw him down by the courthouse early Monday mórning. Well then, by eleven o'clock, I figured he was at my father's. My pappy was sure glad to see him; and do you know, they never did know that I had something to do with that. Well, on a Saturday I had to churn, so I went to the well to get some water to wash the butter down from the sides of the churn. And just as I got to the well I saw a hat through the grape vines and somebody said, "Make haste," and I knew it was Pappy. I was the happiest child you ever heard of. Well, I hurried and got that water and went back to the house, and I asked if Pap had been there, and Ole Missus said, "No, I haven't seen him." Well, I knew he had done gone on by down to the old boss' father's plantation to ask his opinion about taking me to my brother. I didn't say a word; I just went on with my work. Well, he come on back—'course I learned all this later—he come on back and met my own boss man, and they talked and talked; and after a while they both come to the house. When Pappy come in he told me "howdy," and my old marster said, "Vergy, Dave's up yonder with yo' pappy, and your pappy come after you. Do you want to go?" Well, dear, I didn't know what to say, so I just hung my head and said, "I don't know." Well, poor Pap just burst out crying. He said, "I don't want to separate you and Dave till you do yourself." Well, dearie, I didn't know what to do. Pap up and told Mr. John, that was my ole boss, just how Miss Mangy, my missus, had mistreated my mother while she was living; and he told him that was why he had done a heap of things he had. Well, Mr. John said, "Jackson, I have noticed a heap of things you have done, but I didn't know why, then." Well, finally my ole mussus owned up to it; 'course you know, dear, she kinda had to with Pappy right there. So I went on back with Pappy; after I heard how she treated Mammy.

This was the way it happened. You know in those days we had a barrel, you know, and we had to pack water a long ways—that is the drinking water, the fresh water, you see. And in the winter time we had a big sled, something like that flower box there, and we hauled water up to the house in the barrel, on this sled. Well, Pappy used to do all them kinda things to help Mammy, you see. I remember one time the ole missus got mad at Mammy, and my boss was way out in the fields. My Mammy just kept weaving, and Ole

Missus just kept fussing, and you see Mammy didn't pay much 'tention to her, and you know how mad that makes anybody, so she sent me down in the field after the ole marster; so he could come and whip Mammy. I was a small child, of course, and I never did know what the trouble was one way or the other; but I do know then the ole marster, he told his ole lady that he didn't see nowhere to whip her; you see my mammy had carbuncles on her back, and the ole marster just bucked against his own wife and wouldn't hit Mammy a lick, you see. Now, that's why I say she was good and mean, too, in a way, you see.

Mammy finally died and left a little bit of a baby, and do you know? I had sense enough to be glad when the baby died, too. Poor little thing would have to go through the world like I have come; all alone with no mother. Yes sir, I was a child, but I was really glad when the baby died. It was a girl, too; you see that made it even worse. Yes, I couldn't see things like that like I can now, but I guess it was just that instinct or something that made me glad when the poor little thing passed away. Things went on and for a long time after the War, and after Mammy died, and finally they had to hire somebody else to help me with the work. They hired another woman; she had two daughters, and before long she died, too. And she had had an awful hard time in her life; and I was sorry on account of her girls. But you know, dear, even at that she was mean to us, thisaway: Now, she had them two children and she wouldn't give me and brother enough to eat; she would give it all to her children and make us take the leavings. Now in that way, you see, we got in the habit of picking up a biscuit or two and kinda stealing around, and we got one or two whippings about it, too.

Well, it went on that way, and look like the older I growed, little more sense I had. I just continued on that way until way after the War.

Then along a little while later the ole marster went for me to come back for a little visit; and one Saturday they came after me; this was before Ole Missus died, you see. Well, I dressed up and they come after me, and I went back to the old farm just as spry as you please. I was a big girl then, you know. "Well, now, how did you like your new home?" that's the first thing the ole missus said when I come. I was smart and young, you see, so I says, "Liked it well enough to go back." Whew, why Ole Missus nearly had a fit. "Why you ought to get fifty lashes for that," she said. There was an ole white woman working in the kitchen then, and she said, "I'll bet your ole Marse John do give you fifty lashes for that, good as he's done been to you." Oh yes, but I tell you this. When I was gitting ready to leave with Pappy, my white folks say, "Now, Vergy, don't go to stay away from us; you come back whenever you get ready." I come on over with another young girl that was spending the week on the next farm, to see her folks, and we was going back together.

Now as I was going to say, this is what ole Marse John say, "Why she can go back if she wants to; that's her father, and she wants to be with him. No, I ain't gonna give her no whipping 'cause she wants to be with her folks." Now you see that? Then he turned around and asked me all about how I was gitting along, and how was Pappy and my brother, n'everything; you see, nobody had done asked me about them. No sir, he said he wasn't going to separate us; now you think of that! Just goes to show the difference in people. Well, I stayed on that week and they was real nice to me, but all the time I was gitting my things together so that I could take all what I had left there back with me, for good, you see. Well, on Friday, Ole Missus went to town and came back with some real pretty material—they used to call it bird-eyed buff—to make the girl that was cooking for her a skirt out of and she showed it to me, and said she expect she would give me one if I was there much longer. You see, dear, trying to git me to stay. I didn't say nothing but I knew what she was up to, and I knew just as well that I was going back to Pappy. Yes, I thought to myself, they ain't enticing me, 'cause I am going to Daddy.

I got all my things and I remember I had a pretty skirt with five widths in it, and I took and tied all my things up in it and put the bundle on the top of my head, and me and that girl walked seven miles into the country, and got there long before night, too. I stayed with Pappy 'til Christmas and then I went back to the white folks again, and got myself some gifts, he, he, he. That was the last time I saw Ole Missus alive, and she give me some old sorghum molasses to make myself some molasses candy; my ole marster give me two dollars, and I spent one dollar on myself and give the other one to Pappy.

Well, I stayed with my father, and then I married and come up here; but before, I was up here and went into that old Noel school what used to be right over yonder before it was finished. My teacher was a Mr. Atchison, and then there was Miss Molly Tatler, and another white man teacher. I was in the second grade and I married and went across to Jefferson Street one pretty moonshiny night to live with my husband. I ain't forgotten a bit of it.

Then, dear, when I was getting ready to become a mother I went back to the white folks. Then I come back here and had my first child, and all my ole white folks come around to see it, and I remember I held the baby out of an upstairs window so they could look at it, and then I never seen any of them no more until I had my second child; then I went back down there in the country and stayed all night with the white folks.

My ole marster had done been married again, and the last time I went to see them, the new wife died the same week. Then later on, 'bout two or three years later, I went out there and stayed all day with the white girl, and then I sent and got my age; that is how it come me to know exactly how old I am.

That is my old marster's brother what lives out here on Kayne Avenue, you know he runs a coal yard, Mark F. Andrews. Here sometime back I heard that my old boss died several years ago out there at Dolchy Hospital.

Well, I made profession in Christ after I come to Nashville and was married. It was just this a-way. I think like this—seeking for religion is just like anything else; that is, being converted into the grace of the Lord you just got to pray hard, that's all. You can't give up wordly things all at once; it's practically impossible. You just have to live so to speak with man in the hand and God in the heart, don't you dear? You can't change and do that right off, though. You got to have something revealed to you through your soul, you see. You got to push back everything and show that you are really in earnest; dear, you got to give up worldly things, ain't you? You understand, don't you dear: Why, after the Lord converted me, I was a different woman.

I went to church right down yonder on Ninth Avenue. I made a full surrender to the Almighty that night. I remember they were singing, "Why should we wish to die when the Lord God has set us free?" Well, honey, my tongue just cleaved to the roof of my mouth for a while and I got to the place where I couldn't mutter a word. I couldn't have finished that song for the life of me. I wasn't saying nothing, dear, but my heart was singing; the spirit of the Lord was on me. I felt just as light as a feather. I really praised His name that night, I tell you.

Why, dear, even up to the time my last child was born I was a sinner. I prayed and prayed but seem like I just couldn't see and feel that new light in my soul. My baby had done been born and had already done died, and I was sitting here in this very chair one day and just thinking. And I saw my baby just naked like it was when it was born, just as plain as I see you right now; yessir, and that baby was dead. I look down and saw that little naked baby in my lap. The Lord come and put my baby in my lap and I heard him say just as plain as day, "'Cept you come as this little child, you can in nowise enter the kingdom of heaven." Dear, I seen it just as plain as I see you, I tell you. Yessir, that's the truth if I die today.

Then I remember when my oldest daughter died; I was sitting right here sewing on a Saturday afternoon. And I saw her just as plain; she had on one of my old bonnets. Yes, my oldest daughter died, and she was sick—you see, she went to Fisk, too. She came to me over this shoulder and said to me just as plain—you see, she always had a hand for cleaning up and moving things around, and lots of times she has come and told me she was going to move this and that, and I always said it was all right with me. Well, I just jumped up and threw my sewing down, and I said, "Lord, my child ain't dead." Yessir, I sho' saw her just like flesh and blood.

Yes, dear, only those that gone through it know how it is to lose your child, I tell you. Every day for days and weeks, I worried something awful after she went. Lord, dear, you don't know how it worried me. Then after that, seem like the Lord just moved away all my troubles. I felt reconciled, and something just said to me—"The Lord giveth and the Lord taketh away." Yes'm, I've lost two husbands and three children. There is nobody but me and my other daughter what lives here now.

Dear, always be careful about your teeth; don't never have no signs about you when you is having your teeth worked on. No, don't never have a sign near your body 'cause you will go blind or something like that. You ought to have an almanac or something so you can tell. That's one sign I am telling you that I know about sure. Don't you never let no doctor or dentist fool you up to have your teeth fixed at the wrong time.

Well, this is right good for the toothache. Mix up some coal oil and camphor gum and a little table salt, and saturate a little piece of cotton with this and just hold it to your gums, you see. You know Crawford Harwell, don't you. Why, I been knowing him all my life. He says I'm the hardest customer he ever had. I tell him when he come around here, don't you come practicing on me; what's the matter with me? Why that's what I called you for, he, he.

Yes, I remember about the time of the lynching. I had started to market that day; and I got up here somewhere and they told me somebody was about to start a riot 'cause they was killing a man, and I just turned right around and come right back home. That's all I know about it.

I do remember when they hung a man up here at the jail. And he walked out just as unconcerned and stood up on his own coffin, with a cigar in his mouth and his cap tilted back on his head. You know, they used to hang 'em in the jail yard. He told them they were doing wrong, and there was sure something going to happen to them, and sho' nuff it did. When they was taking his coffin to the cemetery the car turned over and one man got his leg broke clean off; and if I remember rightly one man got killed outright. Well, dear, he was just like a heap of other young fool men, he was fooling around with the "po' white trash," and he had been putting up with this old white woman. And you know, it was the queerest thing, the very morning that he was to be hung, this old white hussy come to the jail and said he was innocent.

Dear, don't you never let no white man mess with you, do you hear me: I don't want to see my color mess with them. And I tell you another thing, when the white folks steps in this house, especially the men, I demand respect. I always says, "Won't you rest your hat?" Yessir, just as I feel.

Just like once I was on the street car, and you see my white people that I work for had give me a book to ride on, because I had to come home every Sunday evening to see about my girls. I got on the car, and handed the conductor my book, and he just looked at me kinda mean, and said, "Pay your fare." I kept handing him the book; he kept saying "Pay your fare." He let me go on by to my seat, 'cause I wasn't studying about paying my fare after I had handed him the book. He come on up to the seat I was in and said, "If you don't pay your fare, I'm going to put you off this car," and I said, "Just put me off, put me off, and see if I don't git you put off, too." I turned round to a man what was sitting next to me, and asked him, "What's the matter with this book?" then I asked the coductor, "What's the matter with that book?" And he just kept saying, "Pay your fare." Then some poor old colored man said, "Here lady, here's a nickel for your fare;" you see he was scared, 'fraid the man would put me off, but I wasn't.

Well, I come on home, and when I got back if I didn't tell them white people! Honey, I sure told them all about it, and I asked them "What you got written on that book, nigger or something?" And they sure had that conductor put off.

Didn't Know Nothing, Never Thought of Nothing but Slavery

Mrs. Chapman: I was taken away from my mother when I was seven years old. That was in Hardeman County. I was brought here to Trenton by old man North. He was my guardian. I belonged to a girl but she wasn't old enough and she had to have a guardian for me. I was hired out to make money for that child. I lived about a mile and a half from town. I never was mistreated. They got $100 a year for me and they had to pay my doctor's bill and feed and clothe me. I was the only slave this girl had. After her father died her mother married again and went to Mississippi. They said the Mississippi law allowed the husband to have the wife's property, so I was willed to this child and the husband took my mother. That's how come we was separated. This man what willed me to this girl was name Marshall. Colored people went in the name of their owner then. My father been dead about fifty years. I was hired out to nurse. Some of them had slaves and some didn't. When freedom come I went away for a long time and I come back and been here ever since. I went to Murfreesboro with some white folks and they brought me back here. When I was sick when I was little they would make some kind of tea and put me to bed.

Ben Thomas and his wife and sister was free people and Miss Tenny Smith never was a slave and her sister Ora neither. There was several people round here that was free. After the girl that I belonged to got grown she got married and went somewhere on the Tennessee River. She died. I have white people out in California. Mr. North, my guardian lives in California. I hear from them every year nearly.

I remember once I was hired out and I was trying to say my alphabets backward and forward by memory. I just cried because I couldn't say them backwards by memory. I don't know how I got that book, but I never did learn to say them by memory backwards, but I could say them forward. I was ten years old when the War broke out.

Mr. Chapman: I couldn't tell exactly my age. My fust owner was Luke Thomas; he lived down there between Hiko and McKenzie. I stayed there until he sold me. I worked in the tobacco factory when I was a boy. I have woke up a many morning early and old bread would be laying on the ground and I would pick it up and eat it, and thought it was good. I have always heard that I was taken away from my mother when I was a baby, but I do remember my brother. When we was sold to Chapman, master told him not to separate us 'cause we was brothers, and if he ever wanted to get rid of us to send us to Memphis and he would take us back. They coulda sold me a dozen times, but they couldn't separate us so I wasn't sold. Me and my brother was in the trading yard before the Civil War. We stayed in there three or four weeks. They would fix us all up and carry us in a great big old room and circle us all around every morning and every evening. They would have us up in the show room to show us to the people. They would hit us in the breast to see if we was strong and sound. Monkeys would play with us and see if any boogies was in our heads. They would do pretty well if they found any, but if they didn't they would slap us. They had the monkeys there to keep our heads clean. They made us dance and made us take exercise all the time we was there.

They would give us molasses and bread to eat, and a little meat. We slept in little bunks that was made up side the wall. We didn't know nothing else but slavery—never thought of nothing else. I just know I belonged to the man who provided for me and I had to take whatever he give me.

There was some young ones and some old ones in that trading yard. They had a big time, too. Some of them had fiddles and some banjoes, and they would fiddle and dance. The water that we drunk there was just as black as black could be, but it was as cold as ice. In slavery time they had us in quarters. There was lots of little houses all out from the big house. Luke Thomas was a pretty rough man, but all of them was good to me because they just let me have my way. I always done my work. I was bound out since freedom to a man name Isaac Gritholm. Bound me out when I was 15 years old, and I was to stay till I was twenty-one years old. I was bound out by the Bureau. All orphan children had to be bound out so they give me my choice of two men who wanted me. I went to Isaac, but I seen I wasn't gonna learn nothing so I quit and went on the other side of town and hired out to another fellow. Then I moved back to Trenton. I got $125 a year. Next I hired out to a colored man named William Elder.

My master was pretty good to me, but sometimes he would whip me. I was pretty rough myself. He whipped me a heap of times but it was mostly for fighting. One day he whipped me for running children with snakes. He whipped me one day for fighting a white boy. The white boy had whipped me and stomped me, too, but he didn't see that. Finally, one day that boy got after me again, and I liked to killed him. He hired me out after that to old Bill Cook. I just farmed. I got along well there, too. He give me two suits of clothes, two blankets. I went home every Christmas by myself. One time they had a beef killed for General Forrest's regiment, but somehow or other Forrest didn't get there to eat that meat and it begin to spoil, and they was feeding the slaves that then. I couldn't stomach it, and one day I told marster that I had to quit work 'cause I was starving to death and that I might as well die one way as the other. He asked me what was the matter, that the other slaves was eating all right. I told him that I couldn't stand that meat that I just couldn't stomach it. He carried me to the house and fed me from their table. They tried to get me to tell what the colored folks was doing. They asked me if I see any of them stealing. They give me a dime, quarter and anything to tell on them, but I told them I didn't see them stealing. I had though, and I would eat as much as any of them of anything they had stole. Old Chapman shot one man while I was there with him. John run old man Chapman, for some of the hands told him that Chapman had been after his wife, and John got after him about it. Old Chapman had a gun and John tried to take it away from him and old Chapman shot him in the arm. John taken after Chapman and fell down. Dr. West was the man that doctored on him. He worked on until he and old Chapman had another round. He taken his wife and went to Mississippi, and carried John's wife, too. John kept on disputing with master and master tapped him over the head with his walking cane. Some of the black folks would tell him everything. John was a great big double-jointed man. He had a boy name Henry. We wore great long shirts until we was great big boys. We went to the white folks church with the white people sometimes. They had camp meetings. Whenever the preacher come to the house master would call us up to the house, and the preacher would tell us, "Obey your mistress, be good servants, pray to the Lord not to let the slaves gain they freedom, and that the Yankees won't gain the victory."

They used to have great long knives to cut the Yankees' heads off. I remember the time in the War when there was 350 "homemade Yankees." There was a lot of southern people that fought against the South. A heap of colored people would run away to the Yankees; after they had so many they got them up a company of soldiers. See masters was 'fraid to meet their slaves after freedom 'cause some of them was so mean they was 'fraid they would kill them. The colored people just layed out in the woods all the time if they didn't want to stay at home and didn't want to work. Old Wheeler brought a big pack of hounds to hunt one of his hands, and all the time he was up in the loft. Every night he would come up there and some of the other hands would carry him something to eat. Some of them just wouldn't take a whipping for nothing. I have seen some overseers so cruel. They would slap the slaves and whip them on their naked hide and make blisters on them, and then take a cowhide and whip them. Whenever a darkey got beside himself they would take him down to Louisiana, Mississippi and Georgia. This fellow John Jack wouldn't take a whipping. They was just naturally afraid of him. He was a big stout man.

Me and my brother stayed here a long time, then we decided to go away, and we went to Kansas City, Missouri. He stayed there and died there.

They used to have big corn shuckings, and they had one man who used to holler. A heap of slaves would be invited to come from all around to help shuck the corn. You had a pass to stay so long, and when that pass run out the paddie rollers would come and whip you if you stayed over that time.

After the corn would all be shucked, four men would make a pack saddle and pick up the white man and carry him all around the barn singing:

> Lie low, nigger, lie low
> Bill Hill whoop and the nigger would holler
> Lie low, nigger, lie low.

One night the niggers was going home and heard the paddie rollers coming along way down the road, and they put up a grape vine all across the road and of course they was running fast, and it throwed them every way across the road. By that time all the niggers had run and got out of the way, and you never would know who done it. Some of them niggers was pretty smart, I tell you.

Marster was a regular drunkard. He put my head in the saplings and made me chew tobacco, and mistress got after him about it once. One time he made me drunk, and he come home drunk hisself, and that settled it for that night. She left him and went home. But he went up there after her.

One night the Yankees was travelling all night long and was stealing everything in sight. They stole horses, and they tried to steal the mule but every man that got up on him the old mule would throw him. That mule throwed up to 15 men and not a one could stay on him. One of the soldiers said, "I'm a great mind to shoot him." The captain said, "Don't shoot him, he freed himself." They all said that mule sho' was a good rebel mule. You never saw a gentler looking mule, but he wouldn't let a one stay on his back.

Milton made up a song once, and was singing it and a man heard him singing it one day and asked him where he got that song, and he told him that he just made it up. He said all of that is in the Bible, and he made him sing it for him:

> Shout brother He never said a mumbling word,
> They took my blessed Jesus and taken him to the woods
> And they made him hew out his own dear cross and he wagged up Calvary.
>
> Shout brother He never said a mumbling word.
>
> They taken my blessed Jesus and whipped him up the hill
> With a knotty whip and a raggedy thorn and He never said a mumbling word.
>
> Shout brother he never said a mumbling word.
>
> Two angels come from heaven and brought that mighty loud
> As the heaven door parted, the Israelites squalled and
> The watchmen all fell dead, and the watchmen all fell dead.
>
> Shout brother He never said a mumbling word.
>
> Go tell Mary and Martha the Savior has risen
> Has risen from the dead and will live forever more
> And won't have to die no more and won't have to die no more.
>
> Shout brother, etc.

Massa's Slave Son

I'm 'bout played out now. Yes, I like to look at the ladies sometimes. I don't get out much now. Last night was a cold night, wasn't it?

I was a young man when the stars fell; and you know that was a long time ago. I seen them; they just fell and went out before they hit the ground. How come me to see it, we had just killed hogs and had the meat hanging up on poles and I had to watch it all night. I had a fire out there, you know. It scared a lot of them, but it didn't do no good. Somebody started blowing the horn what you call the dogs with, and they started hollering that Gabriel was blowing his trumpet. I never was a kind of man to worry about any one thing.

I was born right over yonder where Purdy had his school, right over there back of Jubilee Hall. It was woods around here then. My marster's oldest son was my father. My marster never was very mean to me. He knocked me around once. I was driving the calves home, and I tied a can around their necks and made them holler. He whipped me about that. My mother cooked, washed and do things like that around the house. Mistress uster ask me what that was I had on my head and I would tell her, "hair," and she said, "No that ain't hair, that's wool." They wan't mean to none of the slaves. He didn't have but 'bout ten or fifteen slaves. They lived in different little cabins around the yard. He didn't have no overseers. Way after while he had a overseer.

I uster drive my mistress to town, after freedom, and she give me a home back over there back of Meharry.

I uster live mighty bad sometimes—dance, drink whiskey, all night long. I could drink a pint of whiskey at a time. I uster play a fiddle for dance. Sometimes I would play from Saturday night to Sunday morning. They danced 'bout like they do now. They was "wild cats," I tell you. The slaves would get the 4th of July and part day on Saturday, and holidays like that.

I expect I am the oldest man in Nashville. Nearest we can come to making out my age, I am 'bout 120 years old. (A son says 110.) I don't know it exactly 'cause when the War broke out they lost the Bible.

I didn't do much when I was a boy; just played around all the time and pull a little grass out of the pavement. I had a easy time compared to some. Mother didn't have a husband till after the War. She stayed right in the house with the white folks. My wife had good folks, too.

I was out to Fort Negley, and they come and carried me to jail; and I stayed there eight weeks—that's how come I didn't have to go to war. My mother come there and brought me some clothes and something to eat, and the next day they come and carried me home. My mother didn't know where I was at first. I looked like a skallin (skeleton) when I first come out, I was so poor. I was weak and half starved,too. Then it would a took me from now till night to walk to Jubilee Hall. (His owners contrived this means of preventing his running away to the Yankees.)

I don't like slavery nohow. They believe in tramping you like a dog. They used to take a child out and sling it up against a tree and sling its brains out. I never did see that, but my uncle coming from Virginia saw it. They used to stand slaves backwards to the river and shoot them off in the river. (This was during the War). Just meanness, that's all. They did every kind of thing. They used to stand slaves up on a platform down on the public square, and sell them like they was dogs or horses—women and men. It was awful.

We used to raise oats, corn and things like that. Get up at daybreak, went out to feed the stock and come in, eat breakfast, and then out to the field. We used to have hog jowl, cabbage, potatoes and different things like that to eat. Sometimes we would have it for breakfast and dinner, too. Mother worked for them a good while after the War. I didn't have sense enough to feel anyway about it. All I cared about was fiddling and dancing. It was "come day, go day, God send Sunday" with me.

In the summer time we would go around half naked. We didn't wear nothing but one piece—a shirt that come down below your knees. After freedom I used to go hunting a whole lot. Sometimes I would kill fifty rabbits. I wore them long boots, and sometimes I would be bare footed. Do you know Miss Mary Spence? She is a good lady. I go by to see her sometimes now. (He explained that he sold his rabbits sometimes.)

I waited on my marster till he died. He took sick in Arkansas. He inhaled the scent of his brother who was dead, and he took sick and died. That was after freedom. A man killed his brother. They tried to press him in the Rebel army. He told them he wouldn't go and leave his wife and chillen; and they shot him down. It was awful to try to make a man leave his wife and family to go to the army. It's awful to think of slavery anyhow.

I pretended to profess religion one time. I don't hardly know what to think about religion. They say God killed the just and unjust; I don't understand that part of it. It looks hard to think that if you ain't done nothing in the world you be punished just like the wicked. Plenty folks went crazy trying to get that thing straightened out. (The son says his father is an atheist, and never did believe in the Bible or God.)

They used to have corn shuckings and dances all night. It was generally on Saturday night. Oh, no, you couldn't think of going to the white folks' church. Niggers had their own churches, and white folks had theirs. I done wore myself out now; I ain't no count for nothing. I used to work up to Fisk until a few years ago. I did all the carpentry work up there. The last job I worked on was the new Publishing House down town.

There was some free Negroes; nobody bothered them if they had some white man to stand for them. Some of them was carpenters, dig cisterns, and things like that. They would go from one place to another working, sometimes.

"Once a man, twice a child," that part of the Bible is certainly true. I know that to be a fact.

I had straight hair, and my mistress would say, "Don't say hair, say wool." They wouldn't let her mistreat me on account of conditions. (In answer to question of mistress' mistreating him because of kinship, the son says she used to pull out handfuls of his father's hair at times.) My wife's people was good to her, too. She belonged to the Hadleys. We are all related. The Hadleys and Hardings are all kin. I have a cousin, Margie Harding, here, who stays at the Tulane Hotel now. She don't never come out here, though. (Son: I see her—Miss Harding—up town all the time. She stops and talks to me, and always asks me about papa.) (This is the Hadley family who lived in the Hadley Park house. Colonel Hadley here belonged to them.)

After my old marster died old mistress give me an acre of ground for waiting on her. (The son says it was five or six lots.)

One of the old songs we used to sing was:

> Ring a ring a rineo
> Ain't seen a nigger in a mile or more
> You take Sal and I take Sue,
> Ain't no difference 'tween the two.

I used to sing and play "Old Black Joe" a whole lot, too. I don't have no pains much, no headaches, and my appetite is good. (Son: He keeps note on everything you do, too. I have a brother, and he watches every move he makes. You can't put nothing over on him.)

Out at Hillsman's iron works they have shot niggers and chopped their heads off, and stick their heads on poles and throw their bodies in the river. They did everything they could think of. (During a period of fear of slave insurrections.)

I was riding on a street car long after freedom and I passed the cemetery where my father was buried. I started cussing—"Let me get off this damn car and go see where my God damn father is buried, so I can spit on his grave, a God damn son-of-a-bitch." I got no mercy on nobody who bring up their children like dogs. How could any father treat their child like that? Bring them up to be ignorant like they did us. If I had my way with them all I would like to have is a chopping block and chop every one of their heads off. Of course I don't hate them that is good. There are some good white folks. Mighty few, though. Old General Jackson said before he would see niggers free he would build a house nine miles long and put them in it, and burn everyone of them up. A dirty old rascal; now he is dead and gone.

When Ben Brown was hung they carried him out to Brown's Creek to hang him. All at once there was a roaring in the water, and there was lightning, and the horses started running away from folks; and some of them got their legs broke. It sounded just like a storm way off somewhere. I was looking right in his mouth. He walked right out to the hanging ground, smoking a cigar.

They lynched Eph Grizzard about a white woman. I used to go 'round some myself, but I ain't going to say much about that. I've done a little of everything, I can tell you that.

"Knew Lincoln's Cousin"

Well, did you hear me at the Chapel there? I preached that night, the first Sunday night in January. I preached at church there, and went right over from there to Chapel, and I like to have been too late, but when I got there, and had given them a little history relative to the emancipation, they only give me five minutes. Well, I took more than that, and when I got through they patted me back. I didn't go back. The half has never been told. Well, I came back and preached a funeral and went out to the cemetery, and I came back home and went right into "flu" and then into kidney trouble and to bladder and indigestion; kind of a catarrh of the stomach. I can't speak any more because of my teeth; they are sharp and catch my tongue.

I am 88 years old, born March 15, 1843. I am a preacher and a tinner. I was sold four times in my life. First time by my half-brother, and he carried me away from Springfield when I was 7 years old, and when I had come to the age of 12, my half-brother sold me. I was mighty near like Joseph, and my own half-brother sold me. His father and my father and Abe Lincoln was first cousins.

So I was sold four times in Osceola, Missouri. I was sold first time by my half-brother to John Wesley, and second time I was sold to Woods in Osceola. Third time I was sold to Dr. Whitson in Osceola. Dr. Whitson lived at Tullahoma, Tennessee. He bought ten of us in that drove. Brought—if I am talking too fast stop me. I preached 56 years. I am on a pension now. I have been superannuated. Dr. Whitson brought us, from that low, from Osceola to Tennessee, to Tullahoma, Tennessee, in 1860, prior to '61 the beginning of the Civil War. Dr. Whitson started with those 10 to Mississippi to sell when he got to Stephenson, Alabama. He met Ben Harris coming from his farm in Mississippi. Harris met Dr. Whitson, and Harris bought all ten of us, and brought us back to Nashville and my finish of slavery. I was partially reared out here on 4th Avenue. It was known as Nolensville, and I stayed there until '64. In '65 I run away and come to the Yankees. I come here during the Civil War, worked for the Government one month.

A white man can't give the history of the Negro. When I was in Osceola, the man Woods bought me, he carried me to Texas. He had a big farm and he went to Mississippi to his big farm. I suppose he had about 100 Negroes on that farm, and he had a colored woman as foreman or the mistress. In other words, on the farm I left at Osceola, when I got down there, I remember the words just like as if yesterday, "Mary, how do you like the little yeller hellion?" And she said, "He won't do down here, he can't pick cotton, his fingers are too short." He carried the others on that journey. The men were chained.

We had to travel a good deal of the distance on foot, and they travelled 40 and 50 miles on foot. The women, they put them in the wagon and carried them, but the men had to walk. I did go into the sale house where they was, and you could see the women crying about their babies and children they had left. Then they brought us back to Osceola again, and when Dr. Whitson bought us the train had just got into Osceola, and he brought us all to the Ohio River, and put us on a boat, and we travelled two days and two nights, and the second night we were travelling the Ohio River and it was very cold, and froze. The fog was heavy and the water would settle on trees all on the bank. You could see long strips of ice on the trees, just hanging off. We came to Louisville, and the fog was so heavy we had to light up. The fog grew heavier, and we had to stop at Louisville, and the Ohio River frez, and we had to stay for three weeks in Louisville. The whole Ohio River frez, and you could drive over to Jefferson City, which was a free state. While we were there, there was snow, though, on that ice, and the Ohio River riz and the snow melted and made the river run faster. The drifts was about 10 or 12 feet. We found we couldn't get from there—the railroad was running from Louisville, and Dr. Whitson brought us on, on the train, and carried us on to Tullahoma, way to Chattanooga. We stayed all the winter and next spring he packed us up and started the crop, and he took us from there and sold us in Mississippi, to Harris.

We find that the suffering from slavery was plenty bad. Some of us had good owners and some of us had bad. The meanest of all my owners was the last one. Of course I cannot complain much, I was only a boy like, but I knew enough to understand the pressure of slavery, and what the colored went through.

In 1889 I was elected as teacher in the Tennessee Teachers College, to teach electricity. In 1890 I found my mother; and I was gone from her 33 years before I knew anything about her. I wrote letters of inquiry until I found about her. She was no further than Springfield, Kentucky. I went to get her, and she wanted to come, but she belonged to the Catholic Church, and they wouldn't let me have her. She was 73 years old then, and earning wages. They drove me out of there when they found I was a Protestant. It soon spread all over Springfield about what I said and what I did, that I come after my mother and I was a Protestant, and she was a Catholic and she belonged to them; and I never saw my mother again. She died about two years after.

Then I came back home and taught at the Technical School, at tinning and carpentering. At the same time I grovelled with English and struggled with a little science along with that. I learned tinning 'reckly after I came from the Government Service Guarantee. You have heard of Reverend Moore from Fisk University? His father was a tinner from the old school; and when he came out he wanted to learn the trade, and he went to his father and took me with him. I was a grown man then, and arranged myself to learn the trade. I think there was five of us in there learning the trade, and when I came out I was the finest workman of the five. That's when they made all fine tin work by hand, and was no press work. It was all made by hand. At the same time there was about 10 or 12 old workmen, tinmen, working before the War. I served my time with Mr. Moore and then went to Biddleston, for $5.00 a week; and from there I went to $9.00 a week, and wasn't very long before I went to $12.00 a week. I worked at Central Training College. Taught there 8 years, and in that 8 years I issued 5 diplomas. One young man, first one, went out as a Kentuckian. He went out with his diploma. Second one was in Texas; third in Virginia; fourth in Alabama (Montgomery); the fifth one, when he got his diploma, went to Tuskegee to finish himself in other technical work. The same time I was recommended to Tuskegee to teach in the department. Corresponding with Booker T, the man who was in charge of the tinning department was going to quit. He got tired. And after I had sent my recommendation to Booker Washington; if the man had quit I would have had that place, but he didn't quit. The man who had the diploma went down there and stayed 10 years, and learned another trade. So I managed to time the Centennial. This year I was teaching there and I got to Dr. Braddon, to let me make some work for exhibit, and I exhibited hand-made work, and in the hand-made work I got the medal. There was 42 white firms, but they exhibited press work, and I presented there on exhibition hand-work. I got the medal—hand-made work. We had some trouble to get it. The County sent to New York and an old Frenchman was there, and said, "There is the work that is necessary to get the premium. That other that you have isn't hand medal work, it is press work," so I got the medal.

When the Walden building got burned down, the medal was burned. That is when several girls lost their lives. Mrs. Walden, she gave $500 to build that building for her. When Dr. Braddon died they changed that from Central Tennessee College to Walden College; so that is the way they get the Walden.

Now I were here when every school, Negro school, was organized. I know when every one was organized. The first school for colored, McKeeves School. Do you know where Dr. Roman lives? The first school was on that ground. Dr. McKeeve followed the army and then after the War he founded the school. At the close of the War General Fisk bought the Barracks (where the colored library is). If you notice back of the building you will see some frame buildings that was barracks after the war. Where the library is built, that is where the school was. That's why I call that old Fisk University. Dr. White organized the Fisk Jubilee Singers, and that time I was at McKeeves School. I went to school for three weeks, and in the day I was working with Mr. Moore. They organized the Jubilee Singers, and I was in the first crowd. Dr. White took a good deal of pains with me 'cause I had such a good voice. The first $500 that was paid in the building of Jubilee Hall we made it singing round town and places, and we paid it in that. After that Mr. Moore said they thought it would be best for me to learn the trade, 'cause I would break down in the singing troupe, and would not have any trade. Dr. White didn't want to give me up, but I thought it was better, after I was a motherless boy, that I get a trade; so I took up the trade.

Right where the Jubilee Hall stands was Fort Gillam. You remember on the campus, front of Jubilee was an old rock. That is why those stones are there. The faculty ought to have those stones painted and labeled. They tore down those stones when they went to build Jubilee Hall.

Roger Williams was organized right down on Hampton Street, between 12th and 11th, in a big government building. When they got too numerous for that building they moved to another building where there is now a big farm, and they repaired that old building, and that put the school there. They bought a place on Hillsboro Pike, right opposite of Vanderbilt, and built a large building there. It got burned down for some reason, and the white folks would not let them build it back; and they had to go out where they are now.

I got a strong whipping my mother gave me when I was 6 years old, in Kentucky. My mother was picking geese. She only had two boys. She had the geese in a flax house. You know how a flax house is built? Well, you go in, and over you there were some logs what you laid the flax on to dry. You cut the flax and lay it up on the logs and the stems rotted; then you would gin it and get the stems out, and use the bark and get stout cords. My brother and I got to playing with the geese. One goose flew up and went out between the logs through the flax, and when that goose stopped he was way up the Cane River, a mile and a half from home; and my mother whipped me and my brother, and we had to find the goose. We went and got that goose and brought it in, too. It wasn't a hard job because the other geese would call. I remember that just like yesterday.

When I was 7 years old my brother married, in Springfield. They had buggies with seats on the rear. Cullud had to ride on the seats on the buggies. When we got to Bowling Green, I got my first pair of pants. He bought me in Bowling Green. When we got to Bowling Green we got on the train and rode as far as we could. When we got to Osceola City—it is known now as Kansas City—Missouri—we got there and when we got there the country wasn't settled up, and we went out and built log cabins and stayed there. I saw the first train that came to Osceola. They laid the railroad, but it was on poles right across the road like ties are now, and the train run on that there. It was built on a prairie, and you could see the reflection of it like the sun shining on it twelve miles away, because when we saw it coming it would be four hours from when we saw it before the train got into Osceola. The station was built in Osceola out of punching. They used to just scale up logs and the punching was the smooth side of the logs. That's what they made the buildings of in that new country. The roads they had through the new country was made out of punching, called plank roads. You could stand on a clear night and hear horses' feet 10 miles away. No pikes then of dirt; roads were made with punching because on a prairie the dirt was soft and would sink. The water would come to a place in the road deep. The Missouri river is cut through the land. I have seen water in those channels 10 and 12 feet deep.

It is very seldom you can get a colored person to tell you any thing about slavery. The white folks ain't gonna tell you. Women wasn't anything but cattle.

No'm. Yes'm, told him when he left, if he ever got out of money not to sell me; but I got about 12 years old, and he sold me to pay his debts.

Now, you know that I was a first cousin to Abe Lincoln —him and my father was first cousins. In January 1890 I went to see my mother. My folks was a Mudd. My father was a Mudd. Abe Lincoln and him was brother and sister's children. My brother was on the cullud side, carried me to see the old folks; and when I was there I saw a picture on the wall and I said, "That picture looks mighty like Abe Lincoln." And the old woman there looked like she had worn out six or seven bodies with the same face, and said that it ought to because it was Abe Mudd, and they were first cousins. And I went to my mother and I asked her who was my father, and she told me. There was a doctor in Kansas City, and his name was H. G. Mudd, and I asked where was my mother, and they directed me to him. He said, "Well, Charlie, do you know who your father was?" I said, "No, but my mother knows." He said, "I think your father was the killer Mr. Jones had." We was built just alike. When I did come to the place where my mother worked the white woman said, "That must be Aunt Maria's lost boy." And when I came up there they said, "I thought you was Aunt Maria's lost son; you and Kit Mudd walked alike; and I thought you was." When I went to the old mistress' house I had a half-sister, and she was pretty and her hair was as curly as mine was, and she sat and looked at me, and there sat a white brother of mine; and she looked at me, and she looked at me till she got shame and left, and she never did come back. Our hair was just alike, mine was black and curly then. Old Mrs. Mudd looked at me just as hard. I never did go to see Dr. H. G. Mudd to tell him who my father was.

(Family relationships.) I don't know. You know I left when I was 7 years old. I don't know how many there was. She was the mother of 16 children, but there wasn't but two of them when I left. She had 16 children and only 3 girls. The oldest one who lived was six years and the others died when they were babies. Some of them was my father's children. I heard from him when I was in Kansas City, in the drug business, and then when I went after my mother, the old lady tole me he was in the drug business. He was dead then; but he had been. I left him with my mother. He went in the army. He went in the Civil War. But mother never got anything from them. I was told that he was in the Kentucky Cavalry, on the Federal side.

I just took that name myself, 'cause I had so many other names. I was working with Mr. Moore; my last owner was Mr. Harris, and all that lived there was Harris' cullud, and when they left they changed their name. Gib Taylor, do you know him? Now his father and I b'longed to the same white folks, but he went in the name of Taylor. Gib's father's name was Bedford Taylor. He was a preacher, too, but he didn't have the education Gib's got.

Now some of them treated you fairly well, and some of them treated you like brutes. Now while I was with Wesley Mudd they treated me nice, but Mudd, my brother, didn't treat me so nice. I don't know, if the Lord had not been for me I would not have been alive. I know in Osceola the varmints were very bad. The wolves and panthers and bears—very bad, and other varmints. I remember one night a coon got after the chickens in the hen house, along between midnight and day, and it was dangerous to go out. He made me get up out of bed, go down in a thicket distance from here to Jackson Street. The dogs run the coon up the tree. Of course it was in the summer time, and I had to go and keep that coon up in the tree; the dogs and I, till he got up and killed the coon. Then shortly after I had treed the coon up came a bear, and I ran to the house. The dogs gave out and the coon tried to come down; and I kept him up; and then he came down and shot him then. That country was full of varmints —just full. A man could go out and kill a dozen squirrels, they was that thick. Pigeons were thick, too, thicker than hens and chickens. They would come over at night, and they would darken the sun, there would be so many. Wild ducks were numerous; wild ducks came in droves.

He had only one. I don't know whether he hardly had that one; I was sold. The Woods treated me well. He thrashed me or whipped me you know, of course. I was a fighter; they would whip me. The last one I had was the worst one I had. He would kill you. I have had him tie me up to a tree and whip me. He couldn't whip me unless I was tied, and I had to let him tie me, 'cause he had a gun. Didn't anybody whip me on the place but the woman, Mrs. Harris, Granny and Miss Sylvia —she was most as white as the mistress, and Gib Taylor's grandmother would thrash me when I would whip her son. I used to steal sometimes —sugar and coffee. I was the house boy and had to clean up the pantry storeroom. I would cut all the meats up for them to eat. They ate ham. The Negroes' meat was side and occasionally they would give us the shoulder meat. But ham was white folks' meat, and if you got any you would have to steal it; and I was good at that. They would put the hams up in the upper part of the pantry, and there was a hole up there about the size of a brick, and I would cut meat and cut ham and put them through this hole to Gib Taylor's grandmother. Well they'd whip me, and they'd wear me out; and I would get into trouble with men that hire me. I would do some devilment and knock someone in the head. They would tie me up and whip me; the squire and constable. They'd hire me out, and I would have a battle. I never will forget, they hired me to a man and I knocked him in the head, and the squire came and got me and took off my clothes, and they hit me two or three licks, and my young mistress heard me and came out. I b'longed to her; I was her stock of Negroes. I raised so much cain that she came out and told the squire to turn me loose and don't hit me another lick or she would kill him, and she showed him her gun. They said, "Well, we are within the law." She said, "I don't care nothing about the law, you better not hit him." And they turned me loose. It wasn't long before time that the War broke out.

And right where Vanderbilt is, Old Mrs. Taylor, she owned a farm; and they built the Vanderbilt building right on her place. When I came to Nashville in 1856, the capitol wasn't finished then. The walls of the capitol have been finished since the Civil War. And those walls were all quarried on Pearl Street and Jo Hohnson; that was a fine quarry.

Harris had a farm in Mississippi, and a farm out here five miles on the pike. He had about fifty Negroes on that farm. He had one man named Bob. He bought Bob, and they couldn't manage Bob. They carried Bob to Mississippi the third time, to his other farm. Bob wouldn't stay nowhere but at Dr. Johnson's—that was old Harris' grandfather. Bob swam the Mississippi the second time and came back. He lived in the swamps and had to build fires to keep the wolves off him while he rested. He would carry clubs to kill rattle snakes. When he got to the Mississippi river, he was a swimmer, and when he came out he was 15 or 20 miles below. He swum the Mississippi river three times. They couldn't whip him, and when they wanted to whip him he would take to the bushes. He would eat buds.

The white folks would not give us no butter and things like that, and I would go over to the spring house to get it; and I would sometimes bring as much as 2 pounds of butter in my bosom. I would always have something hid in the spring house, and I would prize (pry) the log on the spring house open, and when the white folks would come down to the spring house to get butter and stuff they would be taken out and we would have gotten it and given it to the runaway Negroes. I killed chickens and stuck them in my bosom. I have toted eggs in my bosom. Aunt Letty would make our breeches with short pockets in them; and I would get her to make my pockets large, and I would fill them with strings, and up in the storeroom I would tote sugar and flour and take them to Aunt Letty. I bet I have toted about 20 gallons of blackberry jelly in my pockets to Aunt Letty. I would kill a hen and stick it in my bosom, and she would cook it. We had a big apple orchard. We could have 30 or 40 barrels of apples, and I would tote apples out through the hen house, and get out like the hens came in. If I would want to get out I would look out to see if no one was coming; and if no one was coming I would push them around to the front and let them drop out, and I would come out after.

Yes, we had bacon and cabbages, and they would issue it out. The cook would be at the white house. She had a window, and she would call the boy when dinner was ready. Then we would come up and get it, in pans. We had the fattest meat and thick bread. I was the churner, and sometimes I would churn 12 times on Monday. They would take the butter off the milk, and sometimes I would take the churn and pour the milk to the hogs.

Well, some of them was and some of them wasn't. We had one that was a white as our mistress, and we had one and she was 'bout my color. And there was two others that was dark. They waited on the table, and did the maid work.

No, they allowed them to go to the church. White folks have a morning service, and in the afternoon colored folks would go to the same church. The biggest thing I heard them preach about was, "Servants, obey your mistress and master." They would tell them not to steal. Very few of them told you about religion. They didn't have any time. They would preach to white folks, and they would say, "You ought to be careful and treat your servants right." But to colored they would always say, "Servants, obey your masters." When they had meetings that way they came from other men's farms, and they would slip over and keep the padderollers from getting you, and they would turn the kettle down outside the door, raised so that the sound can get under there and you couldn't hear them. If they heard women pray, the next morning they would hit them fifty lashes for praying.

Yes, right down here when I was brought here in 1856 from Osceola. I was in the sale house right where the Morris Memorial Building is. Going toward the Square a little store was built of white bricks; well that was the sale house, before that was torn down. Right where the Y.M.C.A is there was two sale houses, right down on Cedar, and was another sale house; made four right on the Square, right in front of Market Square. There was a sale block where they carried the Negroes there and auctioned them off. The fellow that auctioned them off, "Ole Pentecost," they called him. He lived, and died about 15 years after the War. Where the auction block was, the A.M.E. Sunday School bought that. They are out on 8th and Lea Avenue, but that was where the African Methodist organized their Sunday School, right there in that building, and when they got so large they couldn't manage it, they bought that place on the corner out there. And right where that old building is now those Irishmen got rich selling Negroes to white folks, and whiskey and beer.

Oh, yes'm, prayed for the children that the time would come when they would be free, and they could serve God under their own vine and fig tree. They sang a song, "Give me Jesus, give me Jesus, and you can have all the world;" and then all those old hymns, they sang them. I used to be very accurate in singing before I got all my teeth out. I was quite a singer. And they used to sing inviting songs, "Come to Jesus," and they used to sing "Dark midnight was my cry." That is all I can think of.

Well, they could have a very good time, but the padderollers would catch them out there and whip them if they would not have a pass. You couldn't go to church without a pass. Wouldn't care whose Negro you were, if they would catch you out they would whip you. Oh, yes, they would have dances; they would have parties at night. They had candy pullings and killings and corn shucking. The man on the adjoining farm; they would have the corn and throw it in a pile, and they would invite all the Negroes over to help shuck out Mr. So-and-So's corn. They had a gallon jug of whiskey, and the Negroes would sing corn songs. No, I can't think of any of the songs. Here was the main song when they was shucking corn. They would pick up the old master that had them shucking the corn and take him around on their backs, and some one would holler:

> If you want to drink Mass'r Frank's whiskey come on
>   men let us shuck the corn
> Come on men let us gather round and throw the trash
>   to the fire
> And go to Massr's table and have a good time.

We would just holler it. After we got through, he would have a good table. His women would cook all day, Irish potatoes, and have a big time. It would be cold, but they wouldn't mind, and they would give us the whiskey. The old man would come round with a jug and you would say, "Pour me half a glass." Sometimes they used to have a lot of jugs.

No, they wouldn't have signs. Afraid one Negro would give the other away to their masters. They had in those days a Hoodoo nigger who could hoodoo niggers, but couldn't hoodoo masters. He couldn't make ole master stop whipping him, with the hoodooism, but they could make Negroes crawl to them. I didn't pay any attention to it till after the War, when a few of those characters lived. They have some of them now; they give you a black bottle, and give you roots.

They was famous for making medicine out of herbs and out of roots. The medicine they gave you was nothing but blue mass and oil and some hot tea, and you would be all right; but you do all that now, and you will be all wrong. I have took more medicine since I have been sick this time than I ever have.

They would get old Brother So-and-So, get an old country preacher, and he could say what he wanted. 'Course an old white preacher wouldn't bother, but you could get an old colored preacher to come. He had to be careful what he said 'cause the white folks were there and listening to him, so that he couldn't have anything to say to cause uprising of his slaves. Yes, they would burry them right with the white people. I have heard of them often (funerals) but I never saw any where I was.

They don't have marriage like that now. I would say, "I want So-and-So's girl." I would ask him, if I wanted his girl; and if I was a Negro that was profitable and would increase other families, I could marry. Then I would ask my master, and if he gave his consent, too, I could marry, but without it, I couldn't. They would get a preacher and say the ceremony. They wouldn't get no license. He would say whatever they wanted to say, it wouldn't matter. But after the War you had to do that marriage all over, and all the slaves had to go and buy license.

When I came to Nashville, Nashville was only a mile and a half anyway. Nothing but cane and thickets, but all that was cut out at the time of the War. 'Course, during the War there was so much killing. Right over there on 7th Avenue there was one of the finest springs the city ever known. Where there was hydrant water you could see 500 wagons getting water, and you could see wagons going round peddling water. All this what you see now, it was nothing but brambles. Pleasant Green was bought in the bushes. I know it just like it was yesterday.

Why certainly, they hung him on the bridge. Yes'm, and I remember long 'fore Eph Grizzard was hung. I know where three or four were hung; one named Alfro was hung. The last person was hung on the gallows, the last person. He was hung in the hollow, Tremals Bottom. There was a old white woman that peddled, went 'round, and she was a milker, and this man was just helping her, and had been helping her for a long time. She was so thick with Negroes, and Alfro was about my color. That was one man that was hung that was innocent. He was tried before a colored squire here. He was the first colored squire here. They used to have a colored squire and constable and lawyer. He was a barber. Alfro was tried before the squire, and he turned him over to the criminal court; and they said the charge was assault, and they hung him. And the day they hung him there was 5,000 persons, and he told them that day he wasn't guilty; and he went on to tell why this woman accused him, and he said she asked him for a chicken and he went and caught it. A whole lot of rumors were centered around it, and they sentenced him to be hung. I thought about the

Apostle Paul. Horses run away and people were wounded, and the squire who turned him over to the criminal court, he got crippled. There was a mighty roaring in the elements when he got hung. They run over him (the squire) and broke his hip, and he never did do no good. He died from the effect of it. That is the last person they hung out in the open. After that they would hang them, but they would hang them on the inside; but they wouldn't hang them on the outside.

Eph Grizzard—there was a white family, and they thought Eph was a little too thick, and they cried out on Eph; and that family just went down to the dogs. They hung Eph over the bridge. For several years they say it has been that a man who came along at night, when it was dark, with a wagon, the horses would stop—Eph would get right in the way, and they cannot pass. It has been that the electric cars wouldn't move, and they had to change that bridge. I lived to see three bridges built over the Cumberland river. The first bridge was a wooden bridge. The Rebels burned that down. The second bridge was wire, and the traffic was too heavy for a wire bridge. And I have lived to see the steel bridge put up. That is the one that Eph Grizzard was hung on.

I was here when there was no street cars. The first cars was horse cars. The colored rode with them, but it wasn't long before they changed and got it. Yes, Negro men and their whiskey; they didn't treat their own women right, and they wouldn't treat the white women right, and they got so bad that Negroes couldn't ride on the railroad, but they saw that they were losing money, and they put a partition in the horse car, just like the railroad. At first, on the horse cars they put the Negroes in the front, but that didn't suit them, and they put the Negroes in the back. I used to tell them when I was travelling on the train, "Well, we Negroes are treated royal all right, you put us right in front and the white folks ride in the back, so that they can smell the the Negroes." Then they started to put the partition on the railroad.

I have been superannuated. I am a natural grammarian. I love botany and zoology, too. I spent eight years in Central Tennessee School studying for the ministry. I went to McKeeve's School, and I was promoted every Monday morning. I used to couldn't come to school but about twice or three times a month, and the teacher wanted to know how I would know so much and be away nearly all the time. I was working for Mr. Moore then. In 1884 I was examined for deaconship, and I only made 45, and to pass I was to make 65; but they let me pass because I was so apt on grammer, and they let me pass; but I saw my trouble, and in eight years from that time I was picked up, and when I was examined for Elder's office I made 85.6.

Kicked Around Like a Mule

I was in the Civil War. Mighty rough time, I tell you. My marster sold me. I was in Georgia, then they brought me to Tennessee. I was on the northern side. The man that bought me brought me from Atlanta to Knoxville; right at the Knoxville branch the Yankees met us and made him give me up; so he lost me.

I got a discharge all right, but after the War I was met one night out in the woods, and some robbers robbed me of all the money I had, which was $2.00, and took my discharge papers. I never thought much about it then, but I have never been able to get a pension on account of not having them papers. Several people have tried for me, but I never could tell what regiment I was with. The regiment was from Wisconsin; I remember that all right, and I remember two names of officers; they were Lieutenant Parker and Lieutenant Hughes. I am 87 years old. The year the Civil War commenced I was a 15 year old boy.

I left long about chopping cotton time. The man who sold me was a speculator in slaves. Buy them just like mules. The Yankees took up I don't know how many boys. I waited on two officers. I kept their clothes clean, boots shined, and would bring water. I was standing right side of them when they give the discharge papers out, and I would be all right now if I coulda just kept them papers. But I just never was able to get on to getting anything. A old lady in Gallatin told me she was going to write about it for me; but I knowed the old heifer wasn't going to do it.

One old man in Gallatin, 'fore I come down here, told me he got $3,000, and said I sure ought to get something out of it.

Well, ladies, I can't tell you nothing 'cept I was treated pretty bad—knocked and kicked arount like I was a mule. They would tie you up to a tree, tie your hands and feet down and whip you. They was awful mean in Georgia. You never was allowed to have a piece of paper to look at. They would whip you for that, 'cause they didn't want you to learn anything. When they would whip you they would tear your back all to pieces. Child, they didn't care for you. We had to stand in fear of them, we had no protection. They would take your clothes off and whip you like you was no more than mules.

When Civil War commenced marster went and stayed two months, but it rained so much he come back. The man who bought me, the Yankees cut him off at Knoxville. That's how I got to Tennessee. I reckon my marster had something like 15 or 16 grown people on his place. Some of them had a hundred men on their farm at once. They would see children and give them candy; if they looked healthy they would buy them and raise them up. They would look at them and say, "That's a mighty fine nigger." Mighty few of them had marsters that would treat them right. The niggers was mighty glad to have the Yankees take them; they wanted to get out from under that rough treatment. Georgia was about the meanest place in the world. They would knock you around just like you was dogs.

You couldn't raise no corn or hogs in Georgia to do no good; the hogs woulda been poor for they didn't have anything to eat. Nothing there but rocks. Sometimes you could grow a little corn near a stream.

But it was so hilly and rocky that you couldn't do nothing but raise cotton. It was a terribly ugly country. Heard it was a good country down there now. I never been back since I left. I never have seen my mother since I left, or my sister or brother. Diana was my mother's only girl. They wouldn't make no difference in the half-white slaves. They would get whippings just like we would. I never seen any colored people who couldn't talk English. I have been as far as Ohio. They talk so curious I just couldn't understand them. We had to go to the white folks' church, and a white man would preach to us. We always sit in the back of the church. My mother had me in her arms and a white man sprinkled me. He pat water on my head. They didn't mind sprinkling then. Colored folks would go to the woods sometimes and have a meeting. Whenever they wanted to marry all you had to do was go ask old marster if you could have So-and-So, and that was all to it. They didn't allow you no license. They wouldn't 'low you to carry a book; reckon they was 'fraid you would learn something. They would let them have parties sometimes on Saturday nights. But the white folks would have to tell the padderollers that we was going to have something, so they wouldn't bother us. In corn shucking time no padderollers would ever bother you. We would have a big time at corn shuckings. They would call up the crowd and line the men up and give them a drink. I was a corn general—would stand out high above everybody, giving out corn songs and throwing down corn to them. There would be two sides of them, one side trying to out-shuck the other. Such times we did have. I never will forget one night the niggers got to fighting and tore down a whole rail fence pulling the rails off, fighting with them. They was full of whiskey then. The ladies would wait on us and give us cakes and pies and all kind of good things to eat. That was the only enjoyment we had, but we sure had a good time then. When we wanted to have a dance, we had to ask marster. They would have a fiddler, and we would tromp around mighty.

You would always have to ask marster and mistress every time you wanted to do anything at all. At Christmas time they would give you something, shoes, hat and one thing and another. Some would do it and some wouldn't.

The man who owned us was right clever to us. He give my mother a little patch to raise cotton, and when he would sell it he would always give her the money. Heap of them was too lazy to work a patch. He would give her a half-day on Saturday to work her crop. On moonlight nights we would work it, too. Every family had a cabin to their self. Hogs was wild, they just roved about in the woods trying to find something to eat. It was a mighty poor country then. There was plenty of grapes, plums and watermelons. Georgia is the greatest place in the world for big watermelons. We would eat them all through the cotton patch. We used to pack watermelons in straw and when Christmas would come we would be eating watermelons for Christmas day.

When a nigger would run away and be caught they would take you and whip you good, and sell you right away; some of them would keep them after they run away.

I didn't get religion until about three or four years ago. I was pretty tough, I guess. I thought I heard something; it look like I heard a voice speak to me when I was seeking religion. Things come like a dream to me sometimes. I feel a change in the body. I tries to do what's right, for I want to get to heaven when I die. I am satisfied to let the world go, so I get to heaven. We got to wait until He come and call, but I want to be ready when he comes.

> I hope to join the army by and by
> I hope to join the army by and by.
> Little bells ringing for the Christians,
> Hope to join the army by and by.

All these old time songs, I can't think of them now. My mind is short. I am looking most any time to be called. My time ain't long here.

They used to give us roots boiled for medicine. For a sore throat they had something called Mobile. It tasted mighty bad, and it would make you holler, but it was good for sore throat. I always wanted to do something. I was raised to it. My mother would make us wash every Monday night. Her name was Sara. She worked all the time. She would go about with her knitting in her pockets, and if she had to walk from the cabin to the house she would always knit wherever she walked to. Sometimes she would sit on top of the mule on her way to the field, knitting. She never got tired of knitting. Sometimes she would whip us for nothing. We always washed the things after she knit them. Marster would take and sell them for her, and give mother the money. He was a right good man in that way.

I didn't know Eph Grizzard; but I knew his brother well. Eph was mobbed.

When time for soldiers to kill a man, twelve of them would have guns, and one would be loaded, and that way none of them would know which one did the killing. Some of the soldiers would be one side, and if things got too hot for him, he would go over on the other side. Once we was trying to get to a little town; men was laying out on the battle field like corn stalks. We was in a little place called Lowden. The niggers come down with the cannons. Little bullets was flying through the woods, niggers was standing on that hill. One man went back and said, "Hell done broke loose in Georgia." We went to a place called Sweetwater, democrats wanted to take us, but the niggers started running, and Lord have mercy, they never did stop. You could hear men all over the battlefield, crying, "Water, Water, somebody please give me water." The ambulance would come and get them and try to do something for them, but they couldn't get them fast enough. It was terrible. That was the bloodiest war I ever saw. I believe gunpowder made them mean. They didn't bit more mind shooting you down than they did a partridge.

From Ole Virginny

Yes, bless God, I was here during the fust war. I come from ole Virginny. They sold me to my old marster's son. I was big enough to plow up ground to plant corn. The Lord hear me telling you the truth. Thank the Lord that he still let me stay here. He took my daughters and sons, and here I am with two of them today. Whenever I go to church one of the sisters always grab me by the arm and say, "Step in and set down and behave yourself." My ole marster sold me to his son. His son come to a country called White County. The son and wife brought me on. There was an ole colored lady who called me to the fence, the kitchen was way down in the yard; she said, "Come here." I don't know how ole I was. I know I was ole enough to plow the ground to plant corn. We stopped some place and stayed all night and, God bless your soul, I sat up in a chair all night. The next morning they taken me and brought me on way out here. The son and his wife both died. I just got tired of setting down and I said, "I am going up and get a job." I went there and stayed two or three weeks, washing, ironing and cooking. I used to plow up the ground, and at dinner time when they would blow the horn I brought my horse up and unhitched him, and put him in the stable and give him some hay to eat. That's been a many years ago. My mother and father was the only slaves they had. They sold my sister Ellen. My mother nearly died when they sold my sister. In them days they make me comb my hair with an old kyard (card) what we used for spinning. My mistress would buy a handkerchief and tie around my head. We would raise a garden with cabbage and beans in it. The Lord has been so precious to let me travel on these many years.

We didn't have churches, just tents. All the little children would sit down in the straw at the mother's feet. The old folks had long wooden benches. A white man would come there and preach to us. He had a ole Bible, brown leather back. He would set the Bible in the middle of a ole bench. They would sing ole hymns like, "Amazing Grace how sweet the sound that saved a wretch like me. I once was lost but now I'm found; was blind but now I see." I belong to Brother Martin's church on Harding Street, Sanctified Church. They don't sing them ole hymns now. Every time I go in the church one of the sisters grab me and say, "Sit down and behave yourself."

Sometimes they would straighten my hair out with a wooden comb, and take a rag and tie it up. They would go out under the tree and set on a bench. I didn't have no colored children to play with around where I lived.

We would go out and pull weeds to make tea for colds. I got that heartfelt religion. I wasn't afraid when I fust got religion. Oh, bless God, I went on and told my mother about it, and went up the road just talking about it. I tell you these ole fashioned songs are precious. Yes, I remember when the soldiers come around with the guns swinging down by their sides. They didn't have roads like they do now, they had red clay hills. Yes, mam, I don't think my ole marster fought in the War. He had a son in the War who got killed.

When my mother died they wouldn't let me go to the cemetery. The sun was just setting red. Don't know why they wouldn't let me go. They buried people in wooden boxes in them days.

They would make me knit stockings, and we wore home-made shoes in them days. They would cook in ashes. We would get old cabbage leaves and wrap the corn pones up in it, and rake back the ashes and put them in the hot ashes to cook. We would wrap potatoes up in cabbage leaves, too, and cook them in ashes.

When they buried anybody they didn't have a funeral; nobody would pray or anything. They just carried you on to the cemetery. Ox would pull the carts, and they would stop at the top of the hill and rest. They buried my mother just about dark. Yes, mam, I remember it. I never shall forget it. They wouldn't let me go. They was mean white folks. My ole marster's son was mean and his wife was mean. I never did see my sister any more after they sold her. I would go out and pull wild salad to cook for dinner.

She would whip me with a ole plaited leather strap. She would whip me if I didn't do right.

We didn't have houses like we do now. They were made out of trees cut down, and clay. Long chimneys, but not brick. We was afraid to make a big fire, for we was afraid the house would catch on fire. We would have big irons to hold the wood on each side of the fireplace. I been here a long time. I just get to thinking how precious the Lord has been to me to let me stay here this long time.

"Niggers Ain't Scared of White Folks Now"

First my owner was a Buford; then she married a Cunningan, and I went with her to him. He's the one that owned me in slavery time. That's how come I don't know my age; they would keep it in the Bible and wouldn't give it to the mothers. I was a great big girl, though, when the War ceasted; it went on four years.

They had cradles for the little nigger babies, and long before the War I was big enough to rock them babies, and old Cunningan would come in and tell ole Miss that they was gonna have a war to free the niggers, and I heard 'em talking, but I didn't know what they was talking 'bout. Mother come in with her steers, from hauling rails, and I told her what they said, and she made like it wasn't nothing, 'cause she was scared I'd tell them if she made like it was important. I said, "Mammy, Old Cunningan come in and say there's gonna be a war to free the niggers, and I didn't know what he was talking about, but old Mistress said, 'I don't want to live to see the niggers free,' and old Cunningan said, 'I want to see how the niggers will act when they're free'." And do you know, the Lawd took that thing away before the war ceasted. She died during the War and he died the year after the War. Mammy and Sis and me was setting out 'taters, and we seed a white shaggy dog come along; we hadn't seed that kind of dog before, and we didn't know what it was, 'cause all the dogs we seed had close cropped hair. Sis and me went to the spring to get some water, and she had done dipped her water up and started to go, and I said, "Hand me a drink," and she handed me the dipper—I mean gourd, we didn't have no dippers then—and just as I started to drink here come that dog. She said, "Little Sis, what is this!" and I run up the fence, and a rail slipped and hit me from behind and knocked my shoulder out of place. It never was put back right, and that's how come it hurts me till today. They took me and tied it up, and call theirselves getting it back; but it wasn't back.

I didn't do nothing but play and pick up chips for old Aunt Fanny. She fed us. They had these round wooden bowls, and Aunt Fanny would take that and pour licker in it, and put bread in it for the chillen to eat. It was a great big bowl, big as that dish pan there. That's what we had for dinner, and milk and bread for supper. Mistress would say, "Go pick up some chips for old Aunt Fan to put on the lid," and I would run and break out to get the chips first, 'cause I was crazy about white bread, and when we all got back with the chips, Mistress would give us some white bread, but she would make me wait till they all got there. I liked it 'cause Mammy 'nem didn't get white bread but once a week—that was Sunday, and the rest of the time they had just corn bread or shorts. I was so foolish! When she died (Mistress) it liked to killed me; I just cried and cried, and Mammy say, "What's the matter with you, gal?" I said, "Ole Miss is dead, and I won't get no more white bread." She said, "Shet you mouth, gal." I thought when she died she carried all the white bread with her. Folks was saying, "Look at that po' little nigger crying 'bout her Mistress," but I wasn't crying 'bout Mistress, I was crying 'cause the white bread was gone.

You know over in Franklin where the Baptist church is on Hardbargain is where the Fort was during the War, and they set right there and spied the rebels in the houses and shelled them. They got old

Cunningan and dared him to say a word. They just stripped him—took everything he had. They camped right there on our place, and when they would blow the bugle I just thought that was the prettiest blowing I ever heard. Ole Cunningan had two girls and one boy, and he was just sitting down this a way (with head in hands) and they was in different rooms. Them Yankees took everything but what Mammy got. She was smart; we had the cradle that would set under the bed, and she pulled it out and filled it full of meat, so Mammy had plenty for her chillen after they left. After they had done took everything from ole Cunningan, Joe watched 'em out of sight and come back to tell his papa they had gone. And he called, "Papa, Papa, get up now, they're gone," and the old man didn't say a word, so he shook him, and he was dead, sitting up there just like that. The doctors said his heart just bursted. I found lots of confederate money, too, when the Yankees left. They took all his money and everything. When I heard they was buying that money I went to get mine, but it had done tore all to pieces down in the bottom of the trunk.

I couldn't tell you how many niggers he did have; he had so many and his wife had so many. The place was full; times sho' was hard, sho' as you born. Chillen was just as lousy as pigs. They had these combs that was just like cards you "card" cotton with, and they would comb your head with them. That wouldn't get the lice out, but it would make it feel better. They had to use larkspur to get 'em out; that would always get lice out of your head. But there wasn't no chillen would get sick before the War. I reckon the lice musta kept 'em healthy.

My husband never did like for me to work; he used to ask me how come I work when he was doing all he could to give me what I wanted. "Looks like you don't 'preciate what I'm trying to do for you." But I'd say, "Yes, I do, honey, I jest help you 'cause I don't want you to break down. If you put a load on one horse it will pull him down, but two horses can pull it jest as easy."

Lawd, the times we did have. I know that when the War got over and we got free they put me in the field to work. I never went to school a day in my life; what I learned to read, I learned myself. My chillen all went to school, though, and my girl that died was sho' smart in her books, too. Yes'm, they're in school (great grandchildren). I wouldn't keep 'em out for nothing.

Oh, I should say so; he was mean as he could be. He had an overseer that went 'round and whipped the niggers every morning, and they hadn't done a thing. He went to my father one morning and said, "Bob, I'm gonna whip you this morning." Daddy said, "I ain't done nothing," and he said, "I know it, I'm gonna whip you to keep you from doing nothing," and he hit him with that cowhide—you know it would cut the blood out of you with every lick if they hit you hard—and Daddy was chopping cotton, so he just took up his hoe and chopped right down on that man's head and knocked his brains out. Yes'm, it killed him, but they didn't put colored folks in jail then, so when old Charlie Merrill, the nigger trader, come along they sold my daddy to him, and he carried him way down in Mississippi. Ole Merrill would buy all the time, buy and sell niggers just like hogs. They sold him Aunt Phoebe's little baby that was just toddling long, and Uncle Dick—that was my mammy's brother.

The way they would whip you was like they done my oldest sister. They tied her, and they had a place just like they're gonna barbecue a hog, and they would strip you and tie you and lay you down. I never seed no buttons like they have now till after the War. We had cloth buttons, and old Aunt Fanny had told marster that my sister wouldn't keep her dress clean, and that's what they was whipping her 'bout. So they had her down in the cellar whipping her, and I was real little. I couldn't say "Big Sis," but I went and told Mammy, "Old Marster's got 'Big Jim' down there in the cellar beating her," and Mammy got out of bed and went in there and throwed Aunt Fan out the kitchen door, and they had to stop whipping Big Sis and come and see about Aunt Fan. You see, she would tell things on the others, trying to keep from getting whipped herself. I seed Mistress crack her many a time over the head with a broom, and I'd be so scared she was gonna crack me, but she never did hit me, 'cept slap me when I'd turn the babies over. I'd get tired and make like I was sleep, and would ease the cradle over and throw the baby out. I never would throw Mammy's out, though. Old Miss would be setting there just knitting and watching the babies; they had a horn and every woman could tell when it was time to come and nurse her baby by the way they would blow the horn. The white folks was crazy 'bout their nigger babies, 'cause that's where they got their profit. A old white woman would come there and look after them. Lawd, there was so much carried on in that place. I don't know whether any of the Cunningan niggers living now, but me or not. Yes, when I'd get tired, I would just ease that baby over and Mistress would slap me so hard; I didn't know a hand could hurt so bad, but I'd take the slap and get to go out to play. She would slap me hard and say, "Git on out of here and stay till you wake up," and that was just what I wanted, 'cause I'd play then.

Them doctors helped me, but they done made me eat Jordan off the cross.

Yes, they took us to the camp meetings; the white folks had the meetings; they would carry you there to show you to their friends. "I'll show you my niggers," they would say to each other, and they would come 'round and look at each other's niggers. They would just shout and sing, and when Mammy would see 'em, she'd say, "Some poor woman is gonna get it," 'cause they would shout like that and then go home and beat anybody that hadn't done things just like they wanted them done.

Aunt Phoebe did (have prayer meetings). She would turn the kettle down and just sing and pray, and sometimes she would be happy and just moan, and I'd say, "Mammy, what's the matter with Aunt Phoebe?" and she'd tell me to hush. I remember one song:

Sleepy creature, sleepy creature,
There's something to do 'sides sleeping.

When the white folks was beating and slashing up colored people; I remember that all right. Old Buford—his darkies had chillen by him, and Mammy wouldn't do it; and I've seen him take a paddle with holes in it and beat her, and everywhere it hit it raised a blister; then he would take a switch and break them blisters. When he was dying they said he was calling Uncle Dick, and just twisting switches in his hand and doing like he was cutting his throat. They said he told them to bring him seven thousand dollars, "to pay my way out of hell," but he couldn'ta got out of hell, the way he beat my mammy.

I look at it now and sometimes niggers so bad; the bad ones ought to be back in slavery; but these niggers ain't gonna take nothing off these white folks. They ain't scared of white folks; some folks thinks that 'cause you been a slave you ought to be scared of white folks now; but I ain't scared of 'em; and I never was scared of 'em, 'cept ole Mistress till she died.

Parents of Martha Harrison were slaves belonging to a family of Bufords in Hillsboro, Tennessee. Father was sold away from the family down into Mississippi, when the children were quite small. Some years later he came back to see them. It seems that he ran away after a fight with the overseer. There were twelve children in the family, of which Martha is the only one living.

Mrs. Harrision was born a slave. She does not know her age, but has a vivid memory of the Civil War and several years before the War. She was perhaps ten or twelve years old when it ended. She belonged, with her mother, to the Buford family. One of the daughters of this family married a Cunningan, and Martha and her mother were given to her as a wedding present. They took the name of Cunningan, which she bore until she married George Harrison in 1877.

George Harrison was born a slave also, in Franklin, Tennessee. He belonged to a family of Harrisons. He was somewhat older than Martha, and was almost a young man when the War ended. Martha met George in Franklin one Sunday when she went there to attend a "Big Meeting" at the church. They saw each other on several occasions, and finally married. They lived in Franklin a while, moved to another town and worked in a family. They moved to Nashville and settled at the same address where she now lives. She brought her mother with her, and she lived with them until she died, at the age of 103.

Three children were born to them—two were stillborn, and one, a daughter, lived to be grown. This daughter, Sally, married an Armstrong, and was the mother of three children. Two died, and one lived to reach maturity. She, Fannie Lou, married a Batey, and also had three children. (Both husband and wife and one child died from tuberculosis, eight years ago.) Charlie, age 11, and Lizzie Lou, age 8, are living with Mrs. Harrison, their great grandmother, and are being cared for entirely by her. Her husband died about four years ago, from heart trouble. He was sick for some time, and at his death left nothing except the home to his widow. She had been married fifty-one years.

Patient was brought to clinic by two of her neighbors. Did not have money to enter, and was allowed to enter and referred to Social Service. She was examined in the clinic. Diagnosis: chronic gastritis; chronic articular rheumatism, chronic valvular heart disease.

(9.15.32) A visit was made to home of patient. River Street is a short, very rough gully through which it is impossible to drive, and almost impossible to walk. Inquiry was made for her. She is well and affectionately known as "Aunt Martha" by children and grown-ups in the neighborhood. Her house is the last one on the street, at the foot of the hill. The yard is small and overgrown with trees and shrubbery, so that the house is partly hidden from view. It is old and unpainted. The ceilings are low, and it is crowded with various old articles of furniture. The three of them sleep in one room, the boy occupying a small bed alone, and the girl shares the large bed with her great grandmother. They seem to be bright, smart children. She says the girl can cook, and helps in many ways. She accuses the boy of being lazy. He was, however, at the time of the visit, washing clothes, and had several of his pals helping him. There were some neighbors to see her. She was worrying because she was not able to keep her house clean and wash her bedding. There seemed to be two other rooms, a back porch, and a front porch. What the other rooms are used for was not found out. She has never asked for charity, and is not known to any of the other agencies.

One of the First Voters in Montgomery County

I was a slave way back in 1856, John Brown's time. They were mighty hard on colored people. They hung two men by the neck right where I was living. That was way before the Civil War. I think the first gun for that was fired in 1861, around Fort Sumter. Back in those days colored people couldn't leave their homes without a written pass from their master and mistress. You couldn't even go to church; if you did you were caught on the highway by the padderollers and beat up. Back there they bought and sold colored people just like they do horses and mules now. Many husbands, wives and children were separated then and never met again. They had contraband camps, and men, women and children had to be guarded to keep the Rebels from carrying them back to the white folks. One time I run away and lay in the woods all day until night. When I got here then I 'listed in the army. Part of my regiment was in Hood's raid in 1864. I was not in it. White people were very hard on colored for being religious. They liked to see you fiddling and dancing all the time. They were hard on them for preaching. Some of them treated the slaves like people, but some of them did not care any more about you than they did for dogs. As for me, I went where I wanted to, but I had to have a pass. Some of them didn't get passes and they would get caught and be sent out to jail, beat up and made come on back. They used to tell you sometimes that they would send you down the river and they would send you to Mississippi, Georgia, and Alabama or Louisiana.

I come down from Virginia to Kentucky with my folks. They were sold when I was about six or seven years old. They used to have a slave market right here in Clarksville.

In Virginia, my white people took care of their slaves, but they had to go when they said so. I was a house boy and when I got big enough to go out to work they let me go anywhere I wanted to go, and if I didn't like it, I could come on back home. But I soon got so I wanted to be free so I run away. I came to Hopkinsville, then to Clarksville, killed my horse and slept in the woods until the next morning. Then I started on into Clarksville, but a pickett halted me. The Rebels wore grey. They asked me where I was going and I told them I was going to Clarksville to join the army, so they told me to stay right there, that they needed a thousand men like me.

When the white folks found colored women and men they would take them away from their children and send them way down South.

Back there they were harder on preachers than they were on anybody else. They thought preachers were ruining the colored people. Back there, even if they thought once that you wanted an education they would kill you. In those days, if a white man did do anything to a free colored man and had to be taken into court, and another colored man saw the act and wanted to be a witness they didn't take his word for nothing. They (the whites) just didn't have any time for a free colored man.

Sometimes the white master or mistress would pay the fee of five dollars to keep their slave from going to the whipping post.

If you wanted to go to church in those days, you had to go and ask, and they would give you a pass, and when the padderollers would meet you and ask for it, if you had it they would let you go on but if you didn't have it they would give you nine and thirty licks and let you go on back. They got me once or twice. I wanted to go somewhere and tried to get by without a pass, but they got me.

It was a long, long time before everything got quiet after the War. On Franklin Street here I saw once 100 Ku Klux Klans, with long robes and faces covered. You don't know anything of them. They were going down here a piece to hang a man. There were about 600 of us soldiers, so we followed them to protect the man. The Klan knew this and passed on by the house and went on back to town and never did bother the man.

One time a colored soldier married a white woman over here at Fort Bruce. The man belonged to my company. His name was Sergeant Cook. About twenty of the soldiers went to the wedding, and they had about five or six white men who said he couldn't marry this woman. Old Dr. Taylor (and by the way this Taylor's Hill here is named for him) came over to marry them. He stood near me and I told him to go on and marry this couple or else someone here would die. He looked around and saw all these soldiers and he knew about us and that we meant for him to do as he had been told. He married them and we guarded their hack over to the war boat on the Cumberland. They went over to Nashville and lived there. They had a daughter whose name was Mrs. Gnatt. When they married was in 1866. Mrs. Gnatt could tell you her father was named Cyrus Cook. Guess you know you can't do that now, no sir; you just can't do that now. At one time a colored man could ride anywhere he wanted to, but now he can't do it. I am one of the first voters of Montgomery County. They told me at one time that I was not to come to the polls or I would be met by 600 men on horses. So about six or eight hundred of us armed and went to the polls with our bayonets. That man that had told me that did not show up. So we voted, and voted for whom we wanted. At that time the Rebels who rebelled against this country could not vote and they said that these Negroes shouldn't vote but we showed them. Of course, they came down and stood and looked at us but they didn't bother us. We went there armed and prepared for fighting so that if they started anything, there would be trouble. When they mustered me out from the army, I brought my gun from Nashville right here to Clarksville and kept it twenty-five years. Finally I let an old soldier have it.

When I first came here we had no teachers here but white teachers. They would call the roll same as calling the roll for soldiers. They taught school in the churches before they had school houses. They used to go to school at night and work all day. Clarence C. White's father, Will White, was the first teacher or principal of the school here in Clarksville. Ed White, his brother, was shot and killed in Topeka, Kansas, and brought here to be buried. He has a daughter in Fisk University now who is a matron or something, I don't know exactly.

In those times some people married just like we marry now, only they didn't get a license but they would get permission from their owner first and then from the girl's parents. Sometimes they got a preacher to marry them, and sometimes they jumped over the broom stick. When they were married by a preacher, they called that a lawful marriage, and when the War come up if a soldier died the wife could get a pension; but if they married by jumping over the broom stick, they didn't recognize that if a soldier died, and his wife could get nothing.

When I was a little boy they would kill us if they caught us in a Sunday School. Then when they did let us go to church sometimes, they would give you a seat way back here, with the white folks in front. Then sometimes they would let you come in the evenings to church and then you would take the front seats, with the padderollers behind, so that if the preacher said something he shouldn't say, they would stop him. One time when they were singing, "Ride on King Jesus, No man can hinder Thee," the padderollers told them to stop or they would show him whether they could be hindered or not. Sometimes the white folks would come in when the colored people would have prayer meeting, and whip every one of them. Most of them thought that when colored people were praying it was against them. For they would catch them praying for God to lift things out of their way, and the white folks would *lift them*.

When I lived down at Cadez, you couldn't be caught out of a yard after sundown. If you did, they would run you in and beat you if they caught you. In 1856 they whipped more colored people to death because they thought the colored people were fixing to rise. Later the rebellion came up, and the Rebels fired the first gun on July 4th at Fort Sumter. But they didn't fire the last one. General Forrest captured Fort Pillar and buried colored people alive. At that time I never thought about dying. I never thought about anybody shooting me; I just thought about shooting them. The War went on four years and then the South did not want to quit then, but General Lee and General Grant decided that the War had gone on long enough. This town used to be full of Rebels and United States soldiers, but they are very few here now. I belonged to a regiment of one thousand men, but now I can't show you another one of them.

Well, when I married I went right here in this court house and got a license. I had five children by my first wife—three dead—one boy is away and one daughter living here. I didn't want to see anybody bring up their children like they did in that day back there. Some of the colored people back there, when punishing their children, would take the children and hang them up in the chimney and smoke them to punish them. I sent my children to school. I had all five of my children in school at one time. They all finished up here in this public school. My baby boy live in Philadelphia. He is married, and been on the road about thirty years or more. I got two boys dead and a girl. I have one grandson who I sent to Nashville to school and took medicine. Now he is a medical doctor up here in Owensboro, Kentucky.

My mother's name was Louisa Harper. Her husband was a soldier in the army with me, and died in '65. She had only two children, Joseph and Abner. Abner died in Topeka, Kansas, in 1893. He was a soldier, too, My parents ran away to get their freedom.

The United States started me with a pension of six dollars a month, payable every three months. Then they increased me eight, twelve, fifteen, twenty, twenty-four and thirty-five dollars at different intervals, and at one time I got seventy-two dollars. But now I get sixty-five dollars a month. I am still hoping to get more. But since Coleridge (Coolidge) came in I got sixty-five dollars. Old Coleridge put that seventy-two dollars in his pocket and called it a pocket veto.

As it is now, I sit down and talk to these old Rebel white people about how they used to do. I treat everybody right; I hold nothing against them. I used to drive a hack here, and would get about as many white passengers as the white hack drivers got. One time a white man came over to my hack and asked me whose hack it was, and I told him that it was Mr. Farley's, and he said, "Well, how much for a trip?" and I told him 50 cents. After I made the trip he said, "Here is 50 cents for your boss and $1.00 for you. He was supposed to be a wealthy man, and I was glad to get that $1.50. Mr. Farley was myself, but he didn't know it, so I didn't tell him nothing but the truth and got $1.50.

One time a white man came to my house and said he was coming to whip me. So when he came I saw a man come loping up on a horse, and I got two pistols, one in my right hand and one in my pocket, and went out to the gate, and he asked me what was the matter with me. I grabbed the horse and threw the pistol in his face and told him I would show him. So he said, "That's all right, that's all right," and when I turned his horse aloose, he galloped off.

Do you all vote? I vote yet, and I believe in voting. When I vote I vote for whom I want to. I never let an election pass. I will be 87 years old if I live to see the first day of April (1930).

My white folks wanted me to learn to read the Bible but not to learn to write.

When the War was over some of the colored returned to their white folks, but I didn't want to be under the white folks again. I was glad to get out. Once, for fifteen years here, I run a saloon and livery stable. One time I worked on a boat. When I was on my first boat, one time I went to vote. A white man told me that if I voted Republican he would fire me, so I told him to fire me then. I just told him he could fire me right now for I didn't want to work anyway. I went on and voted the Republican ticket, and they told me they liked my principle and I could go on and go to work.

I still got my discharge from way back in 1866. I keeps it and I mean to keep it as long as I live. I am proud of it. I will get it and show it to you if you would like to see it. (The name appears as Fowley instead of Farley. When he joined the army and was asked his name they understood him to say Fowley, or perhaps thought that was the way to spell it, according to the statement made by Joseph Farley. On his return the white folks told him that the way to spell his name was "Farley." He said that was the first time he knew just how to spell his name. He said he only went by to see the white folks but didn't want to stay with them any longer, even though they always treated him "pretty well" he thought.)

Owns The House
He Lived in as a Slave

I don't know exactly how old I am, but I recollect far enough back to remember the War. Niggers couldn't have no books then. There wasn't but two colored people there who could read and write—one woman and one man. After freedom, preachers would want to know how to read the Bible, and the others wanted to learn, too, and this woman who could read told them they would have to learn how to spell first, and she told them what they would have to do, so they got about two dozen of these old fashion spelling books. She carried them to Bluff Springs and taught them their a, b, c's. It was two years after freedom before we had any teachers. There wasn't no learning going on in slavery, I can tell you. They wasn't 'lowed to touch a book. If you did you got a good whipping. The colored folks went to the white church; they had a place for you to sit. After freedom there wasn't but one colored church, and that was at Bluff Springs.

I live right in the house now that I lived in when I was a slave. I was born in Murfreesboro but we was moved down here when I was about six or eight weeks old. Mother took the pneumonia and died. I been right here every since. The white folks sold one colored woman to send their boy to school to be a doctor. I remember it as well as if it was yestiddy. They sold her away from her husband. They carried her on down in Mississippi. My marster owned 17 or 20 heads of slaves. He wasn't cruel to his nigger hands. I had a brother who would always slip off and the paddie rollers would run him a many a night, right up under the house he would go, and they couldn't get to him. They come there some five or six times trying to catch him, and then they went to the house and called marster and told him to call his nigger out so they could give him a genteel whipping and make him stay at home, but marster told them he would whip him in the morning. Brother was laying right there listening, and he knowed right then he wasn't gonna get a whipping. The next morning when marster got done eating his breakfast he called brother and said, "Well, I reckon I better see after you this morning. Haven't I told you to stop running around at night? I hope they catch you some night, then you will stay in." His mammy and him neither one wasn't cruel to his colored people. They got a new overseer once and he overheard mistress say to one of the slaves, "I'm gonna have you whipped if you ever do anything again." He got her and whipped her till he cut the blood out of her shoulder. He made her undo her clothes and whipped her. Mistress saw the blood on her and asked her what was the matter, and she told her that the overseer had whipped her. She called him and told him to never whip another one of her slaves again that way, and that she didn't believe in whipping them like that. That made him mad and he said he wasn't gonna fool with any of them again.

Marster died three years after freedom. After so many years I married, and me and my wife bought the place from mistress where I live now. Money was hard to get then, too, but mistress 'lowed me a chance to pay for it. All of my folks dead now—white and black. That tells me that my time ain't long off. My father was a shoemaker. That was his trade. He hardly ever done any work in the fall of the year, but made shoes. People would bring him leather and he would keep busy plumb up to Christmas. Everybody around

63

brought him leather. He made fines ones and coarse ones, and he made them all by hand. Now it is done by machines. He charged them so much for making them. The white folks didn't have nothing to do with what he charged. I can't say much about my father. They told me his father was a white man. He proved that he was right smart kin to the other race, by his hair and build and everything.

The hands got up at daylight and fed the stock first thing. When I was a little boy I drawed water, fed the cows and put them to their place. I stayed right in the house with them until a little over a year before I married the woman I married.

I knew I was a slave after I got big enough to know that I couldn't do the things that I wanted to do. Mrs. James had a sister from the North to come visit her, and she would talk to my father, and she told him once that in a short time he would be free as she was; and told him not to tell what she had told him, but that Lincoln was going to free all the slaves. I have heard a heap of colored people say that all white folks was just alike; that ain't so, 'cause there is some white folks will treat you right, and some will take everything away from you. They ain't all just alike.

I used to be a great fiddler. I fust learned how to play on a long gourd with horsehair strings on it. 'Course I couldn't go very high on it, but it done pretty well. That was the fust of my learning to play. After a while I bought me a fiddle for $1.80, and after so long a time I bought me a fiddle sure enough.

It wasn't but one family of free niggers up here. White people didn't recognize them, and they didn't 'low niggers to go around them. If they knowed they went around them they would cut they backs off nearly. The men woulda noticed the slave girls if the white folks woulda let them. But they wouldn't let the girls go with a free Negro.

We all went to the white folks church, but we had a place in back of the church where we would set. Some of the slaves kept their membership in the white church till several years after the War. Some kept it long as they lived. Two of my sisters married right where I am living now. A preacher married them, just like they do now, only they didn't have a license like they do now. White folks would give them a rooster and an old hen for supper sometimes. You would always have to get a pass to go anywhere, and you had better stop right where that pass say, too; if you didn't the paddie rollers would give you 39 lashes. That was the law. They would whip you with one of these bull hide whips.

Niggers didn't have time to do much courting in them days. White folks would let them have suppers 'round Christmas time, then after that it was all over and no more gatherings till the next summer; then they would let them set out under the shade trees sometimes on Sunday evening, and all like that.

A white preacher would preach to the slaves, and niggers would out shout the Jews. He would let them tell their 'termination and things. 'Course he didn't know what they was talking about, but listened just the same. One said that the hounds run him about a mile and they run him so close to a place he couldn't get out of the way, and he run up a hickory tree and grabbed at the hound as he run up the tree, but he couldn't catch him; and right there was where he was converted. The preacher said, "I reckon you understand what he is talking about brother, shall we take him in the church?" They would all say "Yes, sir." All of the 'terminations would be no better than that one. All of them would be something like that one. They used to sing "Hark from the Tune." That old song has been here every since, I tell you.

Slaves would be in the river washing sometimes, and the paddie rollers would come along and see them, and they would throw their clothes up in the trees; and I have seen them running with not a string around them. They wouldn't have time to put nothing on if they had their clothes, 'cause they was running them so close. Long time after freedom, old Man Vernon who used to be paddie roller said, "I would like to get to hit you 39 lashes when I was a paddie roller." I said, "Yes, but you done lashed you last 39 on a nigger."

Old man James owned more than any man I knowed. He owned 15 or 20 slaves. Nearly all of them was in one family. He would give them meat and bread, milk and biscuits every Sunday morning, and sometimes on Wednesday morning. They would give you much corn bread as you wanted. I have seen more meat in that smoke house than anywhere in the county. They would have 25 to 30 head of hogs.

They had a riot here in '74. The white folks was treating the colored folks so bad that they said they was gonna put a stop to it. Four or five of them was killed, and it made the white folks so mad that they wanted to kill up all the niggers in the county, and seemed like they almost done it, from the amount that was killed in that riot.

When freedom come along, master come out one Monday morning and said, "Well, boys you all is just as free as I am this morning." Nigger was wondering what he was going to do, for he still had to look to the white man, for he didn't know what to do with hisself. They had a debate here some time ago—some said colored folks was better off in slavery and some said they wasn't. They have more privileges now —in some things anyhow. I rather be out of slavery than in, all the time.

"Master Got Good When War Come Up"

Yes, I was here in slavery. I will be 86 years old the 15th of August. My master had 47 slaves. We all lived right in the yard below the white people's house. There was about eight or nine cabins. My mother had eight children; all of us stayed at home. None of us was sold from her. Sometimes they was good and again they was mean. If you didn't do to suit them they would whip you. I have got a many beating over my head with a stick, cowhide, or anything that they could lay their hands on. I was so sassy. I would sass them to the very last. They would knock and beat me again, but I would sass them again. They would whip me 'cause I didn't mind. We would pick wool and have us all sitting around in the house, and I would go to sleep. After a while I would get a lick on my head for going to sleep. Old mistress got sick and I would fan her with a brush, to keep the flies off her. I would hit her all in the face; sometimes I would make out I was sleep and beat her in the face. She was so sick she couldn't sleep much, and couldn't talk, and when old master come in the house she would try to tell him on me, but he thought she meant I would just go to sleep. Then he would tell me to go out in the yard and wake up. She couldn't tell him that I had been hitting her all in the face. I done that woman bad. She was so mean to me.

Well, she died and all the slaves come in the house just a hollering and crying and holding their hands over their eyes, just hollering for all they could. Soon as they got outside of the house they would say, "Old God damn son-of-a-bitch, she gone on down to hell." My mother said she believed I cussed, too, but I didn't. They sho was mean. On Monday morning old master would get up on a big block that was out in the yard and holler for eggs; he would have the niggers bring him all the eggs that was gathered. They would carry you down to the trundle house to whip you. Four niggers was killed in that neighborhood. Old Uncle Henry was hit right in the forehead, and he fell down and never did come to. A woman named Charlotte had real long hair and they cut one side of her hair off and left the other side long. They whipped her one evening for the longest, and told her to get over the barb wire fence, and she said she couldn't, and he jerked her through by the hair, and she never did come to. She was a corpse in 10 minutes after they jerked her through. I never did know how come her to be beat up like that. But they would beat you for anything.

Old mistress had two daughters named Ellen and Nancy; old lady died and Ellen told mother to fix the bed, for since her mother died she believed she was going to die, too. Mother fixed the bed, and she was dead in five minutes.

When the Yankees come I saw them way off in the field, and I didn't know what they was. I run and told master the field was full of buzzards. He filled up a wagon full of bed clothes and things to eat, and was fixing to go away but the Yankees came up there and set fire to that wagon and burned up every one of them bed clothes, and caught old master and tried to make him tell where his money was, but he never did tell that; he never opened his mouth. He didn't even holler.

That was right there in Arrington where we lived. And them slaves was killed right on the next farm from ours at old Payne Buchanan's place. I never been back there but once since I left. I have been here twenty years. When slaves would die they would dig a hole and put you in a box, and take you on up to the woods and burry you. They would burry white and colored in the same graveyard, but the white folks was in the upper part and the colored folks was in the low end. When the white folks would die the slaves would all stand around and 'tend like they was crying but after they would get outside they would say, "They going on to hell like a damn barrel full on nails."

One thing, they give us plenty something to eat and plenty warm clothes. We had red flannel clothes in the winter. In the summer we went about with not a God's thing on but a "shimmy." We always went in our "shimmy tails" in the summer. We had our food put on a table in a kitchen right back of the white folks'. They did feed us good and give us good clothes.

We never did go to no church. White woman took me to church one day with her baby, and I liked to tore them white folks church up shouting. The preacher said, "Let her shout, she is a Christian and got religion." But they never did carry me back no more. They left me home with the baby after that.

One day I was at church here, and a woman come by and give me a awful lick with her fist; she didn't like me nohow, and I knowed she tried to do it, so I just hit her back. She had good sense. Nobody don't get foolish when they are shouting; they just putting on. The War went on four years, and I stayed single, and I was 'gaged to marry the man I did. I never went out with anybody else, for I didn't think it was right since I was 'gaged to him. We got married after he come back. They courted then just like they do now. Only they wasn't fast like they are now. I never in all my born days went out at night by myself and stayed out like these young folks do now. When I went out I always had company.

Whenever a girl had a baby in slavery they never paid no 'tention to it, 'cause they knowed they would have more slaves the more babies they got. Sam Patton come driving up one day with two women in his carriage, and they had veils over they face, and master thought they was white, and he went out to help them and found out they was colored. He run them niggers away from there. Sam Patton was really married to them. We had a girl on the place running out all times of night. I knowed something bad was gonna follow her. You could hear the soldiers after her, and you could hear her scream. They just killed her.

When that happened, mother didn't tell us. I didn't know what had happened to me. I went running to the branch and washed myself. I come on up the road just naked; done been to the branch washing. It never did hurt me, though. The Lord certainly has blessed me.

The white folks would let them sing all they wanted to in the houses. One night they come down and there was three dozen eggs in the fire where they done stole. Mother give me a look, and looked over to the bed, and that meant for me to get up and go to bed; I better had went, too. The fire was hot and one of them eggs popped. Old master looked around trying to see what it was. My mother looked at me for she was scared I was gonna tell. But master didn't stay long, but if he had he would have heard all them eggs. Soon as he left they began pulling eggs out and such a feast they did have. One Saturday night my father and uncle killed a great big mutton. They cooked that mutton and dug a great big hole and put paper over it and put plank across over it and put the mutton there and covered it up. And such another time they did have. They invited company in to help eat it up. They give us nothing, for they didn't want us to know about it, but we knowed it all the time but we knowed better than to tell it. They would kill shoats and have company way in the night. We children would get together and laugh about it. They'd a killed us if we had told.

One day I asked my mother where babies come from; she said the doctor brought it. One day I crawled up under the house when a girl was fixing to have a baby; I heard her holler and after a while I heard the baby crying. I asked my mother why the girl hollered if the doctor brought the baby; she told me to get out of there or she would kill me.

After slavery old master was sitting in the house crying, and he wouldn't tell us we was free, but he sent for his nephew to tell us. The nephew told us to get out, but old master told us we wasn't going to leave. We stayed there four years after slavery. He fed us just like he always did. He sold my father a place right off his place. He fed us and give us clothes just like he always done. He never was mean to us after freedom. He was 'fraid the niggers might kill him. After war come up he got just as good.

I remember once when one of the white folks died old Uncle Albert keeled over on the floor and was just a crying, but when he saw nobody was looking he was just dying a laughing. The soldiers would come and steal all of our butter; we had great buckets of butter in the spring, but the soldiers would come and steal it.

Once they had a runaway nigger, and when they caught him they put a piece of long chain tied on to his ankle and locked it and at night they would put him upstairs. One night old Payne Buchanan come along and put him up, for old master was sick, but he said he saw him go upstairs but he didn't for that nigger got away and stayed away a long time before anybody found him. The flesh was swollen all over that chain when they found him, and it had to be sawed off. He died. Nothing was never done about that.

One night there was a man come and had a little string about a foot long, and he had something on the end of it, and he was swinging it along and when it got to my father it stopped just as still. He said father was going to get whipped the next morning but he would keep him from getting the whipping. Sure enough the next morning they come got him, but they never touched him. They couldn't, for that man had fixed it so they couldn't whip him. This man was a runaway nigger. He just went around keeping people from getting killed. My mother wouldn't let nobody whip her. Old mistress couldn't do nothing with her. She would have the men to tie her, and after she was tied they was 'fraid to whip her.

I remember once a mulatto woman was on the block to be sold and the women would say, "I don't want that mulatto bitch here." Finally one of the brothers bought her. After the War two of her brothers come through, and they carried her away. We had plenty of good food, but at the farm next to us you would see cornbread and meat out on the fence; the slaves would have to get it and eat it the best they could and keep working. He was so mean to them. His name was old Claybrooks. We had a kitchen to eat in, and they just had to eat the best they could. He would make them grab hot dog irons from the fire, and beat them if they wouldn't. Their hands would be so sore from grabbing them that they couldn't open them. He was just mean.

I had eight cards to spin every day. I was good at that. All of us had to spin eight, and sometimes they would be spinning way in the night, and I would be through before night. We made clothes all the time. I used to make the prettiest bedspreads. Men used to shuck corn but the women wasn't there. They would get about forty or fifty men and shuck corn, and they would sing all kinds of songs. We never did have nothing like parties. They would 'low us to make our own quilts.

I got a whipping by my mother every night; I was so bad. Then the children would tell things on me and then I would get another whipping. One day my brother was coming from the spring with a bucket of water, and he said he was sick. I went on up to the house and picked up some rabbit pills that the rabbits had dropped and carried them to him and told him master said take them and he would get well. He swallowed them all like a fool. I didn't think I was going to get a whipping for that but he told mother I had brought him some pills that master sent him. I got a whipping. I used to pick 150 pounds of cotton every day. We would pick cotton and sing, pick and sing all day. A girl would wet in the basket to make her cotton heavier, and she would put rocks in the bottom of it. I told on her, for I didn't want her to beat me. I have been a good worker, but I ain't no good now.

When they wanted to marry they just asked old master, and the squire would marry them. Sometimes they would slip there and sleep with the women and wouldn't marry at all. They would slip just like they do now. They would let us have company, but they couldn't stay no longer than ten o'clock. They couldn't stay until one and two o'clock like they do now.

My mother used to sit on me and whip me. One day I nearly tore a piece out of her and she never did set on me to whip me no more. I caught hold of her with my teeth, and a tried to bite a piece out of her butt.

It's Against the Race
to Talk about Slavery

Yes, I was a slave and knows plenty about it but I don't care to talk about it. Nope, I don't care to give out nothing I know about it; just don't think it would do any good. I been setting down before now and talking to some people about slavery time, and they said it was a damn lie, that white people didn't do any such thing. I was right there and looking right at it, and they was giving me the lash, too. I knows it will just start some sort of disturbance, and I don't care to talk about it. Nobody ain't goin' to believe what you say anyway. I just don't care anything for it at all, 'cause colored people don't see and use sense in anything at all. They don't do that.

My parents are all dead; grandparents all dead. Nope, my father and mother didn't b'long to the same marster. She had two husbands, and they were all in slavery and b'longed to different men. She b'longed to one white man and they b'longed both to another man. They all lived up in Virginia. Sometime they would have two or three men on the same farm, for when one died a second one come in and then another man he got along in his place. When he died they got another supply; sent for three or four more. That's how come she would have two or three men on the same farm. So she had been married to two men who b'longed to the same old white folks. My parents had eight children. I suppose they did have big families in those days. That was the reason my mother had to marry again, because they would carry their husband off to one state or another. White folks when they children married they just give them all they wanted them to have and let them go.

Oh, yes, they allowed them to come from one farm to the other and see each other if they weren't too far from them. No, no, honey, bless you honey, they couldn't come to see them every night. You see the reason I say I don't care to have anything to say is because they disbelieve it anyway, and these white folks here don't like to hear about how they fathers and mothers done these colored folks, and would say they were right and these other niggers believes it and would tell me it was all a damn lie; they never treated Negroes any such way. (What have you been telling them to make them say that?) I don't tell them much at all. I don't want a bit o' scratch made on any book about me. My colored friends ain't got any sense at all and they got just enough education to make a fool out of themself, and all he wants to do is to be right next to the white man and pass the word along the line that "Mr. So-and-So want so and so done." He just wants to stand around and give orders. Of course you knowed that in slavery time. Your mothers and fathers told you that. You might guess from morning till night and wouldn't believe in your own heart that they were really that cruel. I know it would just create disturbance between the two races—white and black ones. White folks, now, some of 'em they were shame for what they fathers and mothers done, and a Negro b'lieves what he says because he is white and got straight hair and blue eyes. So I don't never have any talking with them 'cause they don't know what they are talking about.

I been to Nashville 'fore you was born. I was there 'fore or when the first guns were fired. I was in the battle with Hood's raidin'. Oh, I can tell you that (about being in the War) if you want to know, but I don't care to talk about slavery 'cause most of them slaves are all dead. You don't see no right black folks now. (Did they have black folk in slavery?) The world was full of black folk in slavery. They had about a hundred and fifty, or sixty, or seventy-five working in the field. (How many did your marster have?) About 16 men. I don't care about telling about it sometime because there is always somebody on the outside that knows more about it than I do, and I was right in it, so ordinarily I don't care about talking it.

I was in Hood's raid and men fell and nobody knows how many were killed in it. It was down on Franklin Pike. I was there 'fore the guns were fired. I came on the train from Chattanooga because Hood was so near Nashville; he had got between Nashville and Franklin, Tennessee. Men was slain from Nashville all along, all along the wayside from Nashville to Franklin, and the last gun I fired on the battlefield was at Columbia, Tennessee. They set fire to the bridge and burnt it up, and we had to put in a pontoon bridge. They got over and left some cavalry behind to keep us from putting in a pontoon bridge, but we run them away from there. We whipped around to Chattanooga because there was about seven or eight hundred of them. We had about a year and six months of this. Well, it was in 1865, but don't know what month or day; never thought about keeping dates. Don't know much about education. All I got I got out in the field. That was my fountain pen and pencil, the blade of the hoe, and my slate was the ground. What education I got, ain't a man who come in Clarksville ever seen me set in school a day. What I learnt is self-made. (Did you have sisters and brothers?) Yes, they were young and they went to school while I was out in service. I had one about 14 and one about 9, and I was nearly a young man and went into the army—about 19 years old. I had to run away. They caught me the third time and carried me back home. They wouldn't do nothing but everlasting whip me, my Lord. I fought to free my mammy and her little children all through Nashville and Franklin and Columbia, Tennessee, and all down through Alabama and Augusta, Georgia.

My mother died just about three months before I was mustered out of service, but they stayed here with their stepfather. When a soldier got away and jined the army and he wanted to get off they put soldiers on horses with guns, and sent them with him. I was born in 1842, and I am 90 years this year—oldest one of my mother's children.

There is one person here a little older than me, John Bibbs—at least I think he is older than I am. He was good size up over me when I first knowed him. My old marster just like the balance of the white folks. if they had to give you clothes, they would give you good ones; if it was something to eat, would give you good to eat and if a whipping, would give you a good one. My marster whipped me once and he told me, "Well, it won't be the last one," because he didn't give me over eight or ten licks. But the overseer did the work. He did this while he was able. He give me one lick, and I remember it now, and will for the balance of my days. I just didn't want to take it. I run away when but a chap, and when I got big enough I wouldn't stand them over me. I would fight. If I could get hold of anything, I would go to work and work like I had some sense. If he was about to get too hard for me, I would foot it. I would let him see the bottom of my heels all day. I never had but one or two that I believe could do anything with me. I commenced doing just like the men were doing. (How long did you stay away?) From four or five weeks is about as long as I ever stayed when I run away. (What did you do for food?) I would get in your field, or somebody's, and get roas'n ears and roast them, just cook them in the shucks. When the shucks scortched enough it would dry them out and it was just like roasted corn. I would go by somebody's spring-house where they had their milk, and help myself. Or I would go by somebody's house and I had all the buttermilk I wanted. I would set it back if I wanted. In those days all of them would run away but one or two. There was one who didn't have to run away. He didn't whip him. There were two just growed up that way—he was an old go-head Negro. The overseers didn't like him. His word would go further with the marster than the overseer's. There were no half-white slaves on the place. Not a one. This was all in Christian County, Kentucky.

(Did you court the girls?) Nope, I would just laugh at them sometime. Once in a while I'd go out and the pad-rollers got me sometime. The rule was not to whip you on your marster's plantation, or they would have to pay for it. But I would fool them. When they would say, "Have you got your pass?" I'd tell 'em yes, I had my pass. You see they would say, "John, have you got a pass?" and I would say, "Yes, sir." One time there were three men, and brothers. I told them I had a pass and handed it to them. I never seen them until I was right at them, I was so busy playing with some neighbors' boys. When I looked up, three of them pad-rollers were around me, and I just knowed I was whipped. But while they was looking at the papers I give them, I give them the dodge and when they found out, I was over the fence about six or eight hundred yards. I was running so hard it looked like my heart would bust. When I looked back they were standing looking at me, and would say, "Never mind, we'll get you next time." I would run so I could get over the fence and would be on my own premises and they couldn't bother me. I knowed that.

(How did you court the girls?) Me, I didn't court them. I didn't court them a'tall. All of them loved me; I didn't court. You see, they didn't do like they might do now. They would call one another "Hon," and I would say, "Sweet." And they would say, "Let's go home," and there would be something going on like a quilting, and I would go and take a gal home. They didn't do like they do now. One time I seen a girl have her hand up in the collar of a boy, and she take a small switch off a tree—a black gum tree—and give that boy a whipping. He wasn't no account. He had asked for her company and she granted it. He was too young. They weren't allowed to have company before they was 21 years old; and for a boy when he was just about 17 years old he was just about the right age to be considered a man. I never had nothing to do with any of them hardly (speaking of corn shuckings and quilting parties). They would get drunk just like these Negroes do now, and they didn't sit down and talk about business and laugh and talk, but they would get drunk and do cutting.

(Where did they get the whiskey?) They would get the whiskey from the stillhouse, steal it if they got chance to do it. Me, for my part, I didn't care much about it. I heard my mother and father talking about how much *they* drank. My mother, she drank same as a man. I was 10 or 12 years old, and didn't have nothing to do with it. I heard him say, "Sally (clearing his throat) this here will keep me warm." From what I can think of it now, I guess the snow was about a foot and a half deep. He had to go about two or three miles to a blacksmith shop where he worked, and the old man said it would keep him warm. So I thought maybe it would keep me warm, too. He would pour him out a glass and drink it, and she would drink the half. So I thought to myself I had better drink some after he had gone. I didn't know nothing about it, but just wanted to experience it. Folks ought to be very particular about what they do before children. I know what he said, "I will be just as warm as toast." So I wanted to be just as warm as toast. So I went down and got that jug. It was might near full and I got that jug out from under the bed. There was a bed curtain of fringe tied from one end of the bed to the other end at the foot. You couldn't come into a person's house and look under the bed as you can now. But they would take it off and wash it, and it could be run up on a cord and you could go to one end and pull it to the other. They always had a little more left than she needed, but it would be nicely tied, and they would fix it around there and it would look right nice, and whenever they would come in they would pull out this jug. Well, I got this jug up and the strength was going up into my nostrils, and I had sense enough to know that if I didn't take it down it would go up into my nose. I drank whiskey, and in order to get it down I had to take two or three steps toward the table before I could get it down. I got drunk. I was drunk all that day and all that night. She told the white folks that I was sick—my mother did. The next morning I was no better and she fooled around and got a rag made of sheep wool (don't see none now) and boiled it and poured milk down there and drenched me to death. That was to keep old Mis from knowing I had been drunk all that day. My dad had pitched out for his shop, and I had just wanted to keep warm. I begin drinking and had to drink to keep it from running into my nose. I stay drunk like today and tomorrow and like to have stayed drunk three days. She sent for the doctor and he come. But I was just sick from being drunk, or I was just drunk and sick.

These young people don't know nothing these days. They think they got something but it is only a book knowledge. They start out with rational knowledge. They pass the grammar school and then they turn out to be a fool. Just got ideas and no sense. I can just wrap up some of the high school ones with my sense.

My stepfather was a blacksmith and my mother was a weaver. She weaved most all the time. These white folks where they lived had a very large farm. It was cut into five farms and sold after the War. I have been there. First it was four, and one larger than the others, and that man died and then it was cut into five.

(Were there any churches during those days?)No churches. They went to the white folks church and sometime some old darky would take his text from any place and talk about Sampson slayed the abolitioners, not Philistines. That was what he slayed—Philistines. The white folks would tell this colored preacher that was what the text said. The young white fellows did that in order to have something to laugh about. They would shout and pray. The whites would set there and then go off and laugh about it, about that old uncle So-and-So's sermon. And they'd tell others they ought to hear him preach about slaying 10,000 abolitions. Yes, the colored folks slipped and prayed sometime. They used to go outdoors and they would have a great big old scalding pot—the one that would be used for scalding the shoats in. They would get that pot and take it out to a place and make a fire under it. Then they would come to the house and a while before night would send about two up to the house to kill a shoat and clean him. That was the way they done on our place. They would kill hogs about three or four weeks before Christmas. They would salt him down and smoke it. But these darkies didn't get no fresh meat unless they stole it. When they was singing and praying they would get a little ways off, about half the distance from the house, and would take that pot and bring it in the house, and raise one side up a little from the ground.

You never seed a spinning wheel, I reckon, is you? Well, they would take sheep wool and card it and would make a bat, and they would start that spinning wheel running. You see they used to make our coats then—all our overcoats, too. I never seen but one overcoat until after the War. Even the white people didn't wear them. But these would keep us just as warm as if they was overcoats. We just called them that anyway. They didn't wear overcoats, just wore dress coats. Well, this spinning wheel would be just turning over and over and you could hear that wheel whip from here to a long ways, and it would roar louder than it did when they were spinning. The cloth they used to make would be stout and thick. They would get the cloth spun during the time they were having prayer meeting.

The slaves married like they do now. If you wanted your preacher to marry you, they would but if you didn't, they would have a white preacher. Sometime the white people would give one of the biggest *to-do's* you ever heard of. They would dance and eat and so on. Yes, they would join right hands and the matrimony was said like they do now. Some of the old colored preachers could read and some couldn't. They used to tell experiences and come up and talk about God blessing their soul and some of them would get religion. After the War they asked them all those questions. Some of them said their mother and father were both dead and they would just get to studying about them, and it looked like something would speak to them, and if they would get religion they would see their mother and father again, and if they didn't they would never see them again. All this would cause a person to pray. Like today, I get to studying sometimes about my old people and here I have got so old I am hardly able to ask a blessing for what I eat. Sometimes I feel right good in my heart, feel like if I would die I would go right straight on to heaven and if I would stop at that moment, I would say that. But at another time I might not say that. I might say that I have had religion for a long time but seems like I get so far back and it has been so long since I felt the spirit, I think I made a mistake and had better go back and try it over a second time. When I first embraced a hope in Christ I never have felt that way since. It just looked like to me I had more strength than four or five men had. It just looked like to me I could just pick up a house and tote it.

I prayed on the battle field some of the best prayers I ever prayed in my life. (Why?) Sometimes it looked like the war was about to cut my ears off. I would lay stretched out on the ground and bullets would fly over my head. I would take a rock and place it on top of my head, thinking maybe it would keep the bullet from going through my brain, for I knew that would kill me. I'd just lay out, and I was just as thin and looked like one of these old spreading-adder snakes. After a while they would say, "Forward march." They never say, "Get up." So I'd get up myself and move off and then they would tell me to commence firing. sometimes they wouldn't let me fight at all. The Chaplain or some one of them would pray sometime. They never said nothing about no Lord, they would pray just a little old nigger prayer. They would ask God to "give us the victory this day." Words of praise was not to the strong or to the swift, but to he who held out to the end. For my part, I said every word that I ever heard anybody else say. I wan't giving God no heart. I was just saying what I heard the other people say. But I made God some of the finest promises that ever were made.

Our original home was in Chattanooga, but you would be called out and have to go down to Georgia and Alabama. They all join Tennessee on some part of it—Alabama, Georgia and Arkansas; there is a little point there somewhere that they all run into one another. I believe you can go out of Tennessee into Virginia, Georgia, Kentucky, Alabama and Arkansas. You can go into six of these anyway.

I think it is against the race to tell about how the white people done us back in slavery. I don't want to do anything to tear down; I want to build up. These white people that used to be here before the War, it is just now and then that you can run up on them, and if you do, they are about as old as I am. The law says white and black shan't mix. Now, who made that law? They made that law. I made a law with my hoe that all those weeds must die that I hit.

I want to tell you about what makes people mean now—murdering and everything else. Strong drinks is raging. Do you know how come thay are raging? Because it is a mystery. Whiskey is not natural water and if it wasn't bad it would do you different. Whiskey ain't never done anybody any harm yet, unless they go and drink too much of it that's got deadly poison in it. You drink too much of it with that alcohol that comes from under the earth, and it has just got too much in it. If it didn't heat you up inside, they just didn't put enough to heat you up; it works slow. It is the same as lye. After years man began to get weak nerves and first thing he gives right down at once and dies and I don't believe you could find a sound place in him that wasn't poison. It was not the juice out of the apple nor the corn, but it was the alcohol; that was what it was. These white people say black and white can't mix. Black people had nothing to do with making no law a'tal, but yet they would handle him by the law as if he had part in it. White folks, they will take you to the jail and if he subscribes (describes) you, he will go down and get you out of jail. He made that law himself and he is the first to violation. His race of people is gone Caucasian; they allow everybody but a black one to come in his field and into his vineyard to eat and drink but a nigger. Now watch me now, watch me, I'm almost turned preacher. Well, he is not a nigger at all but he was stolen from Africa. I don't like to get mad because I will sin. Well, they are crossed in and they have got them spottided (spotted) worse than any flower garden. You know how they used to have beautiful calico, all spottided and polkie dotted, but they don't have it now. But that is the way the white race is now; there isn't no Caucasian now; they have all run out. The Irishman come to this country and they crossed in with the Caucasian and he is half a Mongo. I named them that myself; I just give them that name. Just like they used to have a way of calling geese when they were crossed in with the tame ones. Neither one of them didn't have a language, they had a cross. What made it still worse, an Irishman and a Dutch mixes; here comes a Jew and he will marry an American woman. He is not a Caucasian nor a Jew but descended from the Jew nation—one part Jew and one part Caucasian. Then they have children who is part Irish and part Dutch; they grows up and marry another or one of that mixture right back again, and that makes four different bloods. Well, it is the same way with whiskey. That makes a treacherous nation and that begins a treacherous people. They will get mad walking along and some of them will take a mad fit, drink some of that alcohol, go get his pistol and shoot somebody—maybe somebody in his family—all on account of that. But if the white folk sees old *Nap* go into his garner, get out some wheat to make him a little cake, he will go right straight and report him to his company. When the white man start talking with some colored woman I got to let him go; I can't say nothing nor can't do nothing, but it ain't so coming from the other way. I can just keep on talking now if you is got time to listen; yes I can just keep on going.

Fed More White Folks
Than Anybody

I got three children dead but I ain't got nobody now in the world living. I'm just by myself. My father got killed on the battlefield when I was three years old. I got the little dress here now that I wore. I'll get it and show it to you. Here 'tis, ain't it cute and little. My mother used to wash it every week and I washed it after she died till I got so I wasn't able to do it. My mother been dead 44 years. It gives me a pleasure to look at this little dress. Look here at the lace where I tore it going to my mother asking her for tiddy. I never did sew it up 'cause she said I stepped in it going to her.

Pete (a white man who she said boarded with her) been dead about four months now. He went crazy. They took him to the hospital but he didn't want to go. He lived two days after they carried him to the hospital. When he left that morning he says, "I ain't coming back no more, Uncle Jake; I am going on and you come on, too." Uncle Jake died in two weeks after Pete died. I have fed more white folks than anybody. They worked at Phillips and Buttorff's foundry and my table was full all the time. I used to live right next door there and had a restaurant, but I got burnt out. I lost everything I had, ain't even got clothes now. My legs got burnt, too. I used to feed from 16 to 18 white men for dinner. They come down here now to see me and say, "Aunt Liza have you got anything to eat?" I say, "No, I can't work now."

My young mistress is near about as old as me. She's got seven boys, and she lives at Morgantown, Tennessee. Two men come here looking for me and wanted to know if my name was Liza Denton, and I told them that it used to be Denton but I married a Reynolds. Me and my husband come to Murfreesboro and worked at the Jordan Hotel. I left there and brought my mother with me. She never seed a train till then. She never wore nothing but a sunbonnet, a gingham dress and a white apron. I want to be like her. I want to go that way.

I don't never want to see another war. That one I saw was 'ragious. My marster had a lot of horses and fillies and saddles and the Yankees would come in cussing and burn down fences and everything in sight as fast as they could.

The only salt we ever got then was that what drapped down on the ground from the meat that was hanging up. It was just the color of brown sugar. We never knowed about no other kind. I belonged to the Rebel folks. The Rebels didn't have no other kind of salt. We had a great big kettle outdoors that set up on a rack. We used to play around that, but mother used to give us little tasks to do every day. She would make us pick up chips and we better had do whatever she told us to do. She come out one day and say, "Liza Jane, better come in and see 'bout putting the bread on." I acted like I didn't want to do it. She drawed back and struck me here (pointing to face). She had a hard time. Yankees used to beat us and we would dodge. Mother would take the baby and lay her in the cornfield to hide him and then lay down close by him. Mother would be listening. One of the soldiers said, "Don't hurt that little baby." My mother had four children, that was all she ever had. I was the only girl. My mother had a good marster and mistress. I had my wrists burnt once when I was a child and my mistress went to her grave with her hands so she couldn't shut them up, putting me out. Me and my brother was burning one another with broom sage, and I caught fire and went running and hollering. My mistress caught me and her arms stayed like this (bent) all the time. She used to say, "I wouldn't sell her for nothing. I wouldn't take less than a thousand dollars for him (brother) and I wouldn't take two thousand for her; that's my little breeder." Mother said I cussed and said, "Damn you, I won't never be no breeder for you." I don't know how I learned to cuss. They allowed us to have everything to eat they had. They had a big barrel of molasses propped up down in the cellar and I tried to get some of it one day, and pulled the barrel over on me and mashed my foot. Marster told mistress to "give them children enough molasses to eat, there's plenty of it here. They wouldn't have to steal it if you had give them enough." I oughta been whipped. Children then wasn't like they is now. Little girls know more now than I did after I got grown. I work all one day and a half in a hollow stump trying to find me a baby. When the doctor come around with the saddle bags I told him to bring me a baby. I never knowed where they come from. They know now where they come from. I hear these little girls talking about their beaus now. They know more than I know.

My mother worked everywhere, out in the field and in the house, before I got big enough to work. I didn't have sense 'nough to drap corn. They made a cross for me to put corn right in that cross. He got down five or six times to show me where to put it, and then I would put it in the wrong place. I got a whipping for it, and I learned to drap. Yes, you would have to drap it fast 'cause somebody would be behind me to cover it up. I wouldn't know how to drap it now, 'cause they don't have no crosses or nothing now, they just sow it a certain distance apart.

They put my brother on the block and sold him off, and they carried him down South. I cried and cried till marster's brother told me to hush crying that he would go and get him tomorrow. I hushed for a while and break out crying again. But he went and got him and told his brother that he was going to pay for him hisself. He was a good man. He said he wasn't going to have that child crying for her brother.

I was baptized in Caney Folk River, with ice thick enough for wagons to roll over it. They broke the ice and throwed me under it. I have got that same old-time religion today. These children today ain't got the fire I got. None of them ain't raised. Go over there in that house, you can't see where it's ever been swept in the world.

After I got burnt out I joined a little nine-cents a week insurance. I got two weeks insurance money lacking a penny, and the man ain't been around yet. I heard they was gonna cut out all these little insurances like mine. Look like I would get my money back, though, if they gonna cut it out. Mrs. Griffey told me about it today. Last week I looked and looked for him to come, but he ain't come yet. I had 35 quilts to get burnt up and 11 woolen blankets and my burial clothes all got burnt up, too. Mrs. Shaw give me a thick skirt and told me to wear it on Sunday, but I got to wear something now. I'm used to wearing flannel in the winter, but I can't wear it now 'cause I ain't got it. I am insured in the Independent Life Insurance. I done all that when I had money. I got a paid-up policy down there, $200. I took out on a little boy a $225 policy. When he died I couldn't see his mother suffer, so I gave her all but $25.00. Sometimes I don't care if my time was right now.

(At this point one of her white friends came in saying that he had walked twenty miles that day looking for work and couldn't find one thing to do. He said he felt like jumping in the river, and things would just have to get better or he didn't know what would happen.)

Don't talk that way, if you want to talk that way, go outside; don't let me hear you. Why there are thousands of folks just like you, who can't find work to do. I am bothered so much about other folks I don't have time to worry about myself. I tell you people is doing all sorts of things —robbing, stealing, killing and setting houses afire. It's awful. (Visitor: Well, I can't sleep at night now. I just wonder how folks gonna do. I don't eat much, but you got to eat a little to keep alive.)

You all don't know the war is over. There is gonna be another war, watch out; they gonna fight with these booms; that is what they gonna fight with. I reckon charity is doing what they can.

My husband been dead 45 years. He died at Mt. Pleasant. He was robbed and killed; cut his throat. When he sent word that he would be home one Saturday night, I had a big turkey. He was crazy about coons and I had one, a big old fashioned pound cake and a white cake, and you could get a gallon of whiskey for a dollar then. I got that for him. I went down to the First Baptist church and stayed till nearly twelve o'clock, and said I must go on home, for if he was coming it was about time for him to be coming. I hadn't been sleep long when Brother Huddleston, deacon of the church come and knocked on the door. He talked so much like my husband I opened the door before I found out it wasn't him. He came in and said, "Uncle Hy can't come this Saturday 'cause he had so much work to do, but here is $49.00 he sent you, and tell you enjoy yourself. He said you would be glad to get the money anyway." But I was sorry he didn't come. I let the guests come on and let them eat the food anyway. Just about daybreak I heard somebody give one scream after another. Mrs. Solomon's husband got killed and she wanted me to go to the depot with her. I didn't feel like going, for I felt bad all over. I looked up and saw the messenger boy coming, and fell over. The news come to me that my husband got killed. Dr. Murphey worked with me three days, trying to get me to my senses. I couldn't go where he was 'cause smallpox was so bad then they wouldn't let you out if you once got in there. He was a great big fine fat man. He was robbed of $49.00.

My oldest brother died in Warren county. He had malaria fever. My other brother fell out of a tree and died, and my baby brother went away and come back and took pneumonia.

The Yankees had my mother toting water half the night putting water in boots. They told her that was dry bones in the valley. She didn't know they was just empty boots. They told her they wasn't going to hurt her little girl. They camped right there all night. Ain't nobody seen the time I have seen. Old mistress whipped the blood out of me just once. That was the only time she whipped me. Old marster got a hickory stick and whipped her and said nobody ain't got no business with niggers if they don't know how to treat them. He told her if she whipped me again like that he would cut the blood out of her. He was so much better than she was.

My father belonged to Uncle Sam. He fought with the Yankees.

When I had a restaurant I never turned a hobo down. If they would come in hungry I would give them something to eat. I always had a big table full. I had a big dish of hog head, a dish of fish, chitlins and a big dish of chicken, and I always had plenty of cornbread and homemade light bread. I had just plenty of everything, and believe me I had the white people to eat with me. I remember one day a white man come up to me and shook me—I was sitting out in the yard, nodding—and said, "You don't know me, do you? Well, if you don't know me, you will know me. This is the old hobo," and he threw three silver dollars in my lap. That woke me up good, and I said, "Name of God, who is this give me this money? "Then he said, "Don't you remember the old hobo? This is him."

Pete worked in the foundry 35 years. He was a boarder. Every Saturday evening they paid me five dollars apiece. They would come in black; you couldn't tell them from a nigger when they first come in. They would wash up and set down and eat supper.

My mother was bright and her hair was very long. We used to know when she was coming 'cause she would stand up on the draw bars to let us know that she was coming, and sing, "And must I be to judgment brought to answer in that day." When I was a girl if you walked with a girl who had had a baby we would be cut all to pieces. We wouldn't be allowed to speak to her. Now they ain't folks if they ain't got babies.

Young folks ain't got no manners now. One of the school boys up there pushed up against me and knocked me down and he never did say nothing. I was feeling bad about it for three or four days. Brother Watson said he was going to see something about it. He was nice. He used to give me money often, and come to see me.

Proud of That "Ole Time" Religion

Well, chile, I tell you, my mind ain't on old times today but I'll tell you what I kin. When the War broke out I had three little children. You know when I come along we didn't know our ages nor nothing. They stealed just like they stealed now, times ain't changed much, and people ain't changed none, you kin take that from ole sister Kelly. The white folks throwed the book what had our ages in it in the fire to keep us from having it, and none of us never knowed just how old we was.

When I was about 12 years old, just look like one day the stars was falling, and it got just as dark as it could be. If you wants me to tell you what a hard time the po' ole slave had working and gitting whupped, and sech like a that, I knows about that, yessir, and I ain't forgot neither. I never will forget none of that this side of the grave. I have plowed many a field, honey. Sometime, we was in the field time it was daylight, and sometime even before day broke; we would work there all day, then we had to shell corn at night when it was too dark to bend yo' back any longer in the field. Everybody had to shell a bushel of corn most every night, after we had come in from the field.

Well, my old marster was dead when I got old enough to know things. He died and left a widow, and she had all us slaves under a overseer and some guardians. Well, she was good as most any old white woman. She was the best white woman that ever broke bread, but you know, honey, that wasn't much, 'cause they all hated the po' nigger. When she died she said the only reason she hated to die was on account of her children; didn't say a word 'bout her po' slaves what had done wuked theyselves theyselves to death for her. Her name was Mary Booker, and they had a big farm here near Columbia, Tennessee, just 'bout one mile from the courthouse.

Well, we lived and wuked there till she died, then I was hired out; I was 'bout 13 years old then. Yes, you know white folks is always after the money. I tell you, honey, I wuked and lived with good ones and bad ones, too. You got to know something 'bout the Lord to git along anywhere. You don't know nothing 'bout him? Well, you better know him; better learn 'bout him, that's what'll help you. When the War came I married a man by the name of Jim Kelly, and then he died and I come home and lived on the white folks' place. When Christmas come, we would come home; all the white folks would come from New York and places, and there was sho' nuf fine times, I tell you. Them ole red headed yaps would bid us off to the highest bidder and we couldn't do nothin' but pray. Yes, fine times for them, but awful for us po' niggers. Yes'm, they would cry you off to the highest bidder for the next year. One by one, we had to get up on that block, and he bid us off.

Well, we used to have little singing and praying like good ole time revival; and we would take pots and put them right in the middle of the floor to keep the sound in the room; yeah, keep the white folks from meddling. Yes'm, the sound will stay right in the room after you do that. Well, we allus used these old house wash pots like you boil clothes in, you know. Just turn one down in the middle of the floor, that was sufficient.

Let me tell you how I got it. And I sho' got a good one, too; my 'ligion will stand for all time, I'm a-telling you. One Sunday morning I got up. I was just 12 years old. That morning, I commenced to crying and I just couldn't stop; seem like my heart was full of water. Well, I cried all that morning, and when we got dinner done, I went in and asked the old white woman to let me go home. That was when I was at the Brook place. I never said nothin' 'bout why I wanted to go, I just asked her to let me go. She wouldn't let me leave, o'course, 'cause I was hired out to her. You see, honey, that wasn't the Brook place; that was 'bout four miles from there where I was hired out. Well, then, seem like my heart would bust sho' 'nuf. By and by something just said to me, you go but don't stay long. I went on home and cried most all the way. I couldn't help it to save my life. Well, Ole Miss Mary Brook ask me what was the matter, and I said I didn't know. You know in them times folks had little chairs sitting back in the chimney corner; and I went and set back in there and cried some more. 'Pear like to me I couldn't keep from it, and so by and by she says to me, "Honey, time you was goin' home." I don't know what was the matter with me, but I took and got over the fence and started on down the road. Well, I walked along, and by and by I got down into a little flat place right near a pond, and 'pear like to me something said, "You never shall die a sinner." Well, I jest trembled and shook like a leaf. I know what was the matter with me, then. Well, I heard that voice three times, and every time it said, "You never shall die a sinner." It seem like it was inside of me, somehow or other. I said, "What is that talking to me?" Well, chile, I got happy and I jest went up and down, jest shouting and praying and crying for dear life. I said, "Lord what was that talking to me that way?" I jest asked him like that; ooh yes, good God, I 'members it jest like it was yesterday. Something said, like I'm speaking to you right now, "You better gwan, might come back and talk to you again." I stopped right still and started thinking, and seem like a clear loud voice said, "You is jest in God's hands, and you must praise and bless God all the time." Well, honey, you know I was young, and I knowed no more about it than this here rock, but I sho' felt something and I heard something, too.

Well, by and by I kinda got composed and went on up to the house. I didn't know nothin' 'bout it, cept'n I felt funny and sorta light, and I went on in the house and told ole Aunt July. She said, "Chile, jest hold yo' peace, you done been left in God's hands." Well, you know I didn't know what that meant, now you know I was ignorant, jest young, you know. Aunt July told me to pray, pray. Well, I didn't know no more 'bout praying than this here rock. I just cried, 'cause I had nobody to tell me nothing, and nobody what could 'splain the grace of God to me then.

Well, I went on like that for a long time, didn't know nothing 'bout nothin', bless yo' heart, but I jest felt something, didn't know what. I went on my way by myself, and one day I went behind the house and sat down to cry. Well, I got back there and went to sit down, and I tell you the gospel's truth, I kin go and put my hand on the spot right now, where I jest fell face foremost—something just struck me. "Ooh Lord!" I cried, "have mercy on me, a poor hell-deserving sinner." You heard me, I said I didn't know how to pray, but them words jest come to me from nowheres; chile, I fell to crying, jest like I was crazy; I felt right crazy, too, praise God, but I wasn't; it was jest the grace of God I had done been looking for, lo them many weeks. Oooh, merciful Jesus, honey, you ain't never been through all that has you? Why, I went three days and nights without eating and drinking; didn't want nothin', jest was uplifted and free from sin. Somehow or other that morning, I was jest as light as a feather. I got up and I had to go to the foot of the bed to git my clothes, and I stooped down to get 'em, and seem like something jest stopped me, just struck me still, ooh, Jesus, chile, I got right stiff; finally I got my clothes off the floor and wrapped my arms around them right tight, and then, great God, I got upon my knees and prayed the Lord with a prayer that tumbled from my lips, that the Lord had give me to pray hisself—ooh chile, I tell you it's a wonderful feeling when you feel the spirit of the Lord God Almighty in the tips of your fingers, and the bottom of yo' heart. I didn't know then what was the matter with me. I knows now when I feel that spirit arising in my body, yessiree.

Well, I tell you chile, when I got up from prayer, I felt like I was brand new—I had done been washed in Jesus' blood, ooh my great and holy Father! Sometimes I gits to thinking 'bout it and I git happy. Yessirree, chile, if you wants ole sister Kelly to tell you 'bout her 'ligious 'sperience, I sho' kin tell you that, 'cause I sho' been through a great fight with the devil, I tell you, oooh praise God. I didn't know no more 'bout nothin' than this rock, but honey you asks me now, I kin tell you with the very words what God put in my mouth.

That morning, seem like Jesus said to me, "My little one, what makes you so hard to believe, when you know I am the one and only God?"—oooh blessed Jesus, there ain't but one God, honey, and that is the one I am telling you 'bout right now. Yessir, I heard him all on the inside, saying "Come unto me, oh my little one, what makes you so hard to believe when you know I am the one and only God, and there ain't but one God but me?" Seems jest like yesterday 'stid of years and years ago, and I still feels the blessed spirit jest like brand new, ain't like this here rock now, I tell you, oooh praise His holy name.

Well, I still didn't know nothin' 'bout praying, but I says "Oooh, my good and holy Father, what can I say to Thee for Thy blessings," and he said in a voice that shook me like a storm, "Open your mouth and I will fill it with all the elements from on high." Lord, bless his holy name, I never will forget that morning when I was saved by his blood, and changed to the woman you see today. I'm sho' Sister Kelly now.

I tell you, honey, you got to be touched from the inside, and be struck by his hand like I was 'fore you feel that holy uplifting spirit.

Well, the last time the Lord spoke to me, he said, "My little one, I have carried you out of this world, and you is no more of this world, but of another world, the holy world, and they will hate you for my sake." That's the truth, ain't it. I don't fear no man but Jesus. He is my God, do you hear me?

Well, next thing happened to me was when my husband died, and I said, "Lord, why didn't you tell me, why did you take him away from me?" Poor me, I said, "Lord you took him away from me." Well, he spoke to me agin, and he said, "I will forever open the way and provide for you down here on this earth," and he sho' has done it, too, I tell you. The devil tried to cheat me, but I jest held on to His blessed hand. What is written of trouble on the heart is written in His blood, and nobody can take the glory of His name away from you. He sho' guides my trembling feet, I tell you, bless His holy name; He sho' is my heavenly Father, ooh merciful God.

Yes, honey, you jest remember this what Sister Kelly's telling you. This ole world is mighty happy to some of you young folks, but when you is running around having yo' good time, jest remember that you got to stand before the most holy of all, God a'mighty, every deed you done, you gotta give strict account of, you got to know yourself, too, don't never fergit that. When I'm dead and gone on to take my seat beside his blessed throne, you'll 'member what ole Sister Kelly told you.

Honey, right now, you young folks is blind, deaf and dumb to the knowledge of God's name; that can't last, you gonna change, do you hear me? We can't do no good unless we got God in our heart, and our heads, too. Bless God, he holds you in the hollow of his hand, and when he changes yo' soul, you gonna make the world know it, do you hear me? You young folks can't carry on yo' wicked ways without some kinda terrible fall, do you hear me: I ain't caring nothin' 'bout nothing else but God now. He's got me in the hollow of his most holy hand. You youngsters don't understand that, but you mark my word, you will 'fore it's done with. You young folks don't want to humble yourself to the Lord and ask him for these things, but I'm going home to Jesus, yessir, oooh praise His holy name.

After I found Jesus I didn't fool with all these youngsters' pranks. I tell you I'm sorry for you, and you young folks what don't know nothin'. You think this world is all of it, but I tell you it ain't; there's sho' a better world 'n this waiting for all those who trust the Lord, do you hear me? I'm a-telling you, you better get that ole time religion, that's what yo'all better do. You got to stand 'fore God for yo'self, jest like me and anybody else.

Well, you young folks wants to know all 'bout everything but the Lord; now you wants to know 'bout cures for rheumatism. Well people used to get polk root, and sasaparilla for rheumatism. Horehound and catnip and mullin, if you git them and make a syrup, it'll sho' cure a cold. I've tried it lots a times, and it's good.

Another thing, when a dog bite you, if you git some hair from out the middle of his back it will draw the poison out. When you stick a nail in yo' foot, if you git some yarn rag and make a fire, and hold yo' foot over it while the rag smokes, it'll take the soreness out. Hurts something awful, though.

Now what you want to know that for? Lord, you youngsters is awful, I tell you. If you dream something and see it in yo' dream, it's sho' to come to pass. If you dream 'bout a man dying, it's going to be a woman what dies in yo' family, that's the way it go, I believe. Been so long since I heared tell of them kinda things, I done kinda forgot.

There's one thing sho', when you stump yo' foot going to somebody else's house to visit, you kin jest be sure that they don't want you, so you jest turn 'round and go right on back. I 'member 'fore I got sick I started cross the street one day to see one of the neighbors, and they was laughing and talking loud, and jest 'bout time I started in the yard I stumped my foot something awful. I jest says to myself, "I know these here niggers don' want me here, and I'm going right back where I come from."

I seen the last fight they had in the War up here in Nashville. Now, children, I'se tired, and I ain't gonna fool with yo'all no longer, yo'all go on home now. I tell you one thing, I done forgot more'n you young folks will ever know; you mind ain't settled enough to know nothing in these days.

Well, children, old Sister Kelly is getting tired a talking; you see I'se gitting old; yo'all come back agin' and I'll tell you some more 'bout the Grace of God. I kin read you many a line in the Bible by rote and I ain't never read a line or writ a line in my life.

Half-White Slave
Who Defied Master and Overseer

So far as slavery is concerned, I can remember back from '56 on up. In the beginning of slavery, in John Tyler's days as President, he made a speech and died from the effects of it. He was a Whig. He believed in slavery in this way, that the girls should be set free at 16 and the boys at 21, and all over that age should be subject to be taken care of by the states that they was in during their latter days.

Men or mechanics were worth from 12 to 1300 dollars, and boys 8 and 9 years old, 5 and 6 hundred dollars. They had to be a mighty heavy man to be worth that much. The United States would spend eighteen million dollars for Louisiana. Slaves went up.

In Lexington, Kentucky, between Bowling Green and Louisville, was a great place for tobacco and flax. They would raise darkies there and place them in droves along the road having a rope between them like these big cable ropes. They would have the left hands of two people tied to the same rope so they could not run away. A mother would walk along with a child, a suckling, and they would take her and sell her from that child like taking a mother from her pigs. They would have fifty or more in a gang. Sometime these darkies would get away from them. When I was a boy my old master died—when I was 'bout 15 years old. He raised me up in the house with him, and when he died they put me out on the farm to work. I would run away. You see, I was raised up in the house of my master because that was where my mother was; and I hate to say it but I am just going to tell the truth, and that is that my old master was my father. When I used to run away, as I was about to say, they would catch me and carry me back.

I had a sister to die while in slavery and while I was in the army. I worked right here around Hillman's furnace and whenever they got ready to whip a darkey, unless there was a written statement not to draw blood, they would strap them down on their stomach with their hands straight out, fastened feet and legs and with a piece of leather with holes cut in it, the size of a quarter, fifteen or more, and attached to a board, and they would ask how much must I give him. Sometimes they would say three dozen, meaning 300 lashed. Then they had a pot with red pepper liquor, they put salt in it and stirred it up. Then they would rip the blisters and take a rag and rub this liquid on him and grease him with a red pepper mixture. If a darkey refused to be whipped they would take him and send him to Mississippi, Alabama, Georgia, or Louisiany. Way down there, maybe if he ran away the bears and wolves would eat him. About 1861 some of the men and women could read. A woman named Fredonia Gallatin told the white folks that the niggers was going to rise and kill the white folks. One white man said that there was one or more niggers that he wanted to see dead because he thought they had more than he had. He said those that had more than he had, he wanted to see them dead and them that didn't have, he wanted to just see them poor like he was. They took these niggers that could read and whipped one or two to death. Henry King was raised right here. They had him put in jail, then carried him to Dover and a man by the name of "Red Head" Bill Martin knocked this preacher over and cut his head off. They took his brother and brought him out and showed him the head of Henry and told him he would put him in the same fix if he didn't stop talking about being free. Then another white man told Bill Martin that if he didn't take that man's head off that stick and go to bury him he would prosecute him. So he did and never succeeded in life. Them was awful times. It seemed that they would do anything and everything to the niggers. They did so many mean things. things.

One time an old man, a low-laying man in his bed, said there was one more case he wanted to argue before he died, and he sent for a man he wanted to see. The man came and just as he came to this house a wheel came out and run down to where there was a still and stopped. I guessed his sense was in the wheel and had to get out some way. They found the still after he died.

Back in those days the master used to take the mother and sell her one way and the children another. I thought that was a brutal act. I remember once they hired me out to a man by the name of Dave Hutchinson, and they had me out in the field and didn't allow me to have any fire. It was very cold, or cold enough to make one want fire. Then when you wanted fire you could take some flint rocks and rub them together and make fire out of the corn stalks from the sparks you made rubbing the rocks together. One time I went up to the house and after I got in the kitchen the cook told me that Master Dave was going to whip me for burning them corn stalks. Sure enough, he came in about that time and told me to come out and cross my hands, but I told him if he was not ready to meet his God in peace then he had better not fool with me. I looked around me and saw one of those old pots (the kind that people used to boil clothes in when washing; they sat out in the yard.) Nearby there was a cup. So I got me a good cup of this hot water and throwed it on him, and ran across a hundred feet until I got to the Russelville road. This was up in Kentucky. They tried to follow me. I jumped across the road to keep them from seeing my tracks, and I went on across another field to a hiding place I had. Then the next day I went three miles further. I finally got to the house of another man I knew and stayed there a week. In those days people didn't think nothing about walking a long distance; they would walk for miles and miles. Now, people make out they can't walk nowhere hardly. Well, it happened that I had learned to write a little. So one Saturday evening I wrote a letter to Hickman, a great horse man who had a cousin that lived down just below Hopkinsville. He put me on a horse and gave me three dollars and told me to *carry* the letters to Hickman (the letter I wrote and the one he wrote). I did this, and he took me and carried me down three miles further to a swamp section, and I was hired there until the tenth day of December. He paid me, then took me over to the store and bought me an overcoat and a pair of red-top boots (and they was great in that day—just to wear red-top boots). Then I got a hat. Then he gave me a letter and sent me to Elkton. I stayed there until the next day, and then went on back up to the house of my master. I gave him the letter. When he asked me where I had been I told him that I had been working out of the sight of man and healing up my Jesus' wound. They laughed. They said if I was not careful the white folks would kill me, for that was the answer that I gave all of them when they asked me anything about where I had been and so on. I finally went on to the Bibbs' house where the house girl said she was glad to see me. When old Mistiss asked me where I had been I told her the same thing I had told those other white folks. Then old Bibbs came outdoors and I showed him the letter from Dr. King. He looked me over and asked where I got my boots and coat. He thought I stole them, but I told him that I was not a rogue. Then he wanted to sell me for five years, but old Mistiss would not agree to it. So I went back on the farm and finished cutting his tobacco. That was in 1863. I had trouble with the overseer. One time he told me he was going to whip me, but I fought him and ran off and came to Clarksville and hid for three days and nights. I had to ford the river because the bridge was burned down. Then I joined the army here, on November 2, 1863, and was mustered out the second day of April, 1866. We were treated worse than bird dogs. When they commenced mustering out the colored troops they told us to go back as close to the old masters as we could get. I didn't like that much. Then the next hard times that come up was the mobbing and lynching of Negroes. Whipping darkies was the joy of the white man back in those days.

White people, some of them, were religious, and most of them belonged to the Anderson Methodist church. Of the Negroes who finally belonged to such church, it is now called the C.M.E. Church. But that was a long time before this happened. They thought Negroes were cattle and stock and some didn't allow them to go to church and few did. Mighty few niggers learned to read and write. They thought niggers only needed to know enough about reading or writing to know how to count rails or stock or something like that. In fact, they didn't seem to be particular about their reading at all.

When the niggers wanted prayer meeting they turned a pot down in the middle of the floor and sang and shouted and the white folks couldn't hear them. Of course, sometimes they might happen to slip up on them on suspicion.

As I might have said before, my master, my real master, the first one, was my father, and my mother was one of his slaves. She faired pretty good, because the master liked her, kinder. I hate to say these things, but they often happened this way back in those days. The masters were often the fathers.

I had a sister who had two children; one in Canada and one in Chicago. She is dead. I had a brother who is dead, too. My mother died before I ran off during those slave days, so I have been without her a long time. I lived in the master's house with her and ate in the kitchen whenever they got ready for me to eat.

I have three daughters, Katie Goff, living in Missouri, and Birdie Woodard Walters, in St. Louis. Geraldine married Dr. Young. She finished nurse training in St. Louis after she finished the public school here. I have one son in Bowling Green, Kentucky. I was born and raised in Kentucky.

People marry different now from what they used to back in those old days. When people married they had to get an order from one master to the other master, and then set a time. I saw them jump over the broom stick many times. The man used to jump over the brook stick and the woman would stand still.

I am 91 years old, and will be 92 on the first day of August. I still got my discharge around here somewhere another; I don't know where. But I can show you my pension slip, or something that I keeps around here. My cook usually keeps up with these things for me. Sorry you all don't have more time so I could rest a while and then talk with you some more. My chest is beginning to hurt me. It hurts me so bad at times that I can't talk very much at a time. You see, too, I am getting pretty old now. I am glad you all came to see me, and come back again.

Father Gave Her to His White People After the War

Just after the War, or way back there right after slavery, people was treated just as mean and bad as ever. I was born in Morgantown, Kentucky. My mother was a slave, born in Richmond, Virginia. My father was a slave, but I don't know where he was born, because he said when he knew anything he was in a house with the white people, and they never did tell him anything. Where I was born, it is a mighty fine country, and they was awful mean to the colored people in that country. I had six sisters and six brothers and they are all dead except myself. They did not live to be old enough to go to school. I did not go to school because they said it was too far to send me to school. I could spell in the old blue back speller. My father's white people taught me that. I was four years old when my father came from war, and he gave me to the white people, and they took care of me just like I was their own people. They didn't want me to get out with colored people, and they didn't want me to get away from them. My father lived five years after he came from war. His young master was to go to war, but he didn't want to go so they put my father in his place. After he lived in camp three months, in the Confederate army, he stole away and joined the Yankees. My father's name was Frank, and they said Frank was a good nigger; never did but one thing wrong in his life, and that was when he joined the Yankees. They didn't want him to join the Yankees. My mother died after she was the mother of eight children. When my father came back from the War—in the old time way of jumping the broom handle—my mother had married again, so he didn't disturb her, and the little children she had then. He just took me. He was sick, he had scurvy, asthma and all like they would have then after the war. My mother had all her children by her second husband, but me. In those days people married by jumping the broom handle, or marrying with a lamp, or by carrying a glass of water on their head. They would give you a pass to go over on the other farm, and if you didn't have this pass the padder-rollers would cut your head off. Later on, two white men came over to my mother's house and said you would have to have license now to live with your husband. They said a new law had been passed. But mother said she was just going to stay like she was. She died and left a house full of little children. They all died like little sheep. My stepfather left them; he was a mighty ladies' man. The doctor said then that the reason all these little children died like that was because they were half clad and didn't have enough to eat. Of course, I didn't know what they meant then, but I know now that half clad meant they didn't have clothes. I was just raised up in a house to work. I got married and been married so long I done forgot. I was 17, going on 18. When I married I had to have license bought, and that was done right in Morgantown. My mother was supposed to sign the papers, but she would not sign them, but the white people where I was living signed them. I have been married only once. We were just like folks are now sometimes, just living together like cats and dogs. I didn't stay with him but only about three or four years. He didn't work, he didn't do nothing. I don't know why I married him. But I was living up there with those white people, and they never wanted me out. I was raring to get away from white folks. I don't know whether I loved him or not, but I

89

guess I did. After we married it seemed he didn't like dark people, and after we married he talked about my color. He was going with a "yaller" woman, and I whipped all the clothes off her once. I had two children by him. Both are dead now. One lived to be 21.

Back there in those days the people was treated awful mean. For a long distance there were no fences, just field, and you had to work. A white man would ride back and forth and about with spurs and a whip, and you had better not look up from your work. You just had to keep working without looking up for anything.

I sent my child, the one that lived to be 21 years old, to school. My husband left me and went up to Evansville with a "yaller" woman, and after six years sent for me to come and get him. I tried to get the money to go for him and they told me if I did they would whip me. But I told them that he was mine, and if I could get the money I was going to him. I didn't go because I couldn't get the money. I was washing all day for 25 cents, and that was just about as much as you could get for any work in those days. I sure tried all 'round to get the money, but just couldn't get it. Well, he died. They didn't think about bringing a body home back in those days.

I was converted by just laying off everything that looked like sin. I just ran away from everything that looked like sin. You got to get tired of it, go away and leave it, let it alone. Going to shows, dancing, and all those things, and having your name on the church book is not it. You do all these things and then go to church and pay your quarter, or whatever it is, and think that is right, but it is not. My name was on the church book when I was ten years old. Father's master sprinkled me when I was ten months old. Since I been grown, 24 years ago or more, I practiced everything everybody else did. I worked for people that danced, I went with people that danced and paid their quarter in the church on Sunday; but I went and heard the holiness preached. I went to church one night and the preacher just preached to me. He preached all about carrying clothes on your head and carrying them on Sunday. I knew he was preaching to me. I couldn't hardly get home. I never eat nor drank for three days, couldn't do it. I said, "Lord, all these years I been living in church and now going to die and go to hell." He showed me just where I would have went to hell, too. But I know I want to go to a resting place when I am gone. I was tied up in every lodge, club; but those things are rotten to the core. They have all kinds of people in them, and I am just talking for myself; they are no good. Anybody else can go any way they want to, but they say there is only one way to go in, and that is through the straight and narrow. If you see these deacons and all these old preachers doing the things you would do, then you would say that they can't say anything to you, for they are drinking, dancing, going to shows, and everything else. Well, the light came after I fasted three days, and all that burden fell off me. You just got to be sure what you are doing. All that burden fell off me. The man I was living with said that night that I was going to be hungry, naked or out of doors for talking that way. But I said I didn't care. He was Ned Turner; and he put me out of my own house. I was living on his ground but I had built with him, and he said if anything happened I would get my money back. He said he would give me that money back. He died long ago. He asked me if I was going to quit the clubs, lodges, and things, and I said, "You just wait." He was a bad man; he believed in everything going on in his house. I am old now, but I believe in everything going on right.

I have been in Nashville I guess about 18 years. I got crippled and came here to be operated on. I thought I could get a home to live here, but I didn't. They told me that my not being a citizen here, I would have to live here so many days or so long before I could enter the City Hospital. But I got acquainted with Dr. Bright and Dr. Hale and they advised me. I am 73 years old the 15th day of March.

In my father's time and all along my mother's time, that's when they chained the colored people and cut them all to pieces with cat-o'-nine-tails and sprinkled salt and pepper on them. And when I married, that man put me right out in the field. I pulled corn, shocked corn and everything. He was awful mean; so much so I never wanted to go on in his name, Malone. I went on in my mother's name, Holmes; and I am Holmes yet. I haven't done any work now for 12 years. The church pays my rent and everybody here is good to me. People that know me and pass by hand me a little money and send me things. I belong to the Church of God, the Sanctified church on Harding Street, and Reverend Martin is my pastor. He is a mighty fine man, if he is black. 'Course it is all right to be black. Way back, colored people lived more friendly together than they do now. You couldn't go to one's house but what if you stayed there a meal would be cooked and served you. My mother was brought from Virginia when she was ten years old. She didn't know anything more about her people over there. In those days way back there the colored people would do just like they do now, but not as bad. Like when I married, the old folks would make you stay with him. There was no parting among the old folks like they do now. When they married, two would hold a broom, and one time she had a candle on her and jumped over the broom stick, then the next time she had a glass of water and jumped over. It didn't fall off.

There were no doctors back there. If you got sick, you would go dig a hole and dig up roots and fix your own medicine. There was not as much sickness then as there is now. They would make their own pills and syrups, and so on. They were a country full of people who practiced with herbs; white and colored people did this. There were several kinds of bark you could get and make a syrup, poultice, or something. There was not nearly so much dying as there is now.

When I was in Kentucky I went to church with the white people, at the Methodist Church. I sat way back behind. There were three seats in the back and a gate between this part and the other part in front where the white people sat. When they had revival they would open the gate and come back there and ask them some questions and try to have them believe. And if they said they believed, they would sprinkle them. The Baptists did the same thing. At the house, I didn't get to eat at the table with the others, but when the old man got through with his meal or got through eating, I could sit down and eat with the rest of them.

I remember two bad locust years. You couldn't walk on the ground for the locust shells, and couldn't hear your ears for them hollowing "Pharoah." They hollowed "Pharoah" for the old Pharoah plague.

Knows Nothing About Slavery but "Whipping Niggers"

Yes, I was here in slavery then. It is pretty nearly left me now, but I know a whole lot. I was sold when I was 9 years old. I never had no mother or father; white folks raised me. I was sold. She was dead. Wilson County on the Woods Ferry Road. Yes, I have been through a heap. The Lawd has sho' spared me. My white folks who I b'longed to 'fore he died, he sent for his children; he wanted to see them and told them he didn't want the nigger traders to get any of them and they bought them all in. I didn't have to go to Mississippi. So many people what I knowed went to Mississippi. I had a daddy and he had to go. My daddy was sold and sent to Mississippi when I was a little bittie girl, and my aunt. I never did get to see him again. He was killed up on Rangers Hill. You know where that is. A old man took me up to the graveyard on Gallatin Road, and we stayed all day but we never did find my father's grave. I never did find it, but Unc'l Charlie told me he was killed over on Rangers Hill. I don't know where that was, but they buried the soldiers what was killed that day out on Gallatin Road, white and black together. I don't know what his name was when he went to Mississippi, but I looked for him. I knew his name before he left, but I don't know who he b'longed to in Mississippi.

They sold a heap of colored people. They passed right by here, taking them to Nashville sale house. A whole lot of them was sent to Mississippi.

Yes, I was here 'fore the Civil War—a long time. I don't know, he had a lot of 'em, and all of 'em dead what I remember, —all but me. He had women he give to his daughters and men he give to his sons; but it's been so long till I can't place them. Some of them I can remember and some of them I can't.

I have been in the white folks hands ever since I was so high. They took me in the white folks house and kept me there and till after the War, and if I went to any colored folks house I had to come back 'fore night. I cleaned up and toted water and scrubbed and washed dishes. I have washed dishes a long time, and done anything they asked me to. But when my mother died I was just throwed away 'cause she took care of me. I had a half-sister and a half-brother, but they is dead.

No'm, he was his own overseer. He wouldn't have an overseer; they beat the darkies too much, and he wanted to beat his own. He used to beat them right smart. I used to remember about him whipping them. I don't know much about colored folks before the War. I wasn't 'lowed to go to see them. I better not be seen talking to colored people; they would whip me. I couldn't talk to the Negroes in the kitchen. I slept with ole mistiss till I was too big and used to kick her; and then they made me a pallet on the floor, and I never stayed in her bed any more. She told Mary, her daughter, to make me a tick and let me sleep on the floor. The girl said "Why?" and she said, "She kicked me, I didn't sleep a bit last night." And she got some straw and I slept right by her bed. When she died they wrote me a letter, and I didn't go. That was after the War. They had treated me so bad I wouldn't go back. We lived right on the Stuart Ferry Road. I don't remember but one sister and she died right after the War.

93

No, all had houses, and all stayed in the house. The house was built; just a little ole shack. Every family had a little ole shack to stay in. If there was three or four in this family they would stay. They had just one room in the house. Wasn't no cooking done out of the house, it was all done in the house (the white people's house). They gave them plenty to eat.

When the War came all of them ran away and came to Nashville. Nobody stayed but Unc'l Charlie. I had to stay. I stayed in the white folks house and they wouldn't let me out of the house without some of the white children with me. I don't know none of them what's living. One of the grandsons used to come here, and everytime he would come to Nashville he would come here. Well, I used to nurse him when he was a little baby, and he wouldn't mind his mamma, but he would mind me. Yes, he was a grown man, married, and when he would come to Nashville he would always stop to see me and give me a piece of money. The last piece of money he gave me was a dollar bill. He was sick then. I never seed him any more then for a long time, and he come in a wagon and called me to the gate and give me two dollars and say, "Aunty, that's all I can give you. That's all I am able to make; but when I got a dollar you got one." He would always bring me a chicken or butter or something or 'nother. His mother was dead and his father was dead, and he didn't have any friends at all; he said his sister wouldn't care anything about him.

I don't know. I don't remember seeing any of them marry on the place. I don't know anything about it 'cause I didn't get out amongst colored people, and I didn't have anybody to tell me about it.

Till the War had ceasted two years after I stayed there, and they put me out and told me to go on they was tired of giving me anything, and to go on and work for myself. And I started working for some white people—for John Paul and Anne Ridley, and she had a baby and died before she got up, and he took the baby to his mother and that broke them up. They (the slave owner's family) said they wasn't gonna feed me and dress me any longer. Miss Anne Ridley she dressed me up one Sunday and I went to church. I had on a silk dress and a white hat, and I didn't want anybody to touch me. It was the first I had on 'cept cotton dress and cotton bonnet. They was such nice people, but they had to break up; but they wouldn't have but that one chile, and he took that to his mother; and they lived in Davidson County. They sho' was good.

They had a graveyard—they had a place up on the hill and every one died they would dig his grave and put him in the grave. If it was too far, they would hitch the horses and take him on up to the hill. I never heard tell of funerals before the War. I heard of funerals after the War, but I never heard of funerals before the War. Well, what I tell you, there is very few know. People been through what I been through, they certainly would be graduated.

The white folks never would let me pick up a picture and look at it. I would be looking at pictures, you know, and I would get a whipping.

When Dr. Bradden came here after the War, my brother and Unc'l Charlie begged me to go to school and learn, but the white folks had beat all the learning out of me. And Unc'l Charlie said that if I got old I certainly would hate it, and I sho' do.

They had to work in the field and pull fodder and tie fodder and dig potatoes and pull corn; and they wouldn't know anything about church. When I was a girl there was an ole white man, after the War, his name was John Hesley, and he used to have the colored preacher to come to an ole shack to preach, and he would tell them to obey their masters and mistisses. I never will forget it. It was just a little ole shack. He just preached to the Negroes. I will never forget it. Yes, my ole mistiss used to take me behind her and carry me to the Rutledge Church, on her horse, and I had a cotton bonnet and a cotton dress on. This was after the War when John Hesley preached to us. People soon stopped going to hear him. My ole mistiss would carry me on her hoss to her church on Sunday. No, honey, I don't know if they would; if they had them I don't know, 'cause I wouldn't get out amongst the colored people, and I didn't know. There was a man came up from Wilson's farm and came here and got more colored people, and brought them up on that farm, and you know they wouldn't 'low me to say anything to them, and I would get a whipping if I did. Yes, Lawd, there is a mighty whole lot of people today what had they been through what I been through they would be crazy as a bedbug.

No, I never seen any. They used to have nigger whippings. They would be a house sitting about as far as from here to the next street from our house, and every week they would have nigger whippings, and would cry and holler, and if the white people would catch me looking they would whip me. They would whip everyone what was in there. They would whip all those colored people what they would take down there, and they would take a group of them down there. I don't know, all I know is they just had them whippings. I was sitting up on the fence one day, and I was hearing the women cry and I was sitting on the fence watching, and my mistiss, she always teached me how not to sit up and look at folks, and she whipped me, and I never would sit up there again. Yes, they'd have nigger whippings twice a week, and they couldn't run away when they come after them; and they would just have to go. An ole white man I used to get butter from, he used to come in from the country. I said something about going to Wilson County, and he told. He asked me if I came from Wilson County; I said "Yes," and he asked me who I b'longed to, and when I tole him he said, "The meanest man in Wilson County." I knowed him there and I knowed him when he wasn't nothing but a young fellow, but I had forgot him when he come along selling butter and milk. Oh, Lawd, the way that they hollered, it seemed like they was beating them unmercifully, hollering and crying.

(Good times) I don't know whether they would or not. I can't remember those, I wasn't ever out with them, and I don't know nothing.

(Run-away-slaves) Yes, I seen one, one day. I had to tote water a good piece, and I went down to the spring to get water, and I was fixing to reach the spring, and a man said, "Sister, give me something to eat, I am hungry." And I threwed the water down and ran, and I tole the folks that a man had tole me to bring him something to eat, and they went down, and they couldn't find him, but he was up in the thickets, up on side of the hill. They didn't find him, and they said I didn't see anybody.

No, honey, I don't remember nothing, 'cause I heard such a few of them. I can't remember them. All the songs what I remember was those we sang after the War.

Oh, yes, I could just see the cannons when they were shooting, and my mistiss, she wouldn't 'low me to stay in the yard, and one day I was on the fence and some Yankee soldier came and said something to me, and she didn't 'low me out on the fence any more. She said, "They will kill us." But all my white folks dead now. Ain't none of them living. The ole man what brought me butter and milk told me all of them is gone and none of them is living. I never have been up thar since I lived up thar. He said the boy had built a nice house, and he said he was dead, too, and he told me I wouldn't know it if I was to see it. They wouldn't have no houses built like those that was log. They had wide planks on it, and cement put in dar. He said I wouldn't know the place if I was to see it, 'cause it is so much different from what it was. I know he knows, 'cause he lived right in the neighborhood. I spek he's dead now; I don't see nobody from dar.

No, I don't know nothing 'bout no signs. Heard people speak of them, but I wouldn't know any of them.

Honey, I wouldn't know. I don't know nothing they done before the War but whip the niggers. They whipped them all the time. I didn't know nothing before the War but to eat and sleep. Any of them have a little baby down there I could see, but I had to come right back. They wouldn't tell me nothing about babies. I heard them say one day—somebody said, "Don't tell Anne, but the doctor brings these babies." I heard her talking to one of her daughters who had a baby. They wouldn't tell me 'cause I wouldn't know no better than to blab it out; but I did not tell this.

No, they (the colored people) wouldn't say anything before me, 'cause I stayed in the house, and et in there, and slept in there. Yes, they were 'fraid to say anything 'fore me.

I used to have a tin pan and a tin cup—down on the floor, that's where I et. After the War I begun to get out 'mongst people, but before the War I better not go out the house.

No'm, go to nothing, corn shuckings or nothing. They'd have corn shuckings all around in the neighborhood, but I better not say nothing. Yes'm, I was the only one stayed in the house; and I don't reckon I would've stayed in there, but my mother died and after she died I was a little baby and they took me right in the house.

The day of the sale the young mistiss bought me.

"Blacks Have No More Chance Than Slaves Had"

I was a little gal, but I remember how the white folks would come by, way back yonder in the old days, and ask me where was the niggers, and I would tell them, "I don't know." They would keep after me and sometimes I would tell them that they went away. Then they would ask where did they go and I would tell them that they had went away and that was all I knowed. They used to tell me if I would tell them what they wanted to know that they would give me some candy. Of course, I, like other children, liked candy very much, but never could hardly get it. They would give me the candy but I would only tell them that they went away, and I didn't know where they went, just went away. Sometimes they would ask me, "Where is your mammy, little nigger?" and "Ain't you got no mammy?" and "If you will tell me, I will give you some candy." I used to say sometimes, "Will you, sure 'nough?" and they would say, "Yes." They would give me the candy and I would then tell them she had gone to keep the Yankees from getting her. But one time they found her and took her to Hopkinsville and put her in prison. She was carried away in the summer time—I don't remember what time, but she didn't come back until Christmas, and when she did come back we didn't know her. She had three children, two boys and one girl—that was me. They would take niggers and hide them. They would keep them from going to the Yankees. White folks did that. They would ask me, "Little nigger, do you want to go to the Yankees?" and I would tell them, "No, because they would kill me." Just like when I would tell them that my mammy was hiding from the Yankees—they knew that wasn't so. Well, my mind ain't anything now; I can hardly remember, only at times. I have seen such hard times, and it seems like I still see them. Until the last few years I had a stroke and that's what's wrong with my mind. I just can't think half of the time. But I remember when they would take parents away from their children.

My old mammy went to Springfield one time, way back there, and stayed a week, and when she come back I heard her say that the white folks asked her why she came back, and she said to get her children, and they told her that she would not get them. Finally, they kept me and let her have the two boys, and when she got way down the road I hollered, so they told me to go and let the Yankees kill me. But I said I only wanted to go to my mother. Then they said, "Go on to your mammy." I took out and hollered at every jump, and said, "Wait, wait." When she caught my voice she waited, and got her three children and went to the picket post, and the soldiers came and got her out. My mammy been dead a long time. Sometimes I don't think I had a mammy or anything else. All of them are dead but me; all of my old kin are dead. I am the oldest living. As I got bigger the white folks was doing the niggers awful bad. I know one time when I was just a little thing running about, I don't know what come up, I don't know what my mammy done, but something she done did not suit them, and they took her, carried her upstairs and whipped her and whipped her. Every morning they would whip her. So finally they had whipped her and slashed her, so that she went down in a well. They thought that she had run off, but one day somebody had to go after some

97

water, and she was down there sitting crossways, way down in the well, and they called her two boys and me, and old master looked down in the well and talked to her. He took each one of us, and lent us over in the well, and asked her didn't she know that it was a shame to leave her children; just think of her only little girl. He asked her if she wanted to drown herself. He said that he wouldn't whip her any more. We called to her, and asked her not to kill herself; and she agreed to come up. They then drawed her up out of the well. She said she really meant to drown herself, and they had to plead to get her back. Oh, white folks have done everything. I can't hardly hold the tears back. It's just awful to think about it, and it was awful to be there.

I used to sit and listen, and I would sit night and day and hear the white folks plan mean things for the niggers. Sometimes I just can't see—God is a forgiving God, but sometimes I don't think he has forgiven the white people for the way they treated the poor black folks. If I had stayed long enough until I got old enough to have gathered these things, I reckon they would have killed me. But I come out from under all this when I was young.

Sometimes a "big" man would come here to another man and just take all his horses, niggers, food, even take anything else he could get and then burn down the stables and houses. Sometimes when a mother had been separated from her children, they might chance to pass by meeting her children, she going in one direction and they in another; but what could she do? Nothing, the white folks ruled. The Yankees would sometimes come here with a mother, go in or stand out, and tell her to go in and ask for her children. They wouldn't get a rag; they wouldn't get nothing. So the first thing you know, they would go in and take all the white folks clothes and give them to the niggers for their children, and away they would go. I remember a great string of Yankees going through the country taking everything. Once they come to our old master's house and stayed there. They talked of taking the white gal's pony, but finally didn't take it. But next time they come through and took the things out of the house, silver and everything. They carried it off and hid it.

We ain't got a bit more show now than we had then. Let me tell you, child, black folks, black men ain't got a bit more show with white folks than a rabbit sitting before a gun. Just to see how they treat us—we ain't got no law; we ain't got a chance. I ain't been nowhere but here, to Hopkinsville and a few little other places. This gal I stays with is my brother's child, and she come out to see me after her mother died, but she just don't care for me now. I am her own aunt, and after her mother died I helped him with his five children. They didn't go to the dogs; but now this niece what I stays with, she says she don't care about old niggers. She had a car and she never takes me anywhere; not even to church. I wanted to go to the hospital to see her sick sister, but I had to drag there. She had a child, and she wasn't married when she had her. I just like to have died, but when that child come I brought it on here, and she was a good, sweet, loving child, but this one, her mother, hardly ever hands me a drink of water. Sometimes when I am in bed I ask for water and she tells me that I should have got the water before I went to bed. I tell you if it was so fixed that these generations could dwell in what I heard my mammy talk about, it would learn them something; it would make us love, or it couldn't make us hate. She, this niece of mine, says that young folks ain't caring nothing about you, if you live it is all right, or if you die it is all right.

When my mammy died, I had married at fifteen, and I wasn't married more than two years when she died, and I was just as afraid of her then as I was when I was down on the floor. Well, I am not looking for nothing now but God. Every day I aks him to bring me closer to him. I can't think or see all the time what I wants. Sometimes I hum when I want to sing. You can't do nothing with black folks; they are the last race. I helped my brothers with their children, and that black one what came in here to say goodbye to me is the only one who cares for me. She don't stay at this house. The one I stays here with don't care for me. She thinks she is rich. I have been married three times, and all of them are dead now. I didn't have no children.

People were religious back there. They used to say that when some of them would serve the Lord they would turn a pot down in the house, or rather on the cabin floor, and sing and pray, and the pot would catch the voices and keep them from going out. I never was with my grandmammy, but she said they would do this. Old master would cut them all to pieces and the paddy rollers used to get them, too, when they didn't have passes, and were caught going somewhere without them. You see, these were so many white men on horses. If you went from one plantation to another without a pass, the paddy rollers would get you. If you didn't have a pass they would cut you nearly all to pieces, and take you to the master and he would double the whipping. One time, I remember they whipped a man to death. They whipped him and had him tied up and the blood run and went across the floor, and when they took him down he died.

Old Aunt Calline Fletcher used to tell us about way back there when I lived at Peaches Mill. She said that one time she come out to the trade yard, and an old man named Gibson used to carry a string of niggers and when he would get to a place, he would ask the master if he could stay on there all night, and the master would say, "Yes." He would put all of the niggers in a stable, tied together, and the next morning the trade yard would open and when they commenced selling the niggers they would have to strip naked. The white folks would walk around and examine them, and if they saw any scars on the nigger, then some mean white person would say that he wanted to buy him because he was unruly. They would know that these scars were from whippings the nigger had got. When you were sold they would put you way up on a block, and if you didn't suit them they would nearly kill you. It was awful to see the condition of some of the women especially. Some of them were pregnant. It was an awful sight, you can imagine. Old Aunt Calline Fletcher was sold after she come out of the trade yard to old Dick Grinstead. He bought her, and after she had done all she could and yet she didn't suit old Dick's wife, they said she would have to go back to the trade yard. When his wife would get mad she would beat her as long as she wanted to, and she used to lead her around by the ears, and would put hot tongs on her ears, and tell her that these were her earrings. Old Aunt Calline said one time a woman that had to be confined was put into the smokehouse, and they talked about cutting her belly to let the baby come out. A preacher went to dinner there one Sunday, and asked this mean white woman to call her servants in to prayer. She called all of them but one, and he asked her to call the other one, and this woman said, "Oh, she can't come." The preacher didn't get to see her. They were punishing the woman because she had run off after this white woman was so mean. But they had brought her back and had put her in this smokehouse, and in that condition.

I have seen great big balls, you couldn't lift up, locked on the ankles of niggers they would bring back and put in the garden. I have seen this on women. My mother said sometimes when she would run off, she would rub garlic on her feet so the blood hounds couldn't follow her. She said she would run off every time she heard them say they were going to whip her. Sometimes they would give me two or three licks over the head when I would not tell them anything.

I never saw a wedding until I was a great big gal. They said they used to hold a broom and make them jump over it. At one time a man wanted a wife and all he had to do was to ask old Master for the gal, and then if he said "Yes," all they had to do was to go on and go to bed. One old Mistiss by the name of Fletcher would sometimes go and make them get up and tell them that married life was too good for them; and tell them to get up and get out and go to work. I know God didn't like that, and if he forgives the white folks for that, then I don't know what to think. It was considered a big wedding to jump over the broomstick but when you just asked for them and go on to bed after getting the permission, then that was a little wedding. Of course, when I married they had to have license. Sometimes way back there they had big dances and would dance against each other with a glass of water on their head.

I married Elijah Bailey when I first married. I never loved none but him; he was mighty no count, had the "scoflo," but I brought him here from the country until he died. I just married the other two to have somebody to look after me and kinda hold me in my place. My first husband courted me seven years, and then liked to have stealed me for my mother never did say "Yes." She would always say "No," and say "I will never give all the gal I have to a black nigger like you." One time he got me in the notion of going with him, and I was going to run off but I told him if I left that way I never could come back. My brothers would get me if I ran off. We worried like that several years. The last thought my mother had was long about the middle of the fall, after I had got everything I had ready and decided we would marry three weeks before Christmas, and she was so bitterly against it I had to let it alone. So when the thing did go off a week before Christmas, he come and asked me if I had all my things ready, and I said "Yes." He then asked me if I was going to stick to it this time, and I said "Yes." So I said Sunday night I will go out doors and you ask for me again, and when he asked, she said "No," and said, "I will never give her to you; if she is fool enough to marry a nigger like you, then let her go on." I was out of doors. By Monday she told me all about it, and asked me if I was going to marry and I told her "Yes," because I didn't want nobody but him. So my poor little brother Joe would tell me how to do and don't say nothing out of the way to her. First they had me to believe that I had to get 21 before I could marry. But I had such a bad mammy; she would beat me so. When I married she didn't give me anything. The night I was going to marry I was fixing all day and another woman told me to come on to the church and get married and then come on to her house, and she would give me a nice time. We did this and went on to her house. We had ice cream to hand around, and I stayed all night and went home the next day. My mammy used to be mad and walk in and give me the worst whipping with that poker. She didn't hardly allow other people to look at her. If she would whip me she would make me thank her for whipping me and then laugh. That was the way they wanted her to do in slavery. I didn't know she was so mean until I began to grow up. She had been treated so bad during slavery, she just thought she ought to treat everybody that same way. She just had the worst temper of anybody. We used to say that the white folks give her the temper.

I am glad you came to see me. I don't know whether this will do you any good what I have said. I just can't remember everything. Maybe you come back I can tell you something else. I am getting old and feeble, and I'm up in my seventies now. I have sho' seen some bad days, and heard all about them. Times are bad enough now, but you ain't seen nothing. White folks will always be hard on niggers and niggers will never have a chance. I hope God will help the niggers and they will help theirselves. But I ain't never seen how God can forgive those mean white folks for what they done to niggers way back yonder, nor for what they are doing to them now.

Mulatto Whom Owners Treated Like Family Member

My grandmother was stole from Spain and brought here, and they made a slave out of her. I remember mother crying and mistress got in bed with her. She slept right with mother. We had trundle beds then. My mother was kind of the boss around there about things around the house. Mistress' daughter-in-law didn't like it a bit, 'cause mother was bossing things. Mistress finally picked out a place for us and built us a house. We stayed there until after the War come up. We didn't know nothing about hard slavery. We stayed right where mistress did. I was named for her, Margaret Lavine; they call me Maggie now. I was kinda small and I can't remember very much, but I know we didn't have no hard time. I played with the white children all the time.

I can remember when the men was getting ready to go to war, and seeing mother and mistress going off crying. Me and the white children wanted to cry, too, so we wet rags and spit and rubbed it on our eyes to make tears.

Mistress' son had six fine horses. A poor white boy came riding by and said "The Yankees will be here in a few minutes." We was all sitting down on the porch. We didn't pay no attention to him, but mistress got up and looked over the hill and saw them coming. Mother grabbed me in her arms. They had blue coats with shiny buttons, and they had on blue caps, and the coats had capes on the back of them. The soldiers took the horses, cows and everything they could, trying to starve us out. The son kept one horse bridled and hid, so that if the Yankees did come he could run. When he saw them coming over the hill he run and got on his horse that he kept bridled. He had a hundred acre field to run through, and the Yankees saw him and fired shot after shot at him. But they didn't get him. He went to Ringold, Georgia, not far from Chattanooga. That's where the rebel soldiers camped. The soldiers got everything they could and carried them to Chattanooga. The old master wasn't dead then. He sent the family to Murfreesboro, out of the way of the War. We went to Murfreesboro, or we started for it. We didn't know what she was going to do. A man saw us on the train and told mother that the Superintendent of the L. and N. wanted a cook and somebody to keep house for him. We had never been used to no rough life and mother was glad to get that job, for she didn't know what she was going to do. That man was M. H. Smith. He told mother he would give us a home. We stayed there until peace was declared.

I was born about five miles from Cleveland, Tennessee.

I used to play with white children all the time when we was at mistress' house. She used to tell me not to play with the colored children so much 'cause I wasn't like they was. They said my mother was half Spanish and half Indian. She helped drive the Indians away. My father was a white man of course. I just remember seeing him one time, driving by on a horse. When the Yankees come up to our house mistress cried, and master didn't want them to bother us. They said, "God damn, these must be your grandchildren, the way you are carrying on about them." We always had everything the white folks did. Mother was kind the overseer of things. She hired hands, and would see about food and everything. One day a man come by with a pretty clock for sale. Mistress wanted it so bad, and mother told her to get it. She said she would but she didn't have the money. The clock was $12.00, and mother went to her bed and looked under the pillow and got the money and gave it to her. Mistress didn't even know mother had it, and mother had sold milk and things like that, and it really belonged to mistress. But she hadn't even asked her for the money. So you see we didn't know about hard slavery time. Our mistress treated us just like we was in the family. We could have gone back to them after the War, but we didn't do it.

Now Supported by Children She "Raised"

My white folks been dead long time. Lord, chile, I don't know so much; I was born and raised with the white folks. I don't know how old I was; I can find out just 'bout how old I am now when some of the folks comes over. My marsa was a general in the War. Up here at Florence Station is where he was born, and we stayed there years and years. During the War I was nursing the white folks children in Mississippi.

Our white folks was good to us, yes'm, awful good to us. They didn't allow the overseer to whip the darkies. Well, you see, my mother came from the mistress' side; yes'm, she owned my mother. What did I do? Oh, well, I nursed and cooked sometimes, but I liked the field work better than I did the house work. We could talk and do anything we wanted to, just so we picked the cotton; we used to sing and have lots of fun. You know, the man next to our field, he was the meanest white man you most ever saw. No'm, nobody never did run away from my white folks; you see they was so good to us; but they sho' did run away from that other plantation, and you know, they'd have these dogs, bloodhounds, ain't they, after them, you know. Oh it was pitiful; they would jest go up to a tree and bark, and the poor ole' slave had to come down. Wonder how they could tell 'xactly where they was like that?

Ole marsa had a long set of houses, 'bout as far as from here to Belmont, I reckon; big fields, too. Yes'm, we was all real happy; jest as happy as could be. When the War ceasted, ole marsa come to the hotel in Mississippi, and he told Mattie—that was his wife's name—"Well, we have lost all our darkies." They went on home and I stayed with them a while, 'cause they was good to us, but some of the slaves packed up and left real soon; don't know why they did it, 'cause they didn't have nowhere to go; and they didn't have nothin' neither. I didn't know the difference; thought we couldn't do a thing without the white folks. Ole marsa told us we could stay with them as long as we wanted to, so she come down here. Ole marsa died 'bout three years afterwards; she been dead a long time. We said ole marsa died 'cause he lost all his slaves, he, he. Aw, chile, but that man next to our plantation, he just beat his darkies, and wouldn't feed the poor niggers a-tall, sometimes. He was so mean the white folks had to get together and take him to jail. You know it's awful for folks to whip them like that; just put them on the ground and tie them hand and foot and beat 'em. Yes, they did run away; and we could hear the hounds after them jest like they do here when they get out of the penitentiary. Yes'm, a few did get clean away, but it's been so long, I know they is dead now. I know when I was a child I heard my mother talking 'bout it; a boy run away and the white folks was right after him, and he jumped in a creek and got drowned. And they didn't even know he had drowned until 'bout three days after that, he rose. Wonder what makes them rise like that, get full of water? he, he. No'm, when they beat you, you better not talk back, or fight neither; couldn't do nothin'; they'd get mad enough to kill them then; yes'm, they would just kill you then. When the War broke the white folks told us, "Now yo'all starve to death; the Yankees is going to eat everything;" but twarn't a thing to it.

I 'member when the War broke out, Missy asked me if I wanted to go to Mississippi with her. I was so glad I just hopped and skipped, 'cause I was going to git to ride the train; I was foolish, you know. When we got down there she boarded at the hotel; and they sho' is mean down there. Women picked cotton and toted big baskets, just like the men. Everybody had so much a day to do; and if you didn't do it, you got whipped. I couldn't pick fast like some of 'em. Some picked one hundred baskets a day! But they had plenty fun singing and laughing and talking while they was picking. The overseer would watch you good. He'd sit under a tree, and he always knowed who wasn't working. We got a hour for dinner, and we would eat; then we went back to picking, and picked till sundown. We all ate together in a great big kitchen, on a long table clean across the room. We had one lady to do the cooking, and some mo' to help wash the dishes—I say dishes—tin pans. We had right nice things to eat, onions, cabbage, rice, bacon; darkies didn't have biscuits, only on Sunday. For breafas' we didn't have nothin' but meat and bread, oh, yes, and sorghum; that's another thing, the darkies had to tend to the sorghum. Lord, I jest don't like sorghum; guess I had too much of it.

'Nother thing, we had a regular weaving room, and some women to weave and some to spin. They never did buy no clothes like they do nowadays, stockings neither. We had yarn stockings; I don't never want to knit no more.

You ain't never saw them ovens with the handle to them, have you? They used to bake things in them, make what they call corn pone. I kept one of those ovens for years and years. Well, when I moved down here I just threw it away.

(Did the slaves work on Sunday?) Lord, no'm, everybody had Sunday. We did have a little meeting, but we didn't have no schools. Colored men would go round and preach like they do right now. No'm, he warn't free. Wasn't no free folks then among the slaves; better not come and say you b'long to yourself! No'm, white folks never did say nothin' to us 'bout religion. I 'fessed religion after I got grown. Way I found out 'bout religion was once when I went to revival. I found out that you jest got to pray, that's all; and yo' mind got to be on your praying.

(She got up and went over to the radio) 'Wanted to see if there's anything on the radio; what time is it? 'Bout twelve o'clock? It usually start 'bout noon.

(Who stays here with you; do you live alone?) Nobody but me lives here; not a soul but myself. I bought this here house before my last husband died. Well, I got three daughters. One of 'em is in Florida. Who my last husband? Well, I got acquainted with him after the Civil War; he just died three years ago.

(What do you do here all alone?) Well, I did all these quilts this pas' winter by myself. I never sell any of them; my daughter want one. No, I ain't scared to stay here by myself; some folks thinks I oughter be, but I jest fastens up all the back 'bout dark, and leaves this room and the hall open; and goes on to bed. I got a iron bolt on this door, so if anybody tries to git in I won't hear them anyway, 'cause I sleeps good.

(Did they have many love affairs on the plantations? How did they court then?) Well, they courted nicer than they do now. They would come to see the girl they liked, and talk to them at night after the work was done; and sometimes they would ask them to marry; and sometimes they wouldn't. The white folks married you then. Some of the ole marsas used to have the colored folks; and they would take women away from their children just like you would sell a hog or something. Aw, chile, you better be glad you warn't here in them days. You couldn't do nothin' but cry; better not say you didn't want to go, er nothin'. Sho' was awful. You see, the white folks owned you, and you had to say and do way they wanted you to. Sometime you was sold way off from yo' folks, where you couldn't walk back and forth to see them; and then sometime they married again.

One thing, they sho' would make you wear good heavy clothes. Men folks had high boots, and yarn socks. We knitted the socks ourselves. Us women folks had to wear cotton dresses and brown yarn stockings; I never want to see no more brown stockings and things; I never did like brown, looks so dirty, just like mud.

(Did you wear short dresses?) Short dresses! he, he. Lord, no, dresses might nigh dragging the ground. 'Nother thing, we wore hoop skirts on Sunday, jest like the white folks. I never did like them things; if you didn't sit down this-a-way, that old hoop skirt would shoot up like this. I never had no use for them things. Then we wore white waists, and a real long skirt. Then, you know, the style come in of wearing these here long things that warn't 'xactly no drawers—come way down to yo' ankles, and we wore them, too, jest like the white folks.

I like blue and white. We wore white aprons like these men wear in grocery stores, with blue shirt waists; we was awful dressed up then. Poor colored folks; they had a time, but looks like to me they doing more devilment now than they did then, don't you think so? Why, you know, jest the other day, a girl killed that man up in the alley, right down the street; and he hadn't done nothing to her. She took a knife and cut a "leter" in two, and he bled to death 'fore they could get him to the hospital. No'm, ain't nothin' but alleys round here; I wouldn't live in a alley for nothin'.

(When did you slaves know you were free; what did you do?) Well, we come home from work, you know, and ole marsa told us we was all free; and we could all go if we wanted to. Some of 'em left right away, and I ain't never heard no more of them. My younger sister, she married a man and went back to Mississippi; don't know whether she is dead or alive now; we ain't never heard from her no mo'. My mother died soon after I married. I stayed up here in Florence Station during the rest of the War. My father died before the War. 'Nother thing, ain't it funny 'bout names: You see, my father was a Ruby Love, and I went by my white folks name, Anderson; we had to go by the white folks name. Yes'm, my father was owned by a Love, near our plantation; yes'm, my father 'n mother was born here in this county.

(How did the slaves feel about the War?) Lord, well, we jest thought the world was come to the end. Didn't seem like the same place. And then, now everything is so different; jest like I kin pick up that radio, and I kin hear things every which way; even hear things in New York; but if we had that thing when the War was here, we would have been scared of it. Oh yes, 'nother thing, we had hominy a lot to eat, too. White folks had great big barrel that was half full of hickory ashes and water; then it would turn to lye. then they would have a great big iron kettle, and after the corn had done set in the lye, they would boil a whole pot of it for all the hands to eat. 'Nother thing, did you ever eat ash cake? I wouldn't eat none now; folks spit in the fire too much for me. Then they didn't 'low no spitting in the fire. They would rake the ashes back from the fire, and turn 'em over and over, and then they would bake jest like in the oven, and they was good, too. You see, they didn't have no stoves then. We had old time coffee pot, and iron teakettle, too. They would heat the water in the kettle and pour it over the coffee in the pot; and Lord, niggers get down and eat fit to kill. An old woman tended to the children in another room while we et.

(Did they have dances on your plantation?) Lord, yes, they'd pick banjoes, and have big dances. No'm, white folks didn't care; but they had to stop the Klu Kluxes from going and breaking up the parties sometimes. Oh, they would have dances at different houses every week, on Saturday nights. No'm, we wouldn't dress up so much; girls come in clean cotton dresses; we thought we was dressed up enough. 'Nother thing, we used to have big quilting parties; white folks let them have extra food for them. No'm, not on all the plantations; some of the mean white folks, the poor niggers wouldn't get to do nothin' but go to church maybe. Some of the mean white folks poor niggers just couldn't please; they would let on like they wasn't doing nothin' right; they jest love to whip the niggers.

I never know of but one slave to kill another; he just cut him with a knife. He kilt his father; he was gonna whip him. You know it's awful, the way old white men bid off the slaves on the scaffolds. I don't know what made the white folks have such hard hearts; it sho' war awful. 'Nother thing, they would have women that been married long time, two or three years, and didn't have no children; white folks would take them and make 'em marry somebody else, or sell 'em. Wonder what make 'em want so many children like that; make 'em rich, I guess.

Marsa had a brother to have a child by one of the slaves. 'Course he wouldn't own it, but everybody knowed it; he would give it things, but they treated him (the baby boy) like they did all the other slaves; no'm, didn't make no difference toward him. Well, you see, my husband, his marsa was his daddy, there (picture). Well, some of them thought it was an honor to have the marsa, but I didn't want no white man foolin' with me.

(About how many slaves did your master have?) He had five or six families; don't know how many children. I 'member one named Mary; she went to Chicago about three years ago. I ain't never heard of her since. Some said they was going North when the War was over; now what was there up North? They didn't have nothin' as it was. They is all dead by now, I guess; some of them was older'n me. After the Civil War was over, ole Marsa brought some money in a bag and says to his wife that it wasn't no count. What was it they called it? Confederate money? You know when the War ceasted money changed—greenbacks, yes'm. Marsa went to Murfreesboro to a sister named Florence. Then one of them went and married a Yankee; white folks nearly died when one of his sisters went back and married a Yankee. Didn't have nothin' else to do with her; but you know the Yankees did do bad during the war. Yes'm, 'course the Rebels did, too. They stole the pigs and horses and sold them something awful. Wonder what made them do it?

Yes'm, come back any time. You'll always find me the same all the time.

You know, I stayed thirty-nine years down here after I came to town. I come here and hunted a place to stay first; I got this here house, and then I went back and got my children. Then I cooked here for thirty years for Mr. Lee; I raised them children of his'n. They call me "Black Mammy." Best white woman you ever did see. I'd get up 'bout five o'clock, and clean up my room, and cook for the children, and leave it on the table. I always tell them to get to school on time, 'cause I'd be gone when they left. I always got back 'bout nine o'clock, and had lunch ready for them at dinner time. I worked there thirty-nine years. She had six children while I was there. She been dead 'bout twelve years. Mr. Lee jest died here last Christmas. That son out there (picture) is the one what sees after me now. He pays my taxes on my house, and pays my grocery bill, and gives me coal; and he comes and bring my money first of every month. They ain't never stopped my wages; no sireee. Mr. Shultz and all of 'em is crazy 'bout me.

There's an old lady lives down yonder; she change white folks 'bout every week or two; she always saying to me, "What you want to look at them same white folks all the time for; I gits tired." I say, "Oh, I don' know, I'm crazy." What I look in their faces for? Huh, 'cause they good to me. Every Christmas they brings me anything I want. I don't want to dress up, jest so I'm clean. (The Lees own a coal yard, and the radio was one of their presents last Christmas.)

Second Visit

Tha's aright, jest sit down. You know I found a dead rat in the back room, and I had to put down some sugar and burn it, and then I sprinkled around some peroxide; that'll kind quell the odor, you know.

Lord, Hon, I'm too old to think o' songs. We folks didn't pay much 'tention to sech things. The colored folks didn't have meeting only on Sundays; and then they always had it in some ole house; we didn't have no churches in them days, no'm, not a real church, I mean. White folks 'fraid the niggers git to thinkin' they was free; if they had churches 'n things.

One thing, though, they was good 'ligious folks in them days. Now they think too much 'bout killing. They shouted then more than they do now. Folks in them days didn't have education that they do now. Folks would go out and preach, and they would preach what they knowed; but that sho' was good, true, old fashioned gospel. Folks has too much style now to do enough preaching the gospel in these days. Jest like empty wagons; you know a empty wagon sound empty, and a full wagon, you know, it sounds like it full; and that the way they think 'bout 'ligion; less they shout, less 'ligion, that's what I always say.

Well, they'd say the Lord showed 'em where they was free and they got up and told us about it; tell anybody, and everybody; that's the way anybody'll do when yo' soul done been set free, ain't it?

Lord, when I 'fessed 'ligion, it was after I had done heard people talking 'bout it fur a long time. I felt like I had jest got to see the Lord. Yes'm, I viewed the Lord in the spirit; I never seed Him walking around here; you got to give up everything and seek the Lord to free your soul.

Well, I went to the mourner's bench, and people was storming and screaming. And you know I couldn't pray in that; so I went back home, and when I was all by myself, I prayed, and the next night I went back and praised the Lord. You see, I found the Lord all by myself; I used to hear them talking about seeing the Lord sho' 'nuf, but I never seen Him only in the spirit. When I 'fessed 'ligion, I didn't see nothin; I just felt that I was free. Your spirit won't stay happy all the time; but when you begins to feel downcas', you go back and seek the Lord again. The spirit left me after two or three days, and I went back and prayed again. The Lord reasoned unto me, and He called me by my name, and He said "I don't care what you once done; it's done for all the time." Yes'm, that's what He said in a voice to me. He spoke to me so sweet.

Folks say you really see Him. I ain't really seed Him but once, and I viewed Him that one time. He was standing on a high hill, on the steps of a great big white house, and He was standing there jest like a preacher was talking. I ain't never saw Him no more on a building like that; looked something like the capital, with them high white steps, you know. I think if anybody prays and seeks the Lord to change him, and he really means it, but you sho' got to mean it, you got to pray and tell the Lord to do His will, and not your'n; He'll free your soul.

They're having an awful good revival over here at Cain Avenue Church. It been going on about a week. Old Baptist believe in going to the river, you know; but now they done quit going. Brother Green Thompson carry them out here to some creek. They don't have no revival; no'm, they just 'fesses and then they carries them out here to the creek. When I was working for the white folks I used to hurry and get to the Baptism down here at the end of Broad Street where the river is; but now they done built a place, you know, where you unload things, a ferry ain't it?

I been here near on to thirty years. It warn't built up like it is now. It was a small place; now it done stretched way out. When I fust come here there was white folks all in here; colored folks done built it up now; and all the white folks mostly done moved way round here—out yonder round in Inglewood. You know, the penitentiary was here then; over here at the old place out there in North Nashville, but now the town done built up they had to build it further out. There warn't no pavement then; it was all jest like out there in front of the house. All the further the pavement come was Broad and Church streets; you see they come down that far on 'count of the Custom House was there, you know.

You know some folks just rent and rent all their life; but I tell you when you git done renting, you ain't done nothing. When I fust come here, I thought it was awful, the houses was right low on the ground, n'everything; but the wages was better'n I could git in the country, you know, up there above Florence Station; yes'm, up there is where I b'longed to the folks.

(Dreams) Well, I never had no dreams then; but you know that's the way the Lord has of showing you things, did you know that? Yes'm, that sho' is the way the Lord's got of telling you things you ought to know. Some folks say if you dream that you lose a tooth, somepin' sho' gwine to happen; yes'm, some of your close friends or kinfolks is gwine to git in some kinda trouble sho' as you born; yes sir, I 'member I lay down to sleep and I thought I lost a tooth out, and sho' 'nuf, nex' morning first thing, I heard 'bout the lady up the street dying right sudden. She warn't sick no spell at all; well, she had done had a stroke of paralysis 'bout three years before; but everybody thought she had got 'bout all right. Then, 'nother thing, if you hear a kinda ringing in yo' ear, you will hear talk of somebody being dead; I know that's so. You know I was setting down here las' Saturday, and I had that funny ringing in my right ear; and sho' 'nuf, 'bout eight o'clock, a boy jest up and killed his stepfather up here by Bethel Church; they say he was mean to the boy; but he sho' killed him; and I had jest felt that ringing in my ear when the lady what lived down in the lane come by and say, "Miss Catherine, you done heard 'bout that boy killin' his old man, ain't you," and I knew that was why my ear had been ringing.

You know, I sets my clock by the radio; a white boy that I raised fixed it up for me; he said I would be kinda lonesome by myself; yes'm, its lots of company.

(Cures) You know, now they have different medicines and things from what they had in olden times; we used to use this here liniment made out of gympsum weed; everybody used it then; it was sho' good for bad feet and different kinda pains and things. This old worm feud—that's what you call it, I b'lieve—they used to git that stuff and doctor on children for worms n' things. It grows around anywhere weeds kin grow; that was all folks had to cure with before the War. They didn't have no real medicine then like they do now. The darkies and the white folks used them kinda medicine for everything then—most every kind ailment you kin think of; yes'm, that's right. Mullin and gympsum weeds and hohound syrup is good for colds; better'n these patent medicines nowadays; and some of them the doctors still perscribes, too. 'Nother thing, we didn't need so many medicines like they do now; we had more sense. We used to wear boots, and the women wore high top shoes, heavy yarn stockings, and all wool underwear, most all the year round. Folks laugh at all them clothes now. In the summer we put on cotton stockings and underwear; why the darkies thought they couldn't do without their underwear in them days.

Over on Mr. Irving's place some of the darkies did go crazy once in a while; and they said it was 'cause they beat 'em so much. I b'lieve it, too; he sho' was a mean ole man. Well, when dey got like that, they jest put 'em in the 'sylum. Who us? Well, we was 'fraid of them. They would go out in the woods and hide behind trees and things, and they would run from everything and everybody, jest scared, you know; they had been beat so much; why, they would run like a rabbit from a dog. Yes'm, the white people had to 'rest him, ole Mr. Irving, you know, 'cause he beat 'em so. He died long ago; and I wasn't sorry neither; he was jest so awful mean. He wouldn't give 'em 'nuf to eat; and he wouldn't half clothe 'em, and he wouldn't let 'em have no fun at all. Whenever one run off he would git the bloodhounds to catch 'em. Well, he got his pay; he sho' did; he died pretty hard, and you know, chile, when he died I jest couldn't be sorry if I tried; he was so awful mean. We used to make the lye for our own hominy, and we made most everything in them days anyway—soap, n'everything. We used to make the lye with all the good ashes we could find; and it would be nice and sweet as could be; but now you can't make it like that; they don't have no good wood to burn like they used to, or nothin'; things sho' is different to what they was when I was coming along.

(Marriage) Well, there was some colored preachers what married them, too; but most of the time the ole marster jest told them they was man and wife; and they was. Yes'm, colored preachers would preach to them, too; and sometimes, jest as I said, they would marry them right.

Well, they didn't act much different after they was married; they knowed they was man and wife; she knowed he was her husband; and the white folks would build them a little hut to live in; and we would give them a big party; and give 'em some dishes and things to put in the one-room cabin, you know.

In them days the girls was smart; they would quilt, weave, and sew most all their things before they got married; if they was thinkin' 'bout it. The white folks give 'em plenty cotton, 'cause they knowed they was going to have a big family, and you know that meant more hands to work in the fields, to make the white folks rich. Lord, chile, if they had two dishes, four plates, a cup and a saucer, they thought they had something; then somebody might give'm a table, and maybe a homemade safe; and they thought they was the smartest things in the world. They would have quiltings n' sech things; and sometime they would have a big barbecue, and have a big time. Yes'm, the white folks 'lowed 'em to have right nice parties and things if they was good niggers. They didn't have no right to grumble.

Well, they used to have kinda hay wagon parties, like. The young folks would ride in wagons to and from church and have a big time singing songs n' things. Yo'all wouldn't ride in them things nowadays, would you? Why, everybody would laugh. Anyhow, they was happy in them days; only thing, they didn't feel right about was belonging to the white folks; we used to have picnics when the white folks would let us; and jest dance and skip and hop ourselves to death.

They didn't never allow us niggers to mix with what they called the po' white trash; they always said they would learn us how to steal and drink; and it was the truth, too. We used to make cider in them days, from all the rotten old apples that would fall off the trees during the night.

"Stock Was Treated
a Great Deal Better"

I was born in White County, six miles from Sparta. No, my marster didn't have very many slaves. He had just about eight. He treated us very well. He never did whip me any; I was quite a small boy about 14 years old. I was 17 when I left there. My mother, my sister, and my mother's sister and uncle was there. There wasn't much fun to be had in them times. Some of them was pretty mean. They whipped them and done around a good deal. They would half feed them and whip them, too. We would get up every morning 'fore day.

They didn't have no church at all to go to. We didn't have time to study 'bout nothing but work. We would set out under shade trees sometimes. Sometimes we could go to the white church, and set in the back. Stock would be treated better than darkies sometimes. They wouldn't whip horses half as hard as they would darkies.

We would have bacon and corn bread to eat, and sometimes on Sundays we would have biscuits. Not every Sunday, though. Mostly we had was corn bread and buttermilk. A bell would ring every morning for the darkies to get up 'fore day.

I didn't do much. My mother she used to plow. I used to plow, too. My marster raised hogs, horses, and pretty well everything.

We had to wear tore breeches and tore shirts. Never did know what a undershirt was in them days, and no underwear of any kind, summer nor winter. Sometimes we would get some old summer breeches that was wore out, and we would wear them for underwear in the winter. We didn't have much bedclothes. Sometimes we sit around the fire all night. We could have a big hot fire, as much as we wanted, and we would sit up sometimes to keep good and warm.

Sometimes darkies would run off and stay a good while. I was very small, you know, then, and the old folks wouldn't let me hear them talking so much. They didn't want me to know nothing about their business. We used to get whippings with a great long hickory stick about as big as my thumb. They didn't want us to look at a book. Didn't want us to know a thing. We used to plow, hoe corn, cut wood and make rails. Used to keep fences up in winter season. Didn't have no time for yourself. We would have meetings out in the woods sometimes. The preacher didn't know how to read a thing. The white folks would tell us, "Old Uncle So-and-So is going to preach to you all today, go down there and behave yourselves." They didn't aim for us to know anything.

The women would plow, hoe corn, just like the men would.

The white men who had children by slaves would treat them just like the rest. They mighta liked them a little better, but they didn't want to show it.

They didn't have no marriage contract in them days. Colored people didn't know what license was.

Sometimes Uncle Square Wallace would go through some sort of ceremony. But he didn't know a letter in the book. Sometimes Square would marry them on Saturday night. But ten to one, they didn't marry at all.

We all lived in the same cabin; just as many as could get in; men and women all together. They didn't care how we was treated. Stock was treated a great deal better.

Just a few of us had hats. Wore caps all the time. Didn't know what it was to wear a hat or shirt. Yes, they would have dances sometimes. You didn't see any doctors then. Darkies didn't know nothing about castor oil or turpentine. They would give you sassafras tea. Didn't get any medicine. You just had to keep going.

It was a long time after freedom before they had any schools. You see, the white folks wouldn't let Negroes build schools on their land.

I was in the Civil War for twenty-two months. Went in when I was 17 years old. After colored regiment come there they took us to town. I was with Company B, 42nd United States Colored Regiment. We wasn't in no real fighting. We would come to a place and see that nobody would come on it. We would camp there and hold the place. We didn't allow no Democrats to come there at all. General Thomas come down here. We went to Chattanooga, Alabama and Georgia. We would go and clean up the place and hold the places that had been taken. They was pretty sharp, I tell you something like that. One of our officers was named Lieutenant Mittie. Heap of slaves was afraid to go to the army. Everything was done when I come out. If it hadn't, I 'speck I woulda been there till yet. They come right in my house, I walked right out with them, never said a Gods word to nobody.

I never did belong to church. I would go to church with my wife, but I never did join. I thinks about it a heap, but I just never did join. I believe in the church though, but just never got started yet.

Yes, I have danced many a reel. We would have fiddles and banjoes. We had a big time then. The Christian folks would have suppers. They wouldn't dance.

Our mistress had a brother who didn't believe in slavery. He used to tell his sister didn't see how she could be a Christian and own slaves. He wouldn't own a slave. He was a good Christian. Old lady was a member of the church, but was as mean as you please.

We never thought about anything like freedom. My mother and father would do all their talking when I would go to bed.

I have been here in Nashville about 34 years. I come here with a big lumber man, and worked for him about 30 years. I have been living in East Nashville every since I come from Sparta. My son own a lot of property. He built two brick houses and sold them, and now he is building this one.

My wife was always free. She come from across the water. She didn't know what slavery was. Her mother was a slave, but her father was Scotch. She lived in White County. You couldn't tell her from a white woman. Her hair was almost long enough to touch the floor. After I married I went and jined farms where I was when a slave. Stayed there a good long while. I quit there and went to another man and stayed there a good while.

I get $900.00 a year from the Government. The 4th day of every month I go to the bank and get my money.

Every Thursday
Was "Whipping Day" for Slaves

Oh *zam*! It's too much of my life to tell it all today. Well, I were born on Thursday, at seven and a half o'clock in the morning, 1850. There was two of us born in the same house, and the one that was to be born first would git five dollars reward; I got the reward, he, he. Well, you see, I kept the five dollars until I was thirteen years old, in 1863; then I spent that $5.00 for five pounds of bacon. Yes'm, I was coming from Tennessee. Yes'm, we was hungry; we was hoboing, you know. We went in a wheat field and fried that bacon and ate it. You know, it was about that same time that there was measles and mumps sweeping the country, and folks was dying ten at a time; they couldn't build coffins fast enough.

Slavery? Well, during slavery they had whipping day every Thursday. Yes'm, every Thursday was when you got your beating, he, he. They had men hired to do the whipping; everybody got one on Thursday whether you had been bad or not during the week. Well, they had a log and they would tie your hands together and tie you to the log, a hand and arm on each side of the log, and whip you. My father ran off and stayed in the woods about a year to keep from taking them whippings, he, he, he. Yes'm, they finally caught him and the ole marster told him he was going to sell him to the ole nigger seller and he would take him South; but the war broke out and the ole nigger seller never did get to come by.

The War was pretty hot along about then, and finally my pappy come back of his own accord and joined the Yankee army. Yes'm, it wasn't nothin' but that whipping day that made him run away from home.

Well, if you put a frog in your pocket tied up in a handkerchief, you can't have nothin' but good luck for the balance of yo' days.

> *Wife*–We come from Munsey county. My husband's good at telling all 'bout the olden times. You know one thing, everybody's bootlegging nowadays; look like to me I would be scared of God, wouldn't you? Yes'm, everybody is doing it, both women and men. I remember a fellow come here from Seattle long time ago and preached for some time; then he went back; and now they say he's one of the biggest bootleggers you ever heard of.

Well, we slaves worked every day in the week from sunup to eleven and twelve at night sometime, 'specially in the summer nights. We worked in the fields all the light hours, plowing and planting and sech like; then at nights we would shell corn for the fowls, and do other things. When the moon shine some nights we would work in the fields all night. Well, our ole marster was called one of the best marsters in the county. He had five hundred darkies. Everybody had enough to eat; there wasn't no other family of people what done work like we done, 'cause you see, we was well fed and clothed and everything. We did real farm work, good work, I mean.

Yes, I was a house slave; I slept under the stairway in the closet. I was sorta mistress' pet, you know, he, he, he. We house slaves thought we was better'n the others what worked in the field. We really was raised a little different, you know; fact is, I kinda think I'm better'n most folks now, he, he, he, he.

Yes'm, we was raised; they, that is, the field hands, wasn't. They would steal the pigs. I would help them out, too. I never would steal, but if they tell me to say some certain thing, I would always do it, you know, he, he, he. My ole mistress was a high-toned woman. She had a kinda liking for all the poor little nigger slaves on the farm; she kinda took to 'em, you know, and mothered and raised 'em like; that's the way she done me, too; and I is still bred like she taught.

All the field hands had two overseers; and they was around all the time, even when they wasn't supposed to be working. One overseer had 300 under him; and the other had 200 slaves under him; that made 500 in all.

Well, the slaves used to have meetings, two weeks' meeting after the tobacco season were over. Sometime there would be a white preacher, and sometime a colored preacher. Well, since I have learned 'xactly what preaching is, I realizes, you know, that they really couldn't preach, but it were good enough in them days, I reckon, he, he.

Yes'm, they used to git up in the pulpit, these here old preachers, and holler and say, "Oh the heaven above and hell below, run, run, run, sinner." Well, we would have meeting and turn the pots down to keep the sound from the white folks. Well, yes'm, we would pray the Lord to deliver us.

Well, we would sing such songs as "Give me that old time religion." I used to have that there song on my mind all the time.

Yes'm, we used to have dances and parties like they do now; only they would be sho' 'nuf parties, he, he, he. Well, they would give a wedding for you to marry. They never had no license of no kind in them days for us po' slaves. The old marster picked out a wife for you, and you would git a whipping if you didn't stay with her; whether that was the one you liked or not. Well, when they married, they used the same words that they do now. Yes'm, the marster would do all the courting for you, yes sir, he saw to that, he, he, he. Well, the way they do, if you had a daughter, and I had a son, well, you see, when yo'all got married, you would go to one or tother of the homes to stay—that's the way it was, you stayed at one of the parent's home.

(Cures) Well, some folks used gympsum weed a lot for different ails; and then there's catnip for babies; and sheep shat—don't you know what that is? he, he, he. I bet you ain't never heard of bonesat, have you? Well, if you take that—yes'm, it's a kind of weed, and some sassaparilla and burdock, it's real good for the blood; yes'm, make a kinda tea out of it. Poke berries is good for rheumatism; jest take the berries and make a wine like you would make any other kind of wine. Elm leaf, if you stick it on with a little hot water, is good for any kind of swelling, and then there's another kind of plant that grows right on the ground that's good for swelling—lessee, lessee, I can't think of the name of that plant to save my life. For snake bites, if you cut a whole chicken half open and put it on the bite, it'll draw out the poison. Hohound is good for colds, but it's bitter as gall.

Yes'm, it's always been the custom to be what you'd call a good Christian. I never 'fessed religion 'til about 1866. Well, I don't want to see what I saw, no more; that's too much of it. I got that old time religion. Well, you see, I went to church to the revival, and I got to praying and something got out down in me. I jest couldn't git rid of it. I went down to pray on the river side, and God wasn't there; I jest couldn't git no relief seem like; I prayed night and day. I didn't know what to do. I was three years trying to find Christ, then one night I find him, and I served three more years trying to get holy jest like Christ, and then I realized I couldn't be jest like Christ. I went out one day, under a peach tree, and I stayed there praying until midnight. Well, I kept praying and I kept praying, and all of sudden I heard a voice saying, "You rise, you rise," in a voice of mercy. Well, I jumped up and even the house shook; I heard that voice agin, saying, "You rise, you rise," and I took out and run down into the woods naked. When I found myself I was just coming to, seem like. Lord, I don' know what happened; I jest know I sho' was one happy being. Why I jest alarmed the whole neighborhood. Something jest struck me like that; yes'm, it jest struck me. Yes'm, religion sho' comes to you jest like the scripture say, like the wind blows. Why I kin talk with the ants and birds jest like I'm doing with you right now; that's what religion do to you; why now, I wouldn't hurt nothing; I don't need no other religion than the one I got right to this day.

(Signs) Well, if a cow come up and low right in yo' face, it's a sho' sign that somebody is going to die; if she turn her head that way, they going to die up that way; and if she turn her head the other way they going to die that way; jest whichever way she turn her head. Well, now that means the same thing then that it mean now; when a black cat cross yo' path, sho' bad luck, he, he, he. If yo' right eye itch, it's a sho' sign of good luck. If yo' left eye itch, you gwine to have bad luck. When either one of yo' hands itch, you going to git some money. If you sneeze while you is sitting at the table, somebody in the family going to die before the next morning, sho' as you born, he, he, he. If you make a cross mark on a wagon road, and walk backward from it, you'll have lots of good luck.

You know, my ole marster was an administrator; you know what that is; all the people what die was turned over to him.

Well, there was a few smart people in dem days, jest like there is now. Once there was a man, a slave you know, on our plantation what could read and write 'n everything; he was a real good scholar. He would get up at 2 o 'clock and study before he went to the field to work. You know white folks never did like no nigger to act like he was free; and they would whip that smart nigger something awful. They kept whipping him, and finally he run away to the free states. Jones was the man what owned him; I don't remember the slave's name. He sho' was done awful, —half fed, —and his folks owned right smart land, too. They was half fed and tacky; any time we see that kind, we would always say, "There's one of Jones' niggers."

Yes'm, my grandmother come over from Africa down here at Hyde's Ferry, and then they brung her on up here to Nashville. Then she was carried back to Alabama after about two years. Yes'm, they did talk kinda funny; they couldn't understand you, but sometime you could understand a little that they said. They would point to things that they wanted, and you would tell them what it was. She married a Indian man, and he had rings in his nose and ears. Yes'm, he was a slave, but they called him a Crick Indian; he had a way of grunting when he wanted something.

Well, the free niggers was free, and then they wasn't free. They had a guardian over them. When I came to Nashville I came up here with a lot of them kind, you know, the free ones. The guardians hire them out and got their pay, you know. Now if you was a free nigger and did something you didn't have no business doing, you was sent to the penitentiary like anybody else; that was the difference; the slaves never went to the penitentiary for nothin' they did; they was whipped and beat on by the ole marster or the ole overseer. No'm, they didn't allow no po' white trash to light on our place; we wasn't even 'lowed to associate with them.

"They Sold My Sister Right in this Nigger Trading Yard"

We were set free in 1865. I was grown and old enough to be married. Girls didn't marry so fast in those days. They says now that want to have a booth for another colored woman and myself in the World's Fair. The 13th of this last March I entered into my 90th year. I was born in 1842 at Elkton, Todd County, Kentucky. At that time the Yankee teachers were just beginning to come South, and my mother was a cook at the Academy there, and I was born there. Mr. and Mrs. Dickey taught the boys and girls there. My sister was a nurse there at the time—my oldest sister. This lady taught my sister how to read and write, unbeknowingst to the white people. They didn't allow it. After we were set free my sister taught here in Tennessee; her name was Sally Johnson. They taught school right over on that hill. She taught the first free school that was taught here in Clarksville after the Yankees left. At that time we belonged to the Hudsons. My first people was from Culpepper, Virginia—big families, white and colored, and all dead but me and my son. I never left Kentucky until after we were set free over here in Christian County. I crossed over here after Christmas and went to school to a Yankee teacher named Kenny. Him and his son taught a school.

My mistress and master had over 75 slaves. I cut and sewed for them two years before I was set free. I sewed on the first sewing machine that ever come South. I can cut and sew yet. They dressed me awful nice, and treated us all nice. If everybody would work, times wouldn't be like they is. Too many people won't work. My young master married a Miss Nannie Long, and then he give me to her for a maid. They taken me from mother on Christmas, and I was not six years old until March. I never lived with my mother; I lived right in the house with the white folks. I carried a white child on my arm most of the time. Of course I had company, but at nine o'clock I had to go into the house. I was never treated mean.

I intended to go over to Hopkinsville today to see if I could find any of them.

I run off and married right over there in the school house, and then he carried me on out to his house. I had one son, and he is a revenue man in Chicago. I left the farm when he was 4½ years old. His father just got so mean I couldn't stay with him. I took my son to Louisville, Kentucky, and raised him there.

Yes, I went to parties and danced all night on Saturday night, dressed to death. I used to go to parties, and they all treated me nice. I never had a young man, white or colored, to say an ugly word to me, because my young master was very strict with me. Girls don't have to mind nowadays like they used to. My father was white, a Quaker. He wanted to buy me when I was old enough to be taken from my mother, so I could be raised in Philadelphia. His name was Dick Black, but they wouldn't sell me. He owned a store.

When I came to Clarksville all over there was woods. There was a big spring and all of us used to go down there to get water. That was after we was set free. All this place has been cleared off. I been here a long time, and I ain't tired of staying. My mother had eight children. All of them were not my father's children. I was the only one by him. Mother married and her husband's master used to run what was called stages before trains ever come out. The stage would come from Elkton to Russellville and from Russellville

115

to Hopkinsville, and when the trains began coming South his master moved where he could still run his stage. That separated them but she never did marry again. Don't know so much about grandmother—my mother's mother. Aunt Jane would have been over a hundred years old. She nursed mother's children, and then she nursed Robert, my son, until he was eight years old, when she died. I buried her and mother in Louisville. Mother lived to be over 74.

I have always worked hard. I run a lace laundry yet. I have made as high as eight dollars a day up here at my place on 9th Street. My boy was old enough to be called in the Spanish-American War, and was promoted corporal before he come out of that war. He used to run a tailor shop, and then finally went on to Chicago and worked his way into the Post Office, and is a revenue man now. He is about 63. He lived in Chicago about 10 years and just been home about two years. My first husband was Robert Outlaw, and now my boy is named Robert Outlaw. He had three children and lost them all. I go to see them every summer, and stay a while.

During slavery we had to work. Mr. Crab was a mighty good man. His father bought a farm and put them on it, and had these slaves. He was a good man, but everybody had to work. That's what got the country in this condition, people don't want to work. He was very good to his slaves. Of course, I didn't have anything to do with them. It is just like you come here and buys three of us and put a man or woman over us. He was paid so much money a year to run the farm, but he didn't have nothing to do with the women of the house and the house boys. But them on the farm were under the overseer, and if they didn't do their work they got a whipping, a mighty bad whipping. They were mighty mean at that time—some of them. When they commenced running off cross the Mason-Dixon Line, they would catch them, tie them on a barrel and whip them to death sometime. They whipped a young man named Montgomery so hard that he didn't have no skin on his back. When they whipped them they took salt and water and poured it on the backs. They would have you strapped down and whip you from your head down to your feet. I tell you, daughter, it was mighty hard, and colored people oughtn't be so mean to one another. I always cried everyday to see how colored people don't love one another; to see how people have died before they set them free. I never got but one whipping before I was grown, and that was because I whipped my mistress.

Don't you know, I been knitting socks and sewing and piecing quilts every since I was eight years old. I have always been used to work, and wants to work. I been out in the field and worked from Christmas to Christmas. I could do everything, but never could hold a plow straight. They say when I was born they put me in a quart cup; and I have never been much larger. I went up to Chicago the first of July, and Robert weighed me, and I weighed 105 when I got there, and the last of July he weighed me, and I weighed 105, and in August I weighed the same, and he said, "Well, I can't make you weigh any more, I'll have to send you back the same."

What I got this whipping about, the mistress rang the bell and I didn't come right away, and she asked me why I didn't come, and I told her I come as quick as I could, and she whacked me across the head with a broomstick, and I whacked her back, and got a good whipping. When her husband came he whipped me across my shoulders with a cowhide, and Miss Betty had always whipped me with a switch. But I didn't care then if they had killed me. That's why so many colored people got killed; they just whipped them for nothing. I had an uncle, my mother's brother. His name was Nelson, and he lived on the Culpepper line. They wanted to whip him and he didn't let them, and they got another overseer to help them. When they came up to Uncle Nelson they took him out here near the bluff, right by the river. They said to Uncle Nelson, "We are going to get you." Uncle Nelson said, "Yes, we will all go to hell together." And they both were drowned. It was awful hard back there. Girls like you two, they might take you up and sell you for $1000; and they worked girls, and sometimes the work would kill you. They had been offered $1000 for me many times.

My mother was your color—she was dark. My brother and his wife were 33rd degree Masons; Brother Joe died in Hickman, Kentucky. I had no whole brothers and sisters—all halves, and nobody living but me and my boy; even the white people are all dead.

When the War came on we stayed, scared—what else could we do? The men had come to Fort Donaldson. I stayed hid about three days and nights in a corn field. They thought that I had gone like so many women and girls, to cook at Fort Donaldson. I never seen nobody that I could speak to, for so many people would tell on you then. And they do that today. Colored people has got to be more loving. (What did you eat while you were hiding out?) I would go to the orchard and get apples, and I wasn't very far from the spring. I raised a dog and named him Lincoln. I didn't go too near the house, for I was afraid my dog would see me or something. My poor mother was grieved to death, for she didn't know what had become of me. (Did your mother really die then?) No, Robert was about 14 when my mother died; and now he's about 63.

My old mistress thought a lot of me. I was the maid and had to take care of the mistress' children. She had a lot of money, but she never would put it in the bank. When my old mistress died she had four children, and her oldest daughter married and gone up North. She married a Mr. Beatty, and she never seen her any more until she had a grown daughter. Her brother come to see her in ox carts, and had to cross the ferry. While that brother went there to see her she died. When Christmas come we had to be divided out, and straws were drawn with our names on them. The first straw was drawn, you would get that darkey. But the one that drawed mother drew me. My brother Joe was eight years old, and sold for $800. I never did know this old lady—my mistress—to go away from home. She hid all that money upstairs. She had money, and there were no banks, and so people had to hide their money. I laugh a heap of times about an old bureau and a little trunk that she had, and I wanted her to let me put my doll clothes in it, but she would say, "Don't touch it." After she died it was found out that she kept her gold money in it. Then in the bureau she had kept some money so long that it was as black as your dress, and I thought it was buttons, but when it was rubbed off it was money. Girls were hired out for victuals and clothes until 12 years old, and then for money. She was a great weaver. She even had money tied up in fringe on her bedspreads. She used to send me upstairs, but I didn't know anything about that money. I was too little.

Mr. Crab kept Joe because he was my mother's youngest child. Miss Betsy drawed mother and drawed me. Everyone drawed two darkeis and so much money. House slaves and the other slaves got along fine. They all got along nicely. They had what is called nigger quarters; had a great long table set three times a day, and two boys waited on it. These quarters were about as far as across the street from the Big House. They got hats, shoes, clothes and bed clothes, and were well treated. After they were set free many of them stayed there until they broke up. They didn't want me to leave because I was her maid; but sister come after me so I could come over here and go to school. Mother stayed there until after I come here and married. Then her and Joe come here, and lived over here on Franklin Street. Colored people had all that street right after the War. Then white people come here and run them out. We used to have all our dances in the Court House. My sister taught school right up here in the college, and had 125 scholars.

They used to have a song about

"Old master's gone away and the darkies stayed at home;
Must be now that the kingdom's come and the year
    for jubilee."

"Old master, he drilled so hard they called him captain
He got so dreadful tanned he said he's going down
    yonder amongst the Yankees
To pass for a counterbrand."

"His coat was so big, he couldn't pay the tailor,
And it didn't go half around
He's going down yonder amongst them Yankees
And pass for a counterbrand."

Then there was another song about

"Look up the road and seen the cloud arising
And look like we're gonna have a storm
Oh, no, you're mistaken,
It is only the darkies' bayonets and buttons on your uniform."

Once they opened two bottles of champagne, and each bottle was $5.00,
and got to drinking, and then they would sing

"Darkies, did you see old master
With the mustache on his face?
Left here early soon this morning,
Says he's going for to leave this place."

"Coat so big, he couldn't pay the tailor,
and it didn't go half round
He's going down yonder amongst them Yankees,
And pass for a counterbrand."

I have upstairs one of the first coal oil lamps that ever come South. I'll show it to you all before you go, and some other things, too. Had to pay 50 cents for a gallon of oil. One time Mr. Crab told the boys if they would get all the tobacco in before the frost fell they would give them a barbecue, and they did. I come to town and got all these lamps and set them on the table. I told Mr. Crab I wish I had one of those lamps, and he told me I could buy one. I had made a bonnet and he had given me a dollar, and so I bought the lamp with that dollar. I made many and many a dollar sewing by that lamp. I have Robert's little belly band, shoes, underskirt, a dress I paid $5.00 for that come from England, a little hat, and I got them all yet. I am going to put them all on the Fair and leave them there. Then I got a dress that was made the first year after the Civil War. A lady named Mrs. Pritchard taken the premium in Nashville with that dress. It is made Martha Washington style. I have got a pin that I have had ever since all of Clarksville liked to have burned down, and that was in 1872. And it is said that all the fire departments from Nashville came from Nashville, and only the colored fire department put it out. They were going to hang a man out from here, and while they were all out there a darkey set Clarksville on fire; and they ain't never been another attempt at hanging another colored man here since.

You know they call me loud speaker in Chicago. I caught a rich beau while I was in Chicago. He was a City Hall gentleman.

All of the girls on the place, or on our place, were married except me; and my young master would have had a fit if I had married. I wasn't thinking about no marriage. I had my company to come to see me. They dressed me awfully nice. My mistress, she would say, "Go wash," meaning taking a bath, and "then I will come and dress you." She would dress me in her clothes, from skin out. The boys just thought some of the girls were doll babies. That's what they thought about me, with my curls and dressed up so nice.

My sister was brought here from Elkton, and there used to be a nigger trading place right here where the Clarksville National Bank is, right on that place. They sold my sister right in this nigger trading yard. She had a baby, and at first they didn't want to buy her because of the baby, but finally a man from Arkansas bought them, and she never heard nothing of her for 12 years. I mean my mother didn't. Before we were set free there come a gypsy down through Kentucky, telling fortunes. The white people didn't allow them to come in the front door. So they took them around to the kitchen. While one of them was there she looked at mother and said, "I think I can tell you something that you might like to hear." And she said, "Your daughter who you haven't seen or heard from for 12 years is living and doing well, but she has got six other children." That made seven. She told mother all about how well she was living. She said, "Why she goes to the Springs every summer with these children, and has two nurses," And she said, "Well, you will see her; she is living and doing fine." After we were set free, my sister was living right down here on the railroad, by Smith's Alley. I had not been long married and was living in the country. There was a man that used to stay on the station. Sister Emily came and had two children with her, and had to wait for the train to go on to Elkton and to Hopkinsville; and this man told her about her mother. They got to talking, and he told her that her mother and sister were living right here near the railroad. Her husband had let her come to stay three weeks. She had money and brought us things. She had also come to take me back, but she didn't know I was married. The yellow fever broke out, and the man died and all the children but one. She took this one and ran to the train. She said she looked at the place being burnt up and all her children. She took two other children to St. Louis with her. The boy got to be a steward on the steamboat, and always called Sister Emily mother. Once I got to talking about my sister while I was working at the Springs, and a man said if I take care of myself he would take me on to St. Louis to see my sister, and I did. She didn't know me.

During the War we couldn't get starch and coffee. Had to raise sugar corn and stew it down and make coffee out of sweet potatoes. And for salt, we had to wash the floor off where the salt had dripped from the meat, and then let the water dry out. You all ain't seen no hard times, and if another war comes they are going to kill the nits and the old ones. So you all try to be happy. It is nice to live and enjoy, but don't forgit you got to go.

Robert graduated from the Grammar School in Louisville, and graduated at Fisk, and then during the War was promoted a corporal; went from here to Evansville and then on to Chicago, where he worked in the movies, and a fellow got him to try at the Post Office, and he got on there, and is a revenue man yet. He sends me a check the 15th of every month.

Fort Donaldson was the biggest place that the colored people had for their quarters, and I been there many times since.

I remember hearing a toast to General Lee, and I've said it sometimes when I've been called upon, and made everybody laugh because I remembered this one of so long ago.

> "Here it is! to Hancock and to Lee
> And to all those noble officers
> Who fought for the colored race over liberty.
> May the hinges of friendship unite us all together
> And the gray hair upon our heads drag the ground
> And light our souls into heaven."

"I Was Right There When They Broke John Brown's Neck"

I was born in Virginia. I was right there when they broke John Brown's neck. I got some brothers there, and I tried to get in touch with them, but the letter come back. I was raised from a kid up there in Virginia till after they broke John Brown's neck; I was a kid then old enough to wait table. I left an uncle back in that part of the world that was 110 years old, but I can't get any discussion about my own family I left there so young. I don't know whether I'm a lone man or not, but I'm thankful to God. Yes, I was right there looking at them. Jefferson County, Virginia, was my native home, and they broke his neck at Harper's Ferry. From that time I was about ten, twelve or fourteen years old. It wasn't far from where I lived, and they carried me there to see him hung. I've been a slave once, you know, and I had to obey what they told me to do. They hung him on a Friday. No, it was in the daytime, not no night. They hung him because he broke into the navy yard and stole arms. Then Grant and Lee come along, and they had a war. I was in that war all along the Potomac. Oh, I was happy to see a hanging; I never seen one before. No, I don't know whether he ever killed anybody or not, but I know they hung him; and two more with him. Cook, Cooper and Brown was the three men hanged that day. Old master, he was Democrat, and he owned slaves, so he was glad. When the War come, Grant captured 4,000 men and captured old Colonel Harper with 'em. Yes, he got back. He was a very good man to black folks. He married in the Buckner family, and they lived in Berkley County, Virginia. He had about ten or fifteen slaves. We raised wheat, corn, potatoes, and vegetables. That's what makes me such a vegetable man now. I used to be a farmer till I was discharged from the War. Then I got with the Weavers, and they stopped me from farming. Old Captain Harper kept a grocery store, and he sold medicines, too. The slaves lived in cabins; they got up just like folks do now, only they were ordered and whipped in them days. Sometimes they sold whole families for thousands of dollars. They took care of their slaves and would give them anything they wanted; you just had to ask for it. He had black folks on his farm, you know.

We stayed in Jefferson County and Harper's Ferry was one court and Charleston was the other. I guess it's been quite a change there now. Wouldn't hardly know it, I guess. But black folks had more liberty then than they have in some places now. If I had my rights I would have ten or fifteen hundred dollars. I'm suing for a pension now. They said they can't find me, but I won't have that because I was called up since and shouldered a musket. I'm after back time now. It may cause me to have a house and lot of my own instead of living under the roof of folks who won't hardly speak to me.

My mother had four boys and I had a brother-in-law named Elijah. He was a Kentuckian, but he married a sister-in-law of mine named Adeline. My mother had two daughters, but I never heard from or saw any of them since they left. My father belonged to another family of people by the name of McMurry. He owned lots of property, too. My father, he farmed, too. He was a slave, too. He could come there every night, as far as that is concerned. My mother named me Harry. I was named after my mistress' brother.

121

They wanted me to take the name of Harper, but he wanted me to stay on the place and treat me like a slave, and I wouldn't do it. My father was named Robinson, so I kept his name after I got free. That part of the country didn't raise nothing but oats, rye and things like that. I come down here during the War. No, I wasn't on Lee's side, I was on Grant's side. I was old enough to be put in. No'm, I didn't run away (from the farm), I walked away. Grant come there and took us away. Father had a right to be owned by Robinson, his own people, but he was owned by McMurry. I left him back there. I had an uncle, my mother's brother, who was 115 years old. I was a slave near fifteen years; I helped to cook and wait table. Harper was a big man. My mother cooked and cleaned up and things like that. She stayed at the house. He never sold any of her children while I was there, but I have seen folks sold and put up on the block and bidded off like stock.

We had the privilege to go to church, and they would fix us up to go to services, just like we were chillen. Old McMurray was a preacher, too—my father's master. We had the privilege to act like we free almost. Slavery time was just like it is now. Old master built us a church, and we could have prayer meeting when we wanted to.

We had a colored preacher and deacons, too, in slavery time. The whites would come in for revival times sometimes. They would let you do anything you wanted to do, if you ask lief. Now we don't have to ask that way, you see.

Yes'm, they whipped me sometimes if I didn't do what they told me to do, but they'd never break our flesh or anything. There was no overseer on our place, nothing but padderollers. I never been caught by no padderollers, and I ain't never been whipped by them. They had a right to whip you just like the police now. Some black folks was living better then than some white folks now. Grant come through the country to make it so everybody could do as he pleased; that's where it come in at. I didn't know any masters that was mean around there; you just had to ask and he would say yes or no. It was a pretty good time, but they just had us tied so we couldn't get our liberty. No'm, I don't want to go back to slavery. You want your own liberty. You see, children couldn't go to school in them days.

"They Would Tie You Up and Whip You"

That's too far back to dig it up now; what good did that do? About two or three years ago a lady was here talking about it. Ole mass'r had in his will to set all his niggers free, and he wrote it in his Bible, but the Bible got los'; somebody knowed it was in thar and they stole it; and when he died all the slaves was give out to the family. I don't know how old I was. I heard from some of the folks two or three months ago who wanted to know if I was still living. I had the girl to write her and tell her yes, and to send me something, but I knowed she wasn't gonna do it, 'cause I don't 'spect she's got nothing.

I stayed there during the War. My aunt stayed with the Caldwells and I belonged to the McClutchens out there; but after the War she came up and got me and brought me up here. You know Miss Katie died and left her will, and my uncle was sold here and so then my aunty came after me down there and brought me here. I was a little girl then. I don't know about that. How I used to have to get up 'fore day and make fire in the house, feed and yoke my steers. I was big enough to plow. Then they have us scrubbing. That was in the West. I was bred and born here but after the old lady died they took me to the West. White women plowed down there. You know if they worked, we po' culled people had to hit it.

Cut logs, chop, anything. I worked. I look at how these logs are cut on the railroad, and then how I used to chop logs. We had Saturday evening to wash and to clean up our clothes for Sunday. Yes, we had church. White folks church, and sometimes the white preachers would preach in the woods to the darkies. I used to remember, there used to be an old man who was white. What did he say I used to rave about so much? He used to say, "Behold the stranger at the door. He gently knocks and knocks before the bleeding hand and trembling heart. We treat no other friend so ill." I was a child, but I remember the black folks had their virtues then. They used to give white folks sacrament on their side of the church. No, what would they want the Negroes to go up there for? I told Sister Huntsey, "What they want to come up to my house for; what they want to hunt up that now?"

I was cooking for the cullud people over there in West Nashville when they was going to sing to build Jubilee Hall. When they was going across the ocean to build Jubilee. I didn't cook for them, Mrs. Lightner cooked and I set the table for them and did things like that. They were going across the ocean to sing. The Jubilee Hall, I been round it, but I never been in it. I will some time another if I live and get away so I can walk. You know I am very old and can't get around like you people. I thank God I am here to see my young people. I tell them to take care of themselves.

I was looking the other day amongst the weeds they used to use. They would have we children to dig, and the white folks and black made tea out of it. But now they go to the doctor. I got some weeds now. One of my church members was down with kidney trouble. She lives over there where the bed's at.

(Nurse brings her food) Bless your heart—God's got a seat a sitting way back for you. Do you want these things back now? They brings me something every day. Well, I haven't had anything to eat today. I asked them if they had anything over there. When I ain't got no coal I call my church brother, Brother Shep, and he brings me some coal. He sho' is good. I tell you, you don't know, and I tell them this here winter is going to bring something on all this suffering.

What do you call those things going over there? (Speaking of airplanes). Well, they came right over here. That ole gentleman counted them.

When we were under bondage they said we could have prayer meetings out; but I was right young and little then and all I cared was to dance. They had all sorts of dances, quartillions, and quiltings and corn shuckings and everything else. We had good times. I get to thinking about it all the time, and how good they were to me when I was living with my white folks. They were good and I didn't work.

I am gonna show you something that my auntie made, and she was gonna make me one, but they took her away. She used to make everything. My auntie done it. She was gonna make me a spread, too, to go over all my bed, but the white folks took her away. She b'long to this man; I b'longed to the old lady.

If you were a lady and had a chile, they would give you to her daughter, if your miss had a daughter, and where you went you could take this child. Last year somebody come here and took might near everything I have. Everybody wanted this because it is peculiar and everybody wants it. My auntie made a lamp and sold it. Now I have got quilts I am piecing. I tell these children, "Quit racing around here, get down and piece your mama's quilts." A white woman told me the other day if I would carry this to the capitol I could get something for it. I am gonna keep this as long as I live, because my aunt made it, and after I am dead I don't care what becomes of it.

Yes, the pots—skim the grease, that's how she made the lamps. Get some cotton and make a wick and light it. I have made a plenty of them. I used to take the grease on the dinner pot that you boiled and empty the water out of it and put it in the lamp. You would take some meal and make a dough and put this wet dough in the bottom of the cup and let it dry, and take the grease and put it in this dough and make a wick out of cotton.

I used to have a rake and make a garden. I have a garden now out there. I work my garden now. I plant beans and peas and goober peas, and eat them. I can do anything. I cut my own wood. I got my axe in here and all. That man over there plants a tater patch. I was cleaning my house and he was planting a tater patch; and I have an elderberry bush and I can make the best wine you ever saw in your life; and I wanted him to make the tater patch and not move the bush, so I could make wine. Everything has been so tight since Jim left. He used to get rabbits and eggs and everything.

Oh, yes, they is jimson. I make a tea. It is good for most anything. Make a little tea, you can steam the water and pour it over there. When they had the kidney trouble. There was a gal over there what was po'ly; her changes stopped. I went down and got white barking and jimson, and I always keep a little money, and I went and got the money, and she came all right.

Sis Jennie had me laughing about when you were coming, and she said I wasn't far enough back. The young man what lives next door says I wakes him up every morning, and I said "You ought to be glad to be up 'cause I wakes you up in good spirits." You never were in bondage, but you know about it. They would tie you up and whip you. They never whipped me enough to make the blood come out of me. Mass'r whipped me for Miss Polly one day. They would put you over a log and whip you. No, it was the mass'r. I never saw any that they beat so. I heard there was two ole women, they beat them to death here in town, but I don't know. They tied them on a bough; there was two ole white men came long and he saw a cullud man and he wanted to know what the nigger had, and the nigger wouldn't let them see; and they whipped him. Whipped all of them 'cause he wouldn't let them look in his sack. That was about ten miles from me. They were talking about it in the kitchen, but I don't know whether it was so or not.

Oh, yes, honey, yes. I would see them when they were hunting them. When the slaves would run away out in the woods and come around and get something to eat and hide out. They would fix up something to eat and send it by one of the children. They wouldn't send but one, 'cause white folks might suspicion. They was so mean. Uncle Aldridge just layed in the woods, and they catched him and killed him nearly, and they buried him, and the end of the coffin was sticking up and the white folks make them dig them up, and they had buried him in an old meat box. They had to make a coffin for him and bury him right. The ole man was rich and los' everything, and didn't even have money to furnish his house. Here, set your tail on that (addressing investigator); set your rump on that. You are used to running around with rich folks in the parlors and things. I haven't any parlor, this is my parlor, my wash room and cook room and everything, my primp room. I have been here 16 years. It ain't much, but I don't have to run around for house rent. I ain't had no fuss with nobody since I have been here. That upstairs man is a painter, and the one downstairs is a widower, and the one upstairs is a widower. Shep is a widower, but he give me coal.

I knowed them to beat up the overseer. Henry Halfacre killed him out for a while; he come to, though. They run him off and sold him and sneaked him back again. I got his picture, it's so dirty though. This is my brother's picture. My brother's name was Henry Halfacre. He had eight children. I am older than brother. And he died and his wife died since. He was such a scoundrel, as I used to say. He had seven children and was so bad; didn't do like I wanted him to do. He made sixteen or seventeen dollars a week; he was a stone mason. One time he went to the grocery for the other woman and she let him put all the things in the basket, and I reached around after he had got all the things in it, and took the basket. He said, "Sis, what you gonna do?" And I said, "Gonna take it to your children and give them something to eat." He said (I lived on Vine Street) "I am not gonna come in your house any more." Ole sinner, he's dead and gone. He didn't do nothing but go in the alley in the dark part where I couldn't see him, and let the woman get away. Nancy Shout, that was the woman's name. She was a good looking woman, too. I was cooking out for white people then, and when I would come home one of the little fellows would meet me. He would take my basket, and I would say, "Don't take all the biscuits out, leave some in for the other children." He would say that they could do without. I hear from Les,—that's my brother's son. He comes here and preaches down here at this church somewhere down here on Church Street. Les stayed here one time, till his wife come. I have her cup here now; she had a string tied to it so she can get water when she was traveling. I have a niece here in Nashville. The doctor on my leg, he said he knew Jim Halfacre.

The white folks had the ham; after they et what they wanted off it, we would boil the bones. We would get the shorts to make bread, 'cause everybody didn't have it. They had dry head and jowl. Our white folks did give us white bread for Sunday morning, and biscuits. My uncle would come in from town and bring a hogshead as tall as that is. We had a little coffee on Sunday morning. Sure, we had all the vegetables we wanted. We had to plant them, though.

So I am thankful that there ain't none of them 'round me. Shep is so good to me, and he ain't compelled to though, and Shep is a sweet man. He is one out of a hundred; but I do like Shep though I am a heap older than him. I know when all six come here. He had those nice girls and they came out here. We called Shep Mass'r Charles and the girls Miss Anne. I have been in this here house 15 years. Ain't never had a fuss with anybody, and when I tell them all something, they say, "Mammy, you have been a good ole mammy," and I say, "Yes, and you have been a good ole rascal."

Oh, honey, he has been dead since 'fore the War. No, my last one died when the Centennial was here, and I got a dress in my trunk I went up there and bought when the Centennial was in Chicago.

Our folks could have them; everyone did. When they came for them we would pack the rags under the door so that they couldn't see the lights. We could have any (lights) we had, and if a sheep died we would take the taller and make up a big box of candles.

I b'longed to the McClutchens, out 10 miles from town, and the Kumthens lived near. I remember everybody round here, Josh Kumthen and Tom Kumthen.

They would be playing and singing, and I would be dancing. They used to sing, "Hark from the Tomb," and the like. And they used to sing:

> "His hair is white as any lamb's wool
> His body like a marble stone
> His eyes are like a ball of fire
> And his feet like polished brass."

I ain't in no mood for it now, but I wish you could hear me sometimes. I ain't got no voice now. Didn't Jennie tell you any. What good does that do? If they been through what I been through and still doing good as I am doing, they ought to be glad.

We used to sing to the rabbits. Yes, we would be out playing in the field, and turn around and out jumped two or three rabbits, and we would catch the rabbits and sing to them. We would tell the rabbits to "Harken from the Tomb the Doleful Sound." When they would hear us, they would say "What is the matter with you, you had better come here and pick up some chips." She would see us having a good time and she would want us to come and pick up some chips. That was the cook. "Pull some bark off the fence and bring it here to warm ole mass'r's feet." I would say, "I don't care nothing about your feets or nothing."

This leg got hurt. I knocked it up against a piece of wood and it bled a quart of blood. I went around in some rubber shoes, and the white folks would say, "Aunt Lizzie, I don't want you to go like that. Why don't you go to the doctor?" and I say, "I don't want to go see any of those students, they will cut on me, and will say it was my foot." So I went to a doctor in East Nashville, and I told him to bind it so it would be all right. I told him he had bound it too tight yesterday. My leg was swollen up, and when I came home and got the scissors and cut it, and my leg got all right, and I ain't had any trouble but once since, and that was 'cause I drank some whiskey and coffee.

White folks wouldn't learn you how to read and spell. You had to slip and learn it. I have my spelling book here. I went to Sunday School and learned in the reader. Yes, Presbyterian.

Ask your mass'r for you; that is all they would do. Some ole cullud man come round and they wouldn't say nothing else about it. They just asked for you and that was all. Uncle Perry Edmonston come around. My ole mistiss' son's woman married Cotton, and he went down on Saturday night to be a waiter, and waited on them. She married a good looking yellow man. She was a cook. And after they married we had supper and danced. No, they had the supper after they had the ceremony. Uncle Perry married them. He joined their right hands. That's all they did and they said they was married. He just said, "Now you are man and wife" to Cotton and they had cake and wine and a couple of chickens. No, all of them, they didn't get it; just them and that's all. This was my ole mistiss' son's servant. No, they didn't do it in our house, the one who married. She was the weaver, and she wove the clothes. They was great for you to have nice cotton coats.

Yes'm, there was about 25 of them, and they wouldn't hardly have nothing—cheers (chairs) or nothing, sometimes wouldn't have beds. My bed pulled out from under my miss' bed, and the night my ole miss died I jumped out from under this trunnel bed and asked her what she wanted, and she said, "Go and get granddad," and I ran and got him. I never called ole miss nothing but "mother" in my life. When she was traveling and I was her maid, I traveled right with her. If she had a chair I would set down, and if they wouldn't I would stand. She would watch my plate to see that I got everything all right. Ole miss is dead. I went to Holly Springs and all down in Mississippi to Texas. She died before the War. If she hadn't I never would have left here.

Every time you think about Lincoln, and they see you you got scared. When we talked we were way off in the woods. Charlotte, she was laying in with a baby, and she told some of them her dream, and they nearly beat her to death; and she had a baby. I never did get the dream—I don't know what she dreamed. They told us the whole mess. Ole mother was the head of everything. No, I stayed there a while with them, and thought they'd give me a home. I stayed there a while with them, and went to work for some po' white woman, and I rode an ole white horse what the Yankee soldiers had, and he was blind and his name was Ole Captain; and I had my child in my arms and my young mass'r come ridin' the road behind me, 'cause he thought they would come to kill me, but I took another road 'cause that road was so rough, and that's how he missed me. I had my baby, too. I didn't go the rough road 'cause the horse was blind. When I came, the folks was so glad to see me. He was gonna kill me 'cause I was free. I got shame about it, they talked about it so. They left everything they didn't want; just stole what they wanted and left. I was out at ole Bill's Christmas, and they said for us to pack up and go with the Yankees and I said, "No," I wanted to spend the Christmas with them, you know. Jack and Polly Anne, they left and stripped the house. Didn't anyone in our house leave the place to go with the Yankees but Uncle Charlie, and the Yankees had a quick order to go, and the Rebels came and smothered them up. Then the Ku Klux got in there. I went away. I had to leave. I ain't had nobody. Why didn't they help us years and years ago? I know you have heard about plenty hard times.

Some was buried right respectably, but when Scroggins slaves died they went and broke down two yokes of steers that day. They had killed him and they buried him in a meat box and the white folks came and made them take it up and bury him in a coffin and put clothes on him. Oh, no, they didn't do nothing about that.

I danced a pattillion. Vernon, he played everything. They had a bass fiddle and a big fiddle, and a little boy played it, and he had on a ruffled shirt and a scissor or hammer tail coat. When I would go they would say, "Liz, who is your partner?" I said, "I don't know, who's here? Is ole Pat here?" He said "Ole Pat is your partner," and I said, "Sure, I ain't gonna dance with nobody what I got to call figgers for."

(You married somebody who belonged to someone else?) Yes, maybe they were three or four miles away. They would come every Saturday night or every two weeks that way. They had to be out, though, soon Monday morning. That is the way it was, sugar pie. They come in and asked my mistiss for me. I was called your wife, but you couldn't come for me. They wasn't gonna come if you didn't want them to. I would take you in my house and marry you.

Yes, some of them had children for them what wasn't married to you. No, they wouldn't do nothing; they was glad of it. They would be glad to have them little bastards; brag about it. No, I ain't gonna tell you a lie and say they were married. No, he didn't. He wouldn't ask for you 'cause the woman would treat him like the mischief. No, they wouldn't want to marry any more than now. They just want you for a sweetheart nowadays. Yes, they had some look like they were white children. They would get around and whip them just like they would any others. They would take them to town and put them on the block, and he was the father of them. I could take you to the block now, if they haven't moved it. There was a man on the pike. I know when I went off he bought a woman, and this woman came from Arkansas, and this here man got with her and got this boy and she got him, and then she turned round and had a black one, and he turned round and sold it. He bought her from Miss Porter and she got jealous and she turned round and had a dark child and he sold. One died. Joshua is dead now. After she died he went off and bought another yellow woman and one of the servants what had been there to nurse his child. The oldest child died, but I don't know. They gave every one of the children homes. The white folks didn't like it either. I knowed them all. Aunt Margaret cleaned and nursed all these children. He was never married before. Everybody liked his place 'cause it was so much fruit on it.

I had a fellow named Henry. I liked to dance with him. Would not have no courting. They just laughed and talked. Didn't let the boys get around the gals like they do now. He sat over there and you sat over here and do your courting. I never said "No," honey.

Krumthen had children by my Aunt Ann. He had all the children on the place. And ole Bill Scroggins had children by Mary, and there was some others.

"All My Bosses Were Nigger-Traders"

I wasn't very old when the Civil War began. I had just turned into my sixteenth year, I remember when the Yankees come to this town. My old boss hit me that mornin' and he didn't know the Yankees were in town, and when he found it out he come back beggin' me to stay with him, and said he was sorry. We were livin' one and a half miles from the depot. All my bosses were nigger-traders till they married, and then they settled down. I've seen them sell women away from little children, and women would be cryin' and they'd slap 'em about cryin'.

They had guards at the church meetings, waiting for you to come out, to see if you had a pass. Those that had 'em would come out and the others would run away. They had padderollers after night. They came to massa's one night and I was there. They took me out to whip me, and he said "Lay down there right close, so my riggin' won't be in the sun," He had a broad strap and he whipped me fourteen licks. He was counting and I was counting, and at the fourteenth lick I was up. He said, "How come you run?" and I said, "I didn't know your voice, massa. If I had, I wouldn't of run."

When I went to the War I was turning seventeen. I was in the Battle of Nashville, when we whipped old Hood. I went to see my mistress on my furlough, and she was glad to see me. She said, "You remember when you were sick and I had to bring you to the house and nurse you?" and I told her, "Yes'm, I remember." And she said, "And now you are fighting me!" I said, "No'm, I ain't fighting you, I'm fighting to get free."

(Slave Droves) Yes'm, I've seen droves of 'em come through, all chained together. And I laughed; I didn't know no better. I belonged to Jim Caruthers. He was a good man, and he had about one hundred darkies. I was just a little motherless child, kicked and knocked about. Yes, I know Betty (Mrs. Love). The first year I was hired out she was not big enough to wait on the table. The first man I was hired out to was her master. I was nearly sixteen, and she was just a little thing, but she looks older than I do now. Her father died during the War. He was in the hospital when I was. Miles German was her father. He belonged to the same man as my father.

When I was on the farm I was not big enough to do much. I could chop cotton, but I was quite young. I was sick once and Dr. Clifford said, "Let him eat anything he wants, 'cause he can't be raised." Marster told old missus if she could raise me she could have me, and she took me in the house with her and nursed me till I got well.

My old boss never would have his hands up before day. If he had an overseer that was bad the slaves would run away so's he'd have to get another one. They wouldn't suffer it. He wouldn't sell none of them that he raised; but he just wouldn't give them no meat at night. He would expect you to steal what you got at night. If he would read of a reward being out for something that was stolen, he would come around and tell us, and say, "If I catch any of it there, damn you, I'll kill you."

We had beef soup, cabbage, beans and things like that for dinner. Of course we had meat and bread for breakfast; but you could go in the cellar and get all the meal you wanted. We stole so many chickens that if a chicken would see a darkey he'd run right straight to the house. I always wanted some boots and one old lady said, "If you'll kill me a pig I'll get you a boot." I give her three or four pigs, but I never did get no boots. Oh, yes, long in the fall he'd give his darkies shoes, and he'd have 'em half soled once a year. We'd get a coat every other year, and he'd give you a full suit and two pair of pants that winter. And he'd give you two coarse cotton shirts to carry you through the winter. Little children wore what their parents put on 'em.

They'd have to shuck corn at night when they'd come from the field. There was so many of them on our place it wouldn't take 'em no later than ten o'clock to get through. I've been to many a corn shucking at night, five miles from here. There was a crowd from Big Harper and a crowd from Little Harper, and after we got through the shucking they'd give us whiskey, and there'd be plenty of fighting, and the Little Harper white folks would take up for their darkies and the Big Harper white folks would do the same. I used to think them was the best times. They had some kind of biscuit mixed with sweet potatoes and I thought it was the best eating. They would have a big dance, too, and often after the dance they would go to fighting. Sometimes they would have a dance and would turn the pot down to keep the white folks from catching 'em. The padderollers would come there and couldn't find nobody, but they would go away and stay about an hour, and when they come back they'd be pretty sure to catch some.

Slavery was not such a bad time for me. I was young and my mother and father died when I was real young. We'd play marbles and run rabbits, and there was always eighty or ninety little chillen on our place. They had an old woman there to look after them—one that had broke down. When company would come, they would put clothes on them and march them up to the house so they could see his little niggers. We was feared to go up to the house. I 'member once he built a house for young marster and he said he was gonna let the darkies have a dance there, and they thought he was sure 'nough; but he didn't so they decided to have a dance anyhow. It was a moonlight night, and they had this big dance in the field, and the padderollers come and caught one man and threw him right on me, and he come and got me and said "God damn you," and kept his hand right in my collar and held me and took me home to marster. He told marster that he had told me that if I would tell who all was there he wouldn't whip me, but if I didn't he would whip me all day light, and you ought to heard me telling! It was around the time when the niggers was rising, and they asked me did I hear them shooting? "Did you see any guns?" And I said, "No, I didn't see no guns, but I heard them shooting." I hadn't heard a thing, but I knowed what they wanted to hear, so I said I did. They caught Tom Hodge, too, and he had to tell. I couldn't go to none of the parties after that. The niggers would kick me out if they saw me; they wouldn't have me there.

I've seen 'em handcuffed long as from here to the fence out there; women screaming and hollering about leaving their chillen. Yes, I've seen many a one (runaway slaves) and darkies would help 'em round. The Mississippi niggers in our camp used to get to talking, and they told once about a man named Bullens, who had hounds trained to catch the niggers, and they would tree you and carry you back. They say that when anybody would come for the hounds to run a nigger, the hounds would say, "Our Father, I've got a heavenly home up yonder, hallelujah, hallelujah."

My sister was carried away from me, and I went to see her 'reckly after the War. I thought she was dead after that visit, but I met a tramp one day and he said he was from Sheffield, Alabama. I told him I used to have a sister there, and he asked me what was her name, and I told him and he said, "I saw her yesterday." I said, "You're lying; she's been dead for years." But he told me all about them and told it so straight, and how many chillen she had, and everything, that I went to see her, and she was 98 years old, and we had a sure 'nough meeting. She was so glad to see me, and she told everybody, "That's my youngest brother." My sister that's living now stays up on Locklayer in Nashville. She's 84. Clay Farmer lives in that same neighborhood, too. We was boys together. Yes, his marster was a very nice old man; one of his men married a sister of mine, but he was unruly and they had to sell him to Mississippi. Yes, he would fight, fight white and colored, too. Yes, I know Mrs. Glass; 'course she was a slave; slaves don't give as much trouble as the young folks do now. I got two sons, and they never give me any trouble. One is in St. Louis, working in the Post Office and the other is at the Andrew Jackson Building in Nashville. My daughter lives in my other house out on the highway. I have buried many a man out in that cemetary on the Murfreesboro Pike. We had so many to bury a day, and we had to wait 'till the wagon would bring 'em in, and then we would put 'em on our shoulders and take him and bury him; you could hear men cussing and saying,

"Somebody's got my man." They would hide him and go off to see the girls, and then come back going to bury him late that night, and somebody would steal him and bury him. I couldn't do that now.

I never got 'rested but once, and that was in the War. We all got in a contest as to whether I would want a nigger or a white man to arrest me; I said I didn't want no nigger to arrest me 'cause it made him too biggity, and one of the nigger officers told them to take me to a guard house 'cause I said, "Damn a nigger officer." They started after me but I went running to the Captain and told him what had happened. He said to the officer, "You told him to spend his opinion, didn't you? Well, you are not going to take him nowhere." We used to do all kind of tricks in the army, and once a man got shot at a trick. There was a young boy in the picket line, and they made it up to scare that boy, so they went up and the boy shot and hollered at the same time, and it shot that man right in the mouth and the ball come out through his jaw—just done by foolishness. I went out one night to Squire Henderson's to get some apples and a Colonel turned the corner on me. He was with some girls and he passed on a little, but then he said to me, "Did you get permission?" and I said, "No," so he made me double quick back for about half a mile. He said to the Captain, "There's that prisoner out yonder," and the Captain and him et dinner and then he (Captain) come and let me out (guard house). He asked me if I didn't think that we had had 'nough of Squire Henderson's apples and I told him "Yes, but when I joined the army I went to get some medicine for Squire Henderson's wife and he said he would give me some apples for it, and I was just going to get them, and if he hadn't given them to me I wasn't gonna take 'em." That Captain was my friend. I wanted a furlough, and they all said, "You know he ain't gonna let you go, and we got wives and chillen and can't go," but he let me and I come on home. I went in the name of Caruthers then.

The first battle the colored ever got into was Fort Pillow; they buried some of 'em (colored soldiers) alive. Then when they went to Mobile, Alabama, they would just shoot 'em down, and they would just say that he broke to run and they had to shoot him to keep him from getting away. They'd do that any time they got afraid that they would run into the Yankees and they would take the nigger prisoners from them. I saw 'em hanging the Rebels right there in the penitentiary during the War. They tried to hang everyone that was in that battle, for the way they done the colored soldiers. I saw 'em captured just as barefooted, and it was snow on the ground. I've been right to the bridge where I was a guard.

Some of 'em treated 'em mighty tough and some pretty well. The Hodges were good feeders; Bill Mathews was, too. I know a man Bill Mathews undertook to whip him, and he wouldn't let him do it, so the white men were all there in droves to whip him, and he just fought 'em till they shot him down and killed him. Sure, they would kill a nigger; he's no more'n a wolf.

Yes'm, they'd preach your funeral. I can just recollect when my mother died and the funeral was preached right over there by Farmer's Bluff. We had some nigger preachers but they would say, "Obey your mistress and marster." They didn't know nothing else to say. The white preacher would tell you what you had to do, too. If you had prayer meeting you would have it on the sly. We'd sing old time hymns then, but you youngsters have done away with them now. Yes, mam, I've heard them pray for freedom. I thought it was foolishness then, but the old time folks always felt they was to be free. It must have been something 'vealed unto 'em. Back there if they'd catch you writing they would break you if they had to cut off your finger, and still they knew they would be free. It must have been 'vealed to 'em.

Betty's mother, she broke and run and carried her daughters with her, but they caught her. I saw it, 'cause I was working right there. I don't reckon Betty ever seed her father to know him, but I knowed him. I was in there wounded and he was in there wounded and he died from it. When the Yankees got near Nashville, the niggers started running to 'em.

I wasn't big enough to court; I had to slip. I knowed the road she'd come, and I could slip off and meet her sometimes, but we had to dodge the old folks 'cause they would whip me sho'. I'd walk a little piece with her, but I didn't know what to say. Young folks then wasn't like they are now. If I was at some old folks, house and started cutting up they would whip me, and when they'd see my mother they'd tell her and she would whip me again. But you just hit somebody's child now and they'll have you in court. I would just ask her (girl) what was the news, and I thought I was doing big courting then; I would brag to the boys about it.

I'd been better off if I'd bought in the country. I married when I was 21 years old, and I didn't owe but seven dollars on my place. I always wanted a home and a gun, and I got both of them, but my boy took my gun when they had the riot in St. Louis, and I never did buy another one.

'Course I seen 'em marry. We had one to marry right at my boss' front gate. The preacher married them there. They would always give 'em a kind of supper and big dance. They wouldn't marry 'less they could have a dance. Some of them say they don't see why I vote for the Yankees; they say they didn't do nothing for me, but I tell 'em the Yankees done 'nough when they set me free. I had two sisters and they were sent off, and there was three brothers. My sisters were given to my young mistress when she married.

Yes, but there wasn't but one family of half-white chillen on our place. The old lady would be meaner to them than she was to the black ones. Some of them was marster's chillen and old mistress would not have one of them for a house servant. She would get one right black and wouldn't have none of them in there looking as white as her.

I've seen 'em buck and gag 'em; they'd tie your hands here and put a stick there and then roll you about and whip you. The biggest whipping I ever got was from the old women (slaves). Marster would shake my ears, but he seldom would hit me.

(Colored preachers) Old Brother Bill Perkins, Peter Stynes, Uncle Tom Bell—he was the leading preacher; he's a mulatto. Some of 'em learned to read in the books; white folks would let 'em preach. I saw a preacher in Mississippi carry on a revival and he had persuaded the white man's scn to go, and he professed and they would let him have meetings any time, 'cause that white man's son professed under him.

"The Overseer Had a Bull Whip and Marster Had a Strap"

I was in Mississippi, in Juniper County. I belonged to Major Ellison, but I was raised right here in Tennessee till I was eleven year old; then Major Ellison bought me and carried me to Mississippi. I didn't want to go. They 'xamine you just like they do a horse; they look at your teeth, and pull your eyelids back and look at your eyes, and feel you just like you was a horse. He 'xamined me and said, "Where's your mother?" and I said, "I don't know where my mammy is, but I know her." He said, "Would you know your mammy if you saw her?" and I said, "Yes, sir, I would know her; I din't know where she is but I would know her." They had done sold her then. He said, "Do you want us to buy you?" and I said, "No, I don't want you to buy me; I want to stay here." He said, "We'll be nice to you and give you plenty to eat." I said, "No, you won't have much to eat. What do you have to eat?" and he said, "Lots of peas and cotton seed and things like that," but I said, "No, I'd rather stay here because I get plenty of pot licker and bread and buttermilk, and I don't want to go; I get plenty." I was staying with some half-strainers and I didn't know that that wasn't lots to eat. He said, "Well, I have married your young mistress and she wants me to buy you," but I still said, "I don't want to go." They had done sold my mother to Mr. Armstrong then. So he kept talking to me and he said, "Don't you want to see your sister?" I said, "Yes, but I don't want to go there to see her." They had sold her to Mississippi before that, and I knowed she was there, but I didn't want to go.

I went on back home, and the next day the old white woman whupped me, and I said to myself, "I wish that old white man had bought me"—I didn't know he had bought me anyhow; but soon they took my cotton dresses and put 'em in a box, and they combed my hair, and I heard them tell me that Mr. Ellison had done come after me, and he was in a buggy. I wanted to ride in the buggy but I didn't want to go with him, so when I saw him I had a bucket of water on my head, and I set it on the shelf and ran just as fast as I could for the woods. They caught me, and Aunt Bet said, "Honey, don't do that, Mr. Ellison done bought you and you must go with him." She tied my clothes up in a bundle, and he had me sitting up in the buggy with him, and we started to his house here. I had to get down to open the gate and when I got back up, I got behind, in the little seat for servants, and he told me to come back and get inside but I said I could ride behind up to the house, and he let me stay there, but he kept watching me. He was scared I would run away because I had done run away that morning, but I wasn't going to run away 'cause I wouldn't know which way to go after I got that far away.

When we got to the house, my mistress came out with a baby in her arms and said, "Well, here's my little nigger. Shake hands with me." Then he come up and said, "Speak to your young mistress," and I said, "Where she at?" He said, "Right there" and pointed to the baby in my mistress' arms. I said, "No, I don't see no young mistress, that's a baby."

I went in the house, and they had all the glasses around there, and I just turned and looked and looked

133

at myself, 'cause I had never seen myself in a glass before. I heard mistress say, "Po' little thing, she's just like a little motherless child; her mother was sold away from her when she was six years old." They had soft carpets and I was just stepping and stamping up and down with my foot 'cause it was so soft; and then she took me up to a big room and I said to myself, "Lord, God, I got into another fine place!" and the woman in there went in the trunk and got some domestic and some calico and made me a dress and some drawers and a drawer body, and she went to work and made those things for me, and then she told the woman that it was time for her to go home, and she said take them duds and give them to your sister and you comb her head and wash her all over, and honey, she washed me all over and put them things on me and I was never dressed so fine in my life, and I just thought everybody was looking at me because I was dressed so fine; but of course they wasn't paying me no mind a-tall; the dress had some red in it and some big flowers in it, and I was looking at myself in the glass and I would pull up my dress and look at my pretty clean drawers and things, and when I went in the room where my mistress was I pulled it up again and started looking and saying to myself, "Don't I look nice and clean under here," and my mistress said, "You mustn't do that, that's ugly," and so then I went out in the woods where there was lots of cedars thick around, and I got down there and pulled up my dress and just looked and danced and danced. I had never been clean like that before; and staying with them po' white folks I had had a time with those body lice. They would get so bad I would take my dress off and rub it in the suds and rinse it out in the branch; and sometimes I would be rinsing it and Mistress would call me, and I would be so scared I would put it on wet and run to her. I had a time, I tell you; they might nigh eat me up when I was staying there, and I was so glad to be clean.

(In new home) The overseer had a bull whip and old marster had a strap, and I would hear them out in the field beating them, and the slaves would just be crying, "Oh, pray, marster, oh, pray, marster." Ole miss wouldn't let 'em whip me. She was just like a mammy to me; I wanted to die, too, when she died. Yes, she died right here in town. She called me in and told me, "Lu, I'm dying, but you be good to my chillen." and Marse Tom would fan her, but she would always say, "Give it to Lu. You fan to hard, and I don't want you fanning the breath out of me; it's going fast enough without you fanning it away." I stood there and fanned her till she breathed her last, and then I ran in the next room and hugged my arms right around me and held my breath and tried my best to die. I was scared of him (Mr. Ellison) 'cause he cussed so much. I stayed with my mistress while she was sick because they left Aunt Adeline up there to tend to her, and she tried to make her walk when she wasn't able to stand up, and I could lift her up in my arms.

Mistress died on Saturday and they buried her Sunday and on Monday morning Marse Tom called me and Aunt Adeline out and said one of us would have to go home (back to miss) and the other could stay and take care of the chillen. I said right quick, "I'll go home," because I had a little boy down there I was crazy about, and I wanted to go back to him; but marster got to crying and telling me that mistress wanted me to stay with the chillen, and he said, "Stay with my little chillen and I'll never let you want. I'll take care of you and if you are free you can always come to me and get what you need." So I stayed, and I had a hard time, too; they just kept doing me so bad I started cussing. I said, "I'm getting God damned tired of you knocking me round." There was one old woman (slave) and she just kept knocking on me and cussed me and she called me a God damned yellow bitch, and said she was gonna whip me that night if it was the last thing she did, and I told Mary Anne (slave) that she said she was gonna whip me if it was the last thing she did, and Mary Anne said, "If you let her whip you, I'm gonna whip you too." So that night I went to Hannabell and said, "Hannabell hold my baby," and I give her my baby and I come on down there where I knowed she was gonna pass; and I was kinda scared, too, but Hannabell said she would whip me, too, if I let her whip me, so I went on round. She come up and said, "You cussed me, didn't you?" and I said "Yes, you cussed me, too." and she jumped to me and I just grabbed her round the waist and got straddle of her, and her sister come and looked on but she didn't bother us, and I scratched her face and pulled her hair and just beat her up terribly, and her other sister come and pulled me off her, and I started back at her and one of them run and told her husband, and he come running out and caught me by the arm; and I pulled my whole sleeve out of my dress and run back and hit her in the back. Old Perks said he was gonna whip both of us, when he found it out. When we went in the next day he saw my face where she had given me one scratch, and he said, "What on earth's the matter with you?" and I told him that he had always told me to carry up the candle to put the chillen to bed, and Ailse whipped me 'cause I carried it up and didn't bring it back down; and she told him I cussed her and that's why she hit me; and he wanted to know if she cussed me, too, and she didn't say nothing and I said, "Yes, she called me a nasty stinking yellow bitch," and he got up and boxed Ailse round scandless, but he didn't hit me but two licks. He never did hit me no more.

He felt sorry for me 'cause I didn't have nothing to take up for me like the others. I come up here the first year of the War and I never did get back. No'm, he died down there (father of the girl).

I stayed with my white folks three years after freedom, and they tried to make me think I wasn't free. And I'll tell you I made it hot for them when they tried to bother the chillen (master's children). When he'd start to whip them I'd say, "You just let these chillen alone. Miss Janie (first wife) said you was gonna marry some other woman and be mean to her chillen," and he'd say, "Lu, don't tell me that," and I would say, "Yes I is, too; I'm gonna tell you every time you hit one of these chillen." One Sunday I wanted to go to a meeting in Franklin, and I didn't ask; I just told this woman I was going, and she said, "I say you can't go," and I said, "Oh, yes, I'm going," and she called Marse Tom and I told him I was going, and he said, "I say you can't go." So I said, "You look right here, Marse Tom, I'm free, just as free as the birds in the air; you didn't tell me, but I know it," and he didn't say another word. You see, they thought that 'cause I stayed there I was fool enough not to know I was free; but I knowed it; and I went on to Franklin. I was nine miles from town, but I walked there to the meeting.

Later on, they wanted me to go down to Mississippi to live, but I said, "I never 'spect to go to old Sip again long as I live." The chillen kissed me and told me goodbye, and they cried and cried. Later on he bought here, and they moved back and I would go up there every month to see how my chillen was getting along. They would meet me down at a big tree and tell me, "She's (stepmother) just as mean to us as she can be," and they would take me up to the house and give me lots of things to carry home with me. I would tell Marse Tom I come after some money and some clothes, too, and he'd give me a dollar and tell them to give me what I wanted, and they would go to the smokehouse and give me some meat and anything else I wanted. I still can get anything I want if I go to them, but it is hard for me to get way up there now.

(Asked what became of the boy of whom she was fond) He started up here, but the Yankees caught him and took him back. I never did see him no more.

I used to make the chillen cry during the War. I would say "I'm going to the Yankees; Miss Maggie's getting just so mean to me," and the youngest child would say, "We'll go too; I'll tell you which-a-way to go." And she woulda went with me, too; all of them chillen woulda went if I'd run away then. I had a hard time, I tell you.

I married 'reckly after the War ceasted. My old boss married his own niggers in Mississippi; he'd just get the Bible and marry them, and he had the 'surance to marry me after the War, and he had to pay ten dollars for it, too, 'cause he wasn't no officer that could marry me.

(In slavery time) They had a great big table set across the hall, and we would eat, and there was a place to dance like we did on the 4th of July. We did have good things to eat on the 4th of July; and if there wasn't a fiddler on the place, he would hire one to come and play for 'em. That was in Mississippi; and down there they called us Tom Ellison's free niggers, 'cause he was better to us than most of them; but he didn't 'low no visiting. If you did any talking it was through the fence. You know white folks would just as soon kill you as not, and you had to do what they said.

They had a white man that would come over every fourth Sunday and preach to us; he would say, "Be honest, don't steal, and obey your marster and mistress." That was all the preaching we had down in Mississippi. They had benches and planks around for you to sit on and a little table and a chair in the center for the preacher. When I'd come back from church they would ask how I liked it, and I would say I liked it fine. Your marster would whup you for going. You just had to talk through the fence, if you talked; you could go with the folks on your place, but that was about all.

When the War was coming up, I would hear the white folks reading the papers about it, and I would run in the kitchen and tell Aunt Harriet. She would say, "Don't let the white folks hear you talk; they'll kill you," and if I would be going too far she would stop me, and wouldn't let me finish telling it to her.

Me and my sister was the brightest (in color) ones on our place. Yes, I got treated better'n any of them 'cause I stayed in the house; but sister had to work in the field and she wasn't treated any better. They had an old woman to keep the colored chillen, and I would take my chillen (white) and go down to the quarter and I would stay down there and eat, and my chillen would eat down there, too. Marster told missus that that wasn't right, but we kept going and he had to put out meal and meat for us down to the quarters.

He wasn't so mean, but they cussed so much we was scared of 'em. One got to cussing round his little niggers and they ran away. Some of 'em they never did find, 'cept their skeletons where the varmints had destroyed 'em, and they just found one over on a little island, and he had done stayed there so long when they found him he was right wild. They asked him what he had been eating, and he said acorns and bugs and things like that, after he got over it. That man was neighbors to us, and our marster got scared then and got good to his chillen. He had 'em up to the house once a week, and he would give 'em sugar and let them play up there and tell 'em they was his chillen and he wouldn't hurt 'em.

He was sorta mean, though, 'cause sometimes in the evening you would just hear that bull whip crying. He'd tell 'em to pick seven or eight hundred pounds of cotton, and if they didn't do it he would whip 'em. He was so mean they got up a plot to run off, and they never come in till after twelve o'clock that night. They had plotted to go and jump in the Mississippi river and drown themselves; so after that he quit beating and knocking on 'em, and if he got an overseer that was too mean he would turn him off. They said they meant to drown, too, but they thought about their little chillen and come on home.

Yes, she (daughter) is just fifteen years younger'n I am. Her daddy died during the War. No'm, we didn't do much; just dancing and different kinds of plays. I et at the white folks house, and I et what they did, but he fed the others pretty well. He'd give 'em sugar and a peck of flour and coffee and things like that, and they could sell their part of the coffee if they didn't like it. He'd buy their winter clothes, too. Everybody had two pairs of stockings and socks; and he didn't 'low em to work in the rain. He had two barrels of whiskey he kept in the smokehouse, and if they would get a little wet they would have to come to the house and get a dram. He would tell 'em to come, and them niggers would get just a little damp and they would come to the house and say, "Marster, I feel mighty cold and damp," and he'd get up and give them a dram. But he got tired of that, so he bought some castor oil, and he would put that in the cup with the whiskey, but after while they would just drink it all down like they didn't care, and marsa said he wasn't gonna let 'em drink his whiskey and his oil, too, and he stopped putting it in there.

Yes, we had to have coffee and breakfast before we went to the field; just meat and bread. You couldn't have flour everyday down there like they do here, you know. And talk about wild varmings! On a cloudy night you couldn't hear your ears for varmings. And you could see 'em drinking water at twelve o'clock in the day. And fish! You could catch 'em quicker than you could run down a chicken and catch it.

I don't know nothing about my mother and father. She left us and run off, and I was the oldest, and she left me and a little brother and another little suckling baby. She took us to the back porch at Morrison's and left us. On the way there she stopped at Aunt Jenny's and waited till nearly day, and then she took us and made a pallet on Morrison's porch and run away. She told us to lay there till she got back. I remember that Morrison come out of the door and he asked me what we was doing there, and I told him mammy told us to stay there till she got back, and he asked where she went and I told him I didn't know. He went back and said to his wife, "Fannie, Ada's done run away and her chillen's out on the front porch." Then he come back and told me to take the baby and my little brother and go round to the kitchen. Mama, she run away and she stayed right here in town with old Carter for about a year, and after she'd paid him fifty dollars to keep him from telling on her, he 'trayed her; so she found it out and she left the barn where she was staying and come on back home. She seen ole Carter pointing out the barn to a nigger-trader, and she left there. Ole Morrison kept her about two weeks after she come back, and a nigger-trader come along and he sold her. He said it was no good for him to keep her, 'cause if he'd hire her out she would whip the white folks. She had a scar right up over her eye and she got it fighting white folks. I remember it 'cause I remember getting slapped about picking at it when I was little. She would whip 'em and strip 'em naked and carry 'em up to the Court House where marster was.

We was raised up without a mother, and one old woman in the house where we stayed was so mean to us she would take nettle weeds and whip us with them (this was prior to her trip to Mississippi). I had to get up and go to the spring and get water and come back and take breakfast, —and Charlie (brother) was sick, —and we took him out in the yard and let him set up so he could see us play, and after a little while, he said, "I want to lay down; I'm tired of setting up," and I took him and laid him down and just then they called me to the house to get some eggs to make egg bread, and after I got 'em I slipped back down to see how he was, and I called him and he wouldn't answer, and I pulled his eyes open and he didn't say nothing, and I flew up to the kitchen to Aunt Bet (cook) and told her, "Aunt Bet, Charlie's gone to sleep and I can't wake him up." She went over, and he was dead.

Charlotte—the old woman we was living with—was mean to us. She would make the little one (Tobe) get up and go outdoors to do his business (body functions) and he would stay out there till I'd come and get him and bring him his breakfast. I would dip my hand in the gravy and rub it on his toes when his feet was cold, and one morning I brought his breakfast and he couldn't eat, and I tried to open his mouth and I couldn't, so I took him to Aunt Bet. She was my friend—and I said, "Tobe can't eat and he can't open his mouth," and she come back with me and Tobe was sitting there and had lockjaw; so she had to go to the white folks, and they sent for the doctor, but he couldn't do no good, and he stayed all that day, but the next night he died. They made me go to the spring and get some water to bathe that child and it was so dark I couldn't see my hand before me face; and when I got back with the water Tobe was dead; so I didn't get to see neither one of my brothers die. If I live to see this coming March I'll be 89 years old. I can't see and hear so well now. No'm, the girl's father died (her daughter's father). I didn't know the chillen's daddy at all, but they said his name was Riley, and that they named Tobe Riley after his daddy; he was the darkest child mammy had.

I'd go down to my sister's house and do my courting down there. I could go down there and stay till nine o'clock. He'd make 'em marry who he wanted 'em to marry. You couldn't marry who you wanted to.

Mama said she could tell when her chillen died. Everyone of them die, she said her nose would drop a drop of blood; and she said when the two boys died she went over to a neighbor's house and told her that they was dead 'cause her nose dropped a drop of blood. When she come back after freedom, she was here in town a week before I knowed it. I had just had a fight with my husband, and I had just told him that if I had a mammy to go to I would leave and never come back to him, and that night we had gone to bed, and it was raining real hard and I heard somebody holler, and I thought it was somebody coming for him to hunt. He said they could just holler on then; and that was my mother and my little half-brother then. It was dark and they was at the river, and they couldn't find the footlog. So they finally found somebody and asked them how far it was to Mr. May's place, and they told her to turn around and walk three miles back down the pike, and when she got there they told her it was back the way she come, and to go to some of the colored folks house and stay till morning and get an early start. So she went and knocked on a door, but just as soon as she did, they put all the lights out and nobody wouldn't come to the door. So she went back to the white man's barn and got in the hay and stayed all night, and in the morning she got up and come walking up to my house in the rain. It was in February. She walked up to the door, and I had two little girls and I was whipping one of them when the woman come to the door and asked who lived here. I told her Kay Mayberry lived here, and I'm his wife. So she said, "You don't know me?" and I said, "No'm, I don't believe I made your acquaintance before, but come in out of the rain," and she come in and asked me again if I knowed her, and she stepped over to the door. But I didn't know her, and the boy said, "This is your mother, and I'm your brother." I said, "No, my mother's sold and my brothers are dead," and I said, "You're none of my mammy; I know my mammy." Then she took the bundle off her head and took off her hat, and I saw that scar on her face. Child, look like I had wings! I hollered for everybody. I 'larmed out all the neighbors, and it was just like the 'Sociation round there. She stayed with us a long time, and she died right here in this house.

(Courting) We would just sit and talk with each other. I told him once I didn't love him; I hated him, and then I told him again that I loved him so much I just loved to see him walk. You had to court right there on the place 'cause they had padderollers, and if you went out without a pass they would whip you.

"I Can't Forgive Her, the Way She Used to Beat Us"

I don't know anything 'cept what happened when I was a child. I know I was born in slavery, and I know they was awful mean. I was born in 1855, and the War started in '61. My white folks was awful bad and mean. I'm telling you what I know; they was mean; they beat us till the blood run down our legs. When we left here we was naked; my sister was the weaver and she was weaving some clothes for us, and old mistress took that stuff off the loom and took it upstairs and hid it. We went away naked. My mother was the mother of fourteen chillen, but some died and she had seven chillen that was her grandchillen. Their mother was the one that did the weaving.

(Whipped about what?) First one devilment and then another. You know chillen git into mischief, and they get whipped for it. I often told my mother time after time that I didn't blame old mistress for whipping us, but she didn't need to kill us; she coulda just whipped us. We didn't have on but one piece winter nor summer, and she would pull it over our head and whip us till the blood run down, and we was dasn't to holler. I can't remember now like I can back yonder; but I can remember that just as plain as day. We stayed there a year after freedom 'cause we didn't have sense enough to know we was free. My mother took care of the chillen and washing and ironing, and she took me with her to wash socks and handkerchiefs. They used to keep her hired out 'cause she wouldn't let her (mistress) whip her; so they hired her out, and finally sold her. But she come back 'cause they said she only had two chillen and she was sound, and they found out that she had had fourteen chillen, and when she was a girl she had knocked her toe out of place, and she was a little cripple; so they had to take her back. You know if you sold stock and it wasn't sound like you said it was, you would have to take it back; so that's the way they did. I seen mistress come in there with a bucket of water to slosh on my mother, and mother grabbed the bucket and threw it on her, and the old woman hollered murder and all the chillen come running in with sticks and things; then the old woman said she wasn't mad, she was just happy in her soul. One of the boys took the stick he had and hit me a lick or two, but they wouldn't let him hurt me; and he wouldn't touch mother.

You know that old woman was mean. When she was dying she said she was all right, and I said to mother, "Yes, she is all right; all right for hell." Mother said I ought to forgive, but I can't forgive her, the way she used to beat us. Ain't no child what don't deserve a whipping. We'd eat green apples, eat dirt and things like that, and if she caught us we would hide it behind us, and if she asked what we had, we'd say, "Nothing;" you see we done tole a lie right there; and she would whip you! I'm telling you the truth; I can't lie 'cause I got to go before my God, and she's dead and can't speak for herself; but she beat me till the blood run down to my heels. Mother said when she was sold she had a baby in her arms, and her other boy next to the baby was standing by the fence crying. When she come back, she had me. I was her baby. My father was a Bailey, but mother and father separated before I was born. I was born in '55 and that was in slavery time. In '61 I was six years old, and that's when the War started. No, they didn't sell him; he and mother just got mad in a quarrel and separated. He tried to get her back and the white folks tried to get her to take him back, but she wouldn't do it, 'cause he drawed back to hit her with a chair, and he'd never done that before. He woulda hit her, too, if her brother hadn't been there and stopped him.

Mother was put on the block three times after that; and they couldn't sell her. They tried to bid her off for a dime, but nobody would give it. I don't know why they wouldn't but I just know nobody would. Why, in them days they would sell a baby from its mother and a mother from her baby, like cows and calves, and think no more of it.

No'm, we didn't have plenty to eat. We had bean soup, cabbage soup, and milk, with mush or bread in it. The chillen never did get no meat. The grown folks got a little meat, 'cause they had to work; but we didn't. Once a man brought some old hog heads and pieces of fresh meat like that to old mistress in a barrel, to make soap with, and the things was just floating on top; and she got mad 'cause the grown folks (slaves) wouldn't eat it. She give it to us chillen, and 'course we was glad to get it, 'cause it was meat, and we eat it till it made us sick, and they couldn't give us any more. Mr. _____ (man who had given meat) came by and found out what she had done, and he said, "I just brought that meat here 'cause I thought you might want it to make soap. I didn't know you was going to make nobody eat it. I wouldn't give it to my dogs." You know she was mean. When I heared she was dead I couldn't help but laugh, and I was grown then and had a child. She ought not to do me that way.

Marse Jack Barbee, he was so good to we chillen. He jerked her off of us many a time, and he'd say, "Plague take you, you trying to kill that little baby." If he found any of the old rawhides she'd use, he'd cut 'em up and take 'em out to the woodpile and burn 'em. Then she'd go to them old sprouts in the yard. Sometimes I'd rather it been the cowhide, 'cause sometimes the sprouts would have thorns on 'em.

My aunt, she'd slip meat skins through the crack to us chillen till that hole would get right greasy. She had a little hole in the floor that she could use; and we would go down to the orchard and broil them or cook 'em some way. We'd put the little ones in the henhouse, through the hole they left for the hens; and they'd come out with an apron full of eggs, and we'd take them out to the woods and cook 'em someway; and we would steal chickens, too. Me and sister Lottie was the biggest ones in the bunch, and we was real little. The white chillen would help us eat 'em, too, and they would go to the house and get salt, you know.

(When mistress would whip her). I'd squall and squall, and she'd shake me, and tell me to hush; then I'd just jump. I had to do something. I'd go round back of the chimney and cry easy. My mother never did whip me over twice, and I would mind her; I was 'fraid of her, and I always did what she told me. She was part Indian, you know. I said to her after freedom, "It's funny you wouldn't let mistress whip you and yet you let her whip us chillen all the time." She said, "If I'd started that they woulda sent me away and I never woulda seen you no more."

Yes, when we left there we had our dresses pulled round in front to hide our nakedness. Many's the time I had to ask the white chillen for bread, and they'd slip and get us bread, and meat, too. God my deliverer! I despised her! One of her daughters was dying, and I was going to a picnic, and mother said, "You ought to go by and see Miss _____, she's dying," and I told mother I didn't want to go, but you know I had been brought up to obey, and I was grown but I never could tell her I wasn't going. I just left like I was going in that direction, but I went on where I was going and I never did say no more to mother about it. When we was little, she used to whip us and then make us kiss the switch. She was the meanest one of the daughters.

(Courting) No'm, not when I was with her. When we left there I was eleven years old, and I was not old enough to have a big time, and after we got big enough to have a big time mother wouldn't let us go nowhere 'thout and old woman was with us. I didn't have no good time till I married, and I married when I was fourteen years and six months old. I was going to have a good time anyway.

(Songs)

> I'm bound for the promised land
> You see my mother come a-wagging along
> She wags like she don't mind her crosses
> She calls herself a child of God
> Gonna git on to heaven by and bye.

Chorus

Sweet heaven, 'tis my aim
I been a long time waggin' my cross
Sweet heaven, 'tis my aim
Gonna git home to heaven by and bye.

- - - - - -

Chillen, I'm free, chillen, I'm free, chillen.
    I'm free, my Lord
Washed in the blood of the Lamb.

- - - - - -

We will drink out of the well
Where it never runs dry
Oh my glory Hallelu.

Gonna drink the healing waters, chillen, by and bye
Gonna drink the healing waters, chillen, by and bye
Oh my glory Hallelu.

What do you call the healing water by and bye?
What do you call the healing water by and bye?
Oh my glory hallelu.

Pure heartfelt religion, chillen, by and bye
Pure heartfelt religion, chillen, by and bye
Oh my glory hallelu.

We will live with God forever, chillen, by and bye
We will live with God forever, chillen, by and bye
Oh my glory hallelu.

You sing some of the old sings we did, but you don't sing them just like we did. *Steal Away* is one of them. We sang the verse like this:

My Lord, He called me, He called me by the lightning
He called me by the love of God; and I ain't got
    long to stay here.

I know there was one song, and the voice sounded like a woman's, and it was raised up from the graveyard. At first they just thought it was somebody coming through the graveyard for a short cut home and they didn't pay no 'tention to it; but in a little while it come up over the house and then went on back to the graveyard. I've heared white people tell it was well as colored, and it caused quite a stir around there. 'cause the white folks said they couldn't understand it. Yes, it went like this:

I come to pray, I come to sing
I come to do my master's will
By waiting on the Lord.

Just before the War they didn't know what was gonna become of them, and one old colored lady had died on the place; and they said it was her singing, and about a week after that the old white lady died, and they said that song was a token of her death.

My song—I call it my song, they got that in the books—"I heard the voice of Jesus say." It just suited me when I was praying to the Lord to have mercy on me for my sins.

(Asked if she had heard her mother pray) Many a time; niggers in them days turned the pot up and prayed and sung in the pot to keep the white folks from hearing 'em. Our white folks when they have camp meeting would have all the colored come up and sing over the mourners. You know they still say that colored can beat the white folks singing. I think it was just the year before the War mammy said the camp meetings stopped.

I seed one of our young marsters take an old colored woman and pull her clothes down to her waist and whip her with a cowhide. It's a strange thing to me that they would never try to whip my mammy, but I think that old Marster Jack was the cause of that. 'Cause she just had trouble with mistress, and he said he wished they might try to help her out, 'cause she was a woman and Nancy was a woman.

(Asked how they found out they were free) Some other white people tole us; some that didn't have no darkies; they was glad to tell us, you know.

I'm 77 now; I've been here to hear it thunder.

"My Mother Was the Smartest
Black Woman in Eden"

I began to exist in the year 1844, in a small town in Tennessee. Eden, Tennessee, was between Nashville and Memphis, and was located on a branch of the Memphis River. There were no more than four hundred people there, including the slaves. There was a post office, two stores and a hotel in the town. The hotel was owned by Mr. Dodge, who was the uncle of my master.

I was the personal property of Mr. Jennings, who was a well-polished southern man. He was portly in build, lively in step, and dignified in manner. Mr. Jennings was a good man. There was no disputing that. He seemed to always be in debt, and I reasoned that he was too easy, that people took advantage of his good nature. He had married a woman of the same mold, and they had three children.

I did not have the honor or dishonor of being born on a large plantation. Master Jennings had a small farm. We did not cultivate any cotton; we raised corn, oats, hay and fruits. Most of Master Jennings' slaves were hired out. He had four families of slaves, that is, Aunt Caroline's family, Uncle Tom's family, Uncle Dave's family, and the family of which I was a member. None of these others were related by blood to us. My father had several brothers who lived on other places.

Aunt Caroline, a big mulatto woman, was very quiet and good-natured. I don't remember ever hearing her fuss. Each family had a cabin, and there were but four cabins on the place. Aunt Mary, my mother's aunt, stayed with us in our cabin. She had never married or had any children.

My mother was the smartest black woman in Eden. She was as quick as a flash of lightning, and whatever she did could not be done better. She could do anything. She cooked, washed, ironed, spun, nursed and labored in the field. She made as good a field hand as she did a cook. I have heard Master Jennings say to his wife, "Fannie has her faults, but she can outwork any nigger in the country. I'd bet my life on that."

My mother certainly had her faults as a slave. She was very different in nature from Aunt Caroline. Ma fussed, fought, and kicked all the time. I tell you, she was a demon. She said that she wouldn't be whipped, and when she fussed, all Eden must have known it. She was loud and boisterous, and it seemed to me that you could hear her a mile away. Father was often the prey of her high temper. With all her ability for work, she did not make a good slave. She was too high-spirited and independent. I tell you, she was a captain.

The one doctrine of my mother's teaching which was branded upon my senses was that I should never let anyone abuse me. "I'll kill you, gal, if you don't stand up for yourself," she would say. "Fight, and if you can't fight, kick; if you can't kick, then bite." Ma was generally willing to work, but if she didn't feel like doing something, none could make her do it. At least, the Jennings couldn't make, or didn't make her.

"Bob, I don't want no sorry nigger around me. I can't tolerate you if you ain't got no backbone." Such constant warning to my father had its effect. My mother's unrest and fear of abuse spread gradually to my father. He seemed to have been made after the timid kind. He would never fuss back at my mother, or

143

if he did, he couldn't be heard above her shouting. Pa was also a sower of all seeds. He was a yardman, houseman, plowman, gardener, blacksmith, carpenter, keysmith, and anything else they chose him to be.

I was the oldest child. My mother had three other children by the time I was about six years old. It was at this age that I remember the almost daily talks of my mother on the cruelty of slavery. I would say nothing to her, but I was thinking all the time that slavery did not seem so cruel. Master and Mistress Jennings were not mean to my mother. It was she who was mean to them.

Master Jennings allowed his slaves to earn any money they could for their own use. My father had a garden of his own around his little cabin, and he also had some chickens. Mr. Dodge, who was my master's uncle, and who owned the hotel in Eden, was pa's regular customer. He would buy anything my pa brought to him; and many times he was buying his own stuff, or his nephew's stuff. I have seen pa go out at night with a big sack and come back with it full. He'd bring sweet potatoes, watermelons, chickens and turkeys. We were fond of pig roast and sweet potatoes, and the only way to have pig roast was for pa to go out on one of his hunting trips. Where he went, I cannot say, but he brought the booty home. The floor of our cabin was covered with planks. Pa had raised up two planks, and dug a hole. This was our storehouse. Every Sunday, Master Jennings would let pa take the wagon to carry watermelons, cider and ginger cookies to Spring Hill, where the Baptist church was located. The Jennings were Baptists. The white folks would buy from him as well as the free Negroes of Trenton, Tennessee. Sometimes these free Negroes would steal to our cabin at a specified time to buy a chicken or barbecue dinner. Mr. Dodge's slaves always had money and came to buy from us. Pa was allowed to keep the money he made at Spring Hill, and of course Master Jennings didn't know about the little restaurant we had in our cabin.

One day my mother's temper ran wild. For some reason Mistress Jennings struck her with a stick. Ma struck back and a fight followed. Mr. Jennings was not at home and the children became frightened and ran upstairs. For half an hour they wrestled in the kitchen. Mistress, seeing that she could not get the better of ma, ran out in the road, with ma right on her heels. In the road, my mother flew into her again. The thought seemed to race across my mother's mind to tear mistress' clothing off her body. She suddenly began to tear Mistress Jennings' clothes off. She caught hold, pulled, ripped and tore. Poor mistress was nearly naked when the storekeeper got to them and pulled ma off.

"Why, Fannie, what do you mean by that?" he asked.

"Why, I'll kill her, I'll kill her dead if she ever strikes me again."

I have never been able to find out the why of the whole thing. My mother was in a rage for two days, and when pa asked her about it and told her that she shouldn't have done it, it was all that Aunt Caroline could do to keep her from giving him the same dose of medicine.

"No explaining necessary. You are chicken-livered, and you couldn't understand." This was all ma would say about it.

Pa heard Mr. Jennings say that Fannie would have to be whipped by law. He told ma. Two mornings afterwards, two men came in at the big gate, one with a long lash in his hand. I was in the yard and I hoped they couldn't find ma. To my surprise, I saw her running around the house, straight in the direction of the men. She must have seen them coming. I should have known that she wouldn't hide. She knew what they were coming for, and she intended to meet them halfway. She swooped upon them like a hawk on chickens. I believe they were afraid of her or thought she was crazy. One man had a long beard which she grabbed with one hand, and the lash with the other. Her body was made strong with madness. She was a good match for them. Mr. Jennings came and pulled her away. I don't know what would have happened if he hadn't come at that moment, for one man had already pulled his gun out. Ma did not see the gun until Mr. Jennings came up. On catching sight of it, she said, "Use your gun, use it and blow my brains out if you will."

Master sent her to the cabin and he talked with the man for a long time. I had watched the whole scene with hands calmly clasped in front of me. I felt no urge to do anything but look on.

That evening Mistress Jennings came down to the cabin. She stopped at the door and called my mother. Ma came out.

"Well, Fannie," she said, "I'll have to send you away. You won't be whipped, and I'm afraid you'll get killed. They have to knock you down like a beef."

"I'll go to hell or anywhere else, but I won't be whipped," ma answered.

"You can't take the baby, Fannie, Aunt Mary can keep it with the other children."

Mother said nothing at this. That night, ma and pa sat up late, talking over things, I guess. Pa loved ma, and I heard him say, "I'm going, too, Fannie. About a week later, she called me and told me that she and pa were going to leave me the next day, that they were going to Memphis. She didn't know for how long.

"But don't be abused, Puss." She always called me Puss. My right name was Cornelia. I cannot tell in words the feelings I had at that time. My sorrow knew no bound. My very soul seemed to cry out, "Gone, gone, gone forever." I cried until my eyes looked like balls of fire. I felt for the first time in my life that I had been abused. How cruel it was to take my mother and father from me, I thought. My mother had been right. Slavery was cruel, so very cruel.

Thus my mother and father were hired to Tennessee. The next morning they were to leave. I saw ma working around with the baby under her arms as if it had been a bundle of some kind. Pa came up to the cabin with an old mare for ma to ride, and an old mule for himself. Mr. Jennings was with him.

"Fannie, leave the baby with Aunt Mary," said Mr. Jennings very quietly.

At this, ma took the baby by its feet, a foot in each hand, and with the baby's head swinging downward, she vowed to smash its brains out before she'd leave it. Tears were streaming down her face. It was seldom that ma cried, and everyone knew that she meant every word. Ma took her baby with her.

With ma gone, there was no excitement around the place. Aunt Mary was old and very steady in her ways; Aunt Caroline was naturally quiet, and so were all the rest. I didn't have much to do around the place, and I thought about ma more than anyone around there knew. Yes, ma had been right. Slavery was chuck full of cruelty and abuse. During this time I decided to follow my mother's example. I intended to fight, and if I couldn't fight I'd kick; and if I couldn't kick, I'd bite. The children from the big house played with my brothers, but I got out of the bunch. I stopped playing with them. I didn't care about them, so why play with them? At different times I got into scraps with them. Everyone began to say, "Cornelia is the spit of her mother. She is going to be just like Fannie." And I delighted in hearing this. I wanted to be like ma now.

An uneventful year passed. I was destined to be happily surprised by the return of my mother and father. They came one day, and found me sitting by the roadside in a sort of trance. I had not seen them approaching; neither was I aware of their presence until ma spoke. Truly, I had been thinking of ma and pa at the time. I had dreams of seeing them again, but I thought that I would have to go to them. I could hardly believe that ma and pa were standing before my very eyes. I asked myself if I was still dreaming. No, I was not dreaming. They were standing over me. Ma was speaking to me.

"Puss, we've come back, me and pa, and we've come to stay."

"Oh, Ma," I exclaimed, "I was a praying to see you."

She and pa embraced and caressed me for a long time. We went to the cabin, and Master Jennings was there nearly as soon as we were.

"Hello, Fannie. How did you get along?" he asked.

"Why, Mr. Jennings, you know that I know how to get along," she answered.

"Well, I'm glad to hear that, Fannie."

Ma had on new clothes, and a pair of beautiful earrings. She told Aunt Mary that she stayed in Memphis one year without a whipping or a cross word.

Pa had learned to drink more liquor than ever, it seemed. At least, he was able to get more of it, for there were many disagreements between pa and ma about his drinking. Drinkers will drink together, and Mr. Jennings was no exception. Pa would have the excuse that Master Jennings offered him liquor, and of course he wouldn't take it from anybody else. It was common to see them together, half drunk, with arms locked, walking around and around the old barn. Then pa would put his hands behind him and let out a big whoop which could be heard all over Eden.

My temper seemed to be getting worse and worse. I was always fighting with my younger brothers, and with Aunt Caroline's kids. I went around with a chip on my shoulder all the time. Mrs. Jennings had me to nurse Ellen, her youngest child, for a while, but I was mean to her, and she stopped me. I could do plenty of work in a short time, but I had such an ugly temperament. Pa would scold me about being so mean, but ma would say, "Bob, she can't help it. It ain't her fault because she's made like that."

Our family was increased by the arrival of a baby girl. Ma was very sick, and she never did get well after that. She was cooking for Mistress Jennings one day when she came home and went to bed. She never got up. I guess ma was sick about six months. During that time she never hit a tap of work. She said she had brought five children in the world for the Jennings, and that was enough; that she didn't intend to work when she felt bad.

On the day my mother died, she called pa and said, "Bob, what time is it?" Pa went to the window and pushed it back and looked up at the sun. "It's four o'clock, Fannie."

"Well, I'm going to leave you at eight o'clock. Go tell Master Jennings to come in, and get all the slaves too."

Pa went and returned in five minutes with old master.

"Fannie, are you any worse?" said old master.

"No, no, Master Jennings, no worse. But I'm going to leave you at eight o'clock."

"Where are you going, Fannie," Master Jennings asked as if he didn't know that ma was talking about dying.

Ma shook her head slowly and answered, "I'm going where there ain't no fighting and cussing and damning."

"Is there anything that you want me to do for you, Fannie?"

Ma told him that she reckoned there wasn't much of anything that anybody could do for her now.

"But I would like for you to take Puss and hire her out among ladies, so she can be raised right. She will never be any good here, Master Jennings."

A funny look came over Master Jennings' face, and he bowed his head up and down. All the hands had come in and were standing around with him.

My mother died at just about eight o'clock.

"I Stole My Learning in the Woods"

I am about 85 years old. I wasn't old enough to go to the Civil War, but I was such a big boy they thought I was old enough to go. I have seen colored people treated all kinds of ways in my life. I have seen them beat till the blood run out of them. I could do any kind of plowing. I was playing marbles when they took me to the war. I wasn't old enough to go, but I was big enough. The War broke out in 1861. I was born in Henry County, near Paris, Tennessee, and been round 'bout there most of my life.

My mother had twelve children—four boys and eight girls. She was a cook. Her owner set them at liberty about three years before the Civil War, and give them a home as long as they lived. They had worked her enough, I reckon. Before her mistress died she liberated all of her people. She never did sell none of mother's children from her. Her son was a lawyer in that town. My father was foreman over all her slaves. We had pretty good treatment. When they carried me away they fooled me on the horse. I didn't know nothing 'bout where I was going, for I was nothing but a boy. They carried me off somewhere near Nashville. I was there about two years. I remember before they carried me off we was down on the ground playing marbles, and we saw some soldiers coming, and we started running, and they caught us and wanted to know what we was running for, and I told them we was running from the Lincolnites. He said they wasn't gonna hurt us. It was right funny, I was talking to a Lincolnite and didn't know it. I could hear the colored people talk about they was gonna be free, but I didn't have sense to know what they was talking about. It wasn't any way for the colored people to get away, for they always had blood hounds to catch you if you started running away.

We played marbles then, just about like the boys do now, only we had four square rings, and I think they have diamonds now. We played Molly Bright and Three Score and Ten. My mother stayed in the house all the time. I never knowed her to get out of my sight.

I remember once mistress had a big red apple setting on her table, and I had planned to steal it, and I bit down in it, and it wasn't nothing but soap. That was a good one on me. They let us go to the table to eat after they got through eating. They raised all kinds of vegetables. She had a fine carriage, and she went to Memphis every fall. I worked in the field, and at night we used to play marbles in the house. We would make a ring on the floor by candle light. Some times they would wait till you was ten years old before they put you to plowing. I used to chop with the hoe, and plow. I would get a nice little whipping sometimes when trying to plow, cause I wouldn't do it right. They had a great deal of hogs. They used to send me to feed the hogs and horses. I never went to but one wedding while I was little, I slipped off and went to that one. My father whipped the fire out of me, too. The preacher said some kind of ceremony out of the Bible, but they didn't have no license.

Boys wasn't like these now. We didn't pay no 'tention to people courtin'. We had a little trundle bed, and when we was put in it we didn't see no more till the next morning, and we had better keep quiet, too.

We never did see daylight after we was put in that bed until the next morning. Their beds was high enough to roll our's under their's. They had hemp rope across their bed to keep from falling in on us.

We had a cellar to keep potatoes and things like that in. We used to draw things out of it—that was our elevator. (He explained that they would tie a rope around one of the children and let him down in the cellar to get what they wanted, then pull him up.) Mistress had one under her parlor. She had steps running down to it. Mistress had a fine flower garden, carriage, and a driver.

I never did see no colored man whipped. I seen one colored lady whipped—I didn't see her either, but they said she had just had a whipping when I saw her. But she whipped nearly everybody else she run into, white or colored. Our white folks was pretty good to us. They would let the slaves have a garden, and let one build a little chicken house and sell chickens. He had more chickens than the white folks did. Some of the slaves would go away up to Canada where there was some free slaves.

Colored people didn't get sick and die like they do now. They had little things, but not serious diseases. I don't know why, but they just didn't do it.

Mistress was a mighty church member. They told me mostly what I know. When her husband died, they bought 12 candles and burnt six of them and kept the other six until she died. The colored people used the white folks' church after they preaching was over. The ladies all wore long skirts and used bamboo briars to make them tilt. When boys got pretty large they wore body breeches. They wore a shirt and nothing else until they got a certain age. They wore something kinda like these cover-alls they wear now. Old lady used to make that old fashioned hominy so many times a week. She had one ot these cockle shells just like a snail shell that she blowed for the hands to come to dinner. I kept it a long time after she died. Old man Peter blowed his first; he was the kind of leader in blowing, and my mother would blow her's then. The white folks would eat in the dining room, and the hands would eat in the kitchen. I think they treated the house slaves a little better than they did the others. Some of them was bright and some was brown skin. My sister said that my old mistress' father was my mother's father. The children take some after him in color, and some after her. Speculators used to come round every week after slaves, but they didn't never sell none of them. It was a long time after the Civil War 'fore I knowed where babies come from. They used to tell us that Aunt Sarah brought babies, and I didn't know no better.

These ladies can get what they want without me telling my age. They know when the War started, and they can count from that. I don't need to tell my age. Yes, they had parties sometimes, but you would always have to get a pass to go anywhere, 'cause if you didn't have one the paddie rollers would catch you and whip you. Dancing was their main things. One fiddler used to pat his foot out of this country. Sometimes I think a nigger was happier then than he is now. They used to have corn shuckings, and when all the corn was shucked they would pick up old marster and carry him all round the room singing. They used to sing, "Rock me Julie, rock me, hey, hey, I'm going way to leave you."

I had a brother who got to the line of Canada. We all had freedom in our bones. "Give me liberty or give me death" was in my bones. I read that since freedom. Patrick Henry said that. I stole my learning in the woods. When I was a little boy I always wanted to know what was on a piece of paper. I got a spelling book, and in the night I would try to get my lessons. One night I was down on the floor trying to spell when marster come in and asked me what I was doing, and I told him I was trying to spell. He made me spell "farm" and told me that he didn't want to catch me spelling no more. After that I had to steal what little learning I had.

I had a brother-in-law who was going to buy my oldest sister for $900, but freedom come just about the time he was going to buy her. He was a barber. There was a right smart free folks around here. Jane Randall and her three daughters and one son was free. I knowed a man name Wyatt who was free, and he wanted to marry a slave girl name Carrie, and he gave himself to Carrie's master, to marry her. That love is an awful thing, I tell you. I don't think I would give my freedom away to marry anybody. What I woulda done was to go off and send for her later on. He was crazy to do that. They treated the free colored people pretty rough. But after all they had better privileges than a slave if they didn't go crazy about some slave girl and give hisself away.

I didn't know I was a slave until once they cut darkies heads off in a riot. They put their faces up like a sign board. They said they was going to burn niggers up by the hundreds. I have heard a heap of people say they wouldn't take the treatment what the slaves took, but they woulda took it or death. If they had been there they woulda took the very same treatment.

Say, is there any danger in this talk? If so, I want to take back everything I said. See that fellow over there (speaking of an ex—slave visitor), he was one of the best fiddlers in this part of the country. He can tell you all about it, too.

"My Old Marster Was a Methodist Preacher"

I was a slave until I was twelve years old. I married two years after I come here. I married when I was fourteen years old. I had six children and raised them without a husband. I been a widow forty years. All my children died, but they got grown and married before they died. I ain't got no people at all. Nobody but me here. Three of my daughters died inside of three years. My last son owned this home. I had one granddaughter. She died with consumption. She was the only grandchild I had. Nobody in the world but me. I am getting along fine, though. Somebody always coming to see me and giving me something. The folks are all mighty nice to me. Of course I get lonesome sometimes and need children to do little things for me, but the neighbors helps me out just as well, I reckon. There was a man here this summer taking my testimony, and when he left he and the girl with him gave me a quarter each. He come back to see me one night not long ago.

Well, my old marster was name Billy Shaw. He was a Methodist preacher. He didn't do us like he was a preacher, though. I was born in Robinson county. They moved us here in covered wagons. My mother was sold from me, and they kept me. They sold her to some people here in town. My old marster was right good to us—that is, he wasn't as mean as some of them was. He would knock and beat us. Lord, I said if I ever got away from that place I would never go back again. I belonged to my marster's daughter. I just had to knock around the best way I could until my mother sent for me. They hired me out when I was only six years old. They said they hired me out to pick up things after the child and see after her. But they carried me to the corn field and put a bucket on my arm, and I dropped corn all day in the hot sun. If I missed any rows he would take the hoe and beat me. I had to go just as fast as he could. If he got to the end before I could get there, well I would get a beating. They made me tote fodder after night. They made me go out there after night with them men. Sometimes we would tote it all night. I used to hear runaway niggers running in the field at night.

My old marster used to have a lot of slaves before his son broke him. But after he got broke, he didn't have many. I don't know whether his son broke him while he was running on the river, or some other way. They sold my mother, but not me. They would let me come to see my mother sometimes, and stay three or four days. The white folks I stayed with treated me so mean that my mother got a man to slip me away from them. He brought me on here to her. He come and got me about 12 or 1 o'clock in the night. He told me he was coming to get me. They brought me here to the Picket's, here in town. They was talking about sending me South, but if they had done that I would never have got to see my mother. They never did whip the blood out of us like they did a lot of them. Some of them would get whipped until the blood would run down they heels. I used to go to the spring to get water, with a bucket on top of my head, and one in each hand. I was about ten years old then. When the War come up I was just 12 years old. Lord, honey, I had to do everything. I was just working all the time.

Yes, mam, he was mean to them, even if he was going with them. If his wife find it out he would have to sell her (Negro concubine). He would sell his own children by slave women just like he would any others. Just since he was making money. In slavery, niggers and mules was white folk's living. They would sell for $500 and $1,000. My mother sold for $1,000.

They didn't 'low you to eat watermelons and cantaloupes then. I went through the patch one day and pulled a muskmellon and throwed it way over in the weeds, but they found it and measured that melon against my mouth, and measured my feet in the dust, and said I done it, and I sure did get a beating for taking that melon.

In the winter time they would give you two suits of underclothes, and one pair of brogan shoes. If you wore that pair out before winter was over, you just had to go bare footed, that was all.

No, mam, they wasn't allowed to have prayer meeting or nothing like a meeting. If a nigger got religion they said you was crazy. Sometimes I would go to church with the white folks, to see after the children, but the niggers wasn't allowed to go to church. Sometimes they would give us about a hour on Sundays to play, but after that we would have to go to work. Sometimes they would leave me to cook when they would go to church. I remember once I tried to turn a custard over and it fell in the ashes. You know they made me eat that custard? Some of the slaves got religion anyhow. White folks in the country had camp meetings. I never saw slaves go to church; sometimes they would carry one along to wait on them.

I seed a heap of things when I got religion, but I never heard nothing. I seed the Lord when he opened a cloud and looked down on my heart. He opened my heart and I could see it. It was just as black as could be. That was the sin in it. He took it out and put it right back in my body. I never have heerd nobody say nothing, though. He looked just like you see him in these pictures. Long white robe and long hair and beard. I don't like to hear people tell nobody that they heard something, for that throws some people off from getting religion, for they would be expecting to hear something.

When they got ready to marry, they would just come to the marster and tell him that he wanted one of his women, and he could just take her. They didn't have no ceremony. They wouldn't let a scrubby man come in among them; but if he was healthy he could just take her and start living with her. They jump over the broomstick in them days. I never seed nobody marry until I was free. Niggers never knowed about marriage, for they couldn't read. If a neighbor's man got a child by your woman, that was your child. He couldn't take it away. When your marster had a baby born in his family they would call all the niggers and tell them to come in and "see your new marster." We had to call them babies "Mr." and "Miss," too. They would hire the nigger children out to work, then they could sell them. I used to hoe cotton just like a man. I never had nothing to do with horses, but I did everything else. I never did know much about horses.

If anybody had corn they wanted to get shucked, well, they would give corn shuckings. They said they had a good time. Anyhow, that was the only good time they had. They would pass around cider to them. The women would have quiltings. They would have little suppers sometimes at the quiltings. They would have dances sometimes and turn a pot upside down right in front of the door. They said that would keep the sound from going outside. Look like people had better times in some things than they do now. But their good times was so long between times. At Christmas they would let them have a little fun. But that was just on Christmas day.

They was colored carpenters on the place, just do work around the place, but you couldn't hire yourself out to do work for other people. If a man was free and come to that country, he had to get some white man to stand for him, just like he owned him. There was just a few free men. I don't know much about the Dungey's, but they wasn't slaves, I know. Charley Dungey is the only one living. The old man kept that place all the time. His sister let some one mortgage it and she thought it was all paid off. When she found out it was not and that she was going to lose it, she just died right in her tracks.

Did anybody ever tell you about old General Jackson? He was mean. Old Andrew Johnson, well, his man's wife was real sick, and he would ride with him to see his wife, and he would just let him go in to see her for just a little while and then he would ride on in front of him again. Heap of women had to build fences just like the men. In General Jackson's old place they had a whipping room, and they say now you can hear strange noises out there in that old house. I used to wash out there, after the War, but I never would go to the room to try to hear anything. People rent that place now in the summer, for a summer home. It is a fine old place. The wood and everything in it is fine, but it is old. That house was built for his two daughters, but they married so rich they didn't need to live there. Nobody don't stay there in the winter. All the servant's rooms was in a row.

I never knowed anybody who was whipped to death. But I have heard of it.

When anybody died, they didn't have no funeral or anything. One man would just go and bury you. You was nailed up in a big box and put in a wagan and carried on to the graveyard. You could stand and watch them go, but you couldn't go. They buried you at a place called Mill Creek. The graveyard was out there for the country folks. I never seed nobody buried until I come to town. When colored folks died in summer, they would put elm bushes over the body to keep flies from getting to the body.

Yes, I can remember the War. When I was out in Flat Rock, I could hear the bullets flying all around, just whizzing by. The Yankees would come and take everything they wanted—corn, horses, and anything they wanted. They would have brought me to town, but I was afraid to come. I just stayed out there until my mother sent for me. I lived down in a little house all by myself. Nobody never bothered me. My uncle fought in the War. There was a lot of colored men fought in the War. There was a lot of fighting all up and down the Franklin Pike. The Maxwell House was the barracks. They would bring the wounded soldiers there. I was living right on Cherry Street Pike.

If the Rebel soldiers would come, well I would have to go and cook them something good to eat. After the War, niggers would run away, two and three every night. That's the way they got away after they was free. After you run away and they would catch you, they would put you in the caliboose until your marster would come and get you out.

Lord, yes, I was here when they lynched Eph Grizzard. Some of them say he got away, that when he was throwed over the bridge they didn't look to see his body, but that some doctor helped him get away to Kansas.

There was a old white woman named old Miss Bruce who had two men hung right in front of her house. The white folks was against her for having them men hung. The white woman told her it was a plumb shame. That's been near forty years ago.

They would give us castor oil and sage tea. We never had a doctor hardly ever. We would just take what the white folks would fix up at the house.

Old people had signs for everything then. I don't know much about them. You had better be up when day broke and be on your way to the field. You had to work in the field until dark. Then you would put the horses up. When I was little I milked two cows and sometimes I would have to go to the woods in the dark and find them cows, too. I would churn, wash and iron. If I didn't do the right thing then I would get a whipping. I would chop enough wood on Saturday evening to last till Monday morning. They was Methodists and didn't want me chopping wood on Sundays. I would carry it to the house and put some of it on the fire for a back log. Every one of them folks is dead and I am here yet.

They never know what it was till it come on. Nobody would tell them. When it first come on I ran to the branch trying to make it stop. It's a wonder it didn't kill me. But it didn't bother me. I was trying to stop it for I didn't know whether I was going to get a killing for it or not. I didn't know what it was. I was living with these white people. She told me what 'twas.

Whenever white women had babies they would make us stay out. I never did know then where the babies would come from. First thing I would know the baby would start to holler. We never seed nothing. People was very particular in them days. They wouldn't let children know anything like they do now. The children now know everything.

I never heard my mother say she went to camp meeting but once in my life. They wouldn't let them have church. My mother was married in Robinson County. Her marster married her. He was a squire. My father come from Clarksville. He was a carpenter. His name was Jack Hale. He belonged to a man named Hale down in Clarksville.

A Sister and Two Brothers Who Were Not Separated During Slavery

I was born right here in this county. There wasn't none of these houses here then, neither the jail house or the court house. Just had horses and wagons and plenty of dust. You couldn't go nowhere without a pass, did you would get your shirt took off and get a whipping. Darkies would go to church after the white folks got through. You had to stay at home and cook dinner for them and after everything was over you could go to the white folks church. My mother was a mother of 10 children. My father was born free. They said his mother was a white woman. He didn't remember his father. He was free but lived right on the place with my mother and she was a slave. He hired hisself out and had a little garden and a water—melon patch. On big days in town my mother would always make some ginger cakes and he would carry them on the square and sell them. Old Virginia was his home. He never did see his father. The last 'count I had of my age I reckon I am between 96 and 97 years old. My father lived to be 110 years old. I got 10 great-grandchildren.

Brother: I will be 73 years old my next birthday. I remember when the Yankees come through stealing everything in sight. Young master was in the War and he used to slip back to see his people in the night to keep the Yankees from catching him. Many a night you could hear them protectors running around all night looking for men who would slip off and they would be right up there in bed sleep. I could hear them cannons way 'cross at Fort Pillow bellowing out. They would be so big that it would take 25 or 30 horses to pull them.

White folks used to have overseers riding up and down the field to see that you would keep working. If they caught you loafing they would tie your hands with a chain or anything like that and whip you. Master sent our older sister off down to Mississippi. He slipped her off at night but mother couldn't do nothing 'bout it but set down and cry. They would drive slaves off just like they do hogs now. A great big nigger like me would bring four or five thousand dollars but a little nigger wouldn't bring nothing hardly. Nobody didn't want a little puny nigger. Our white folks wasn't so good and wasn't so mean. He wasn't as mean as some of them.

There was one or two families of free niggers around. Sarah Powell was free all her days. We used to call her "free Sarah." She hired herself out to the white folks.

We wore good clothes cause mammy spun and wove them. We wore brogan shoes with brass tips on them. Mammy would knit our socks; she would have one stran of wool and one stran of cotton. Mammy was the cook and she would do all the weaving.

Older brother: I was born in 1854. I was nine years old when the War started. I toted water during the War. Me and old master's daughter used to play together all the time and one day we was out in the field playing together and old boss come out and slapped her jaws and give me a hoe and from that time on I was in the field. Guess he thought I had got big enough to work then. Master just had one man outside of our family. It was 13 of us. Every one of us lived together and got grown before any of the family died. Father was born before the Revolutionary War. Sometimes I think we was a little better off then than now. Then we didn't have to worry 'bout nothing to eat and wear and now it is a little tough on you and making no money either. I remember just as well when master come out one morning and said, "Well, you all is just as free as I is this morning." He didn't tell us till a year after freedom was declared though. I said, "We been knowing it all the time but just been waiting for you to tell us." He said "I want you all to stay with me if you will." When Christmas come he made my oldest brother drunk and said he would give us $700 if we would stay and my brother made the deal. But we done well if we got $75.00 out of it. He just made promises. Our father was old and feeble when he died. He was 104 when he died.

Master hired my mother out a whole year and she didn't get a thing for it. Old master borrowed from my father and he owed me $1000. The Yankees camped near where we lived and I found a roll of money that they had dropped as big as my arm. Master said he was going to send it back and get some good money for me and I never got none of it a-tall.

We all went to church after the white folks come home and eat dinner. The preacher would tell us if we wanted to get to heaven to mind our mistress and master and not steal their things and we would shore get to heaven.

We used to rip and romp and play. If we could get a pass you could go to see somebody else but if you wouldn't carry that pass with you the paddle rollers would get you and give you a whipping.

We didn't court much in them days. A boy had to be near 'bout grown. The fust girl I went with I was nearly 18 years old. When you got ready to marry all you had to do was for the girl to ask her mother and you had to get permission from the master and that was just about all to it. You want to learn how we courted so you can do it? If a boy went with a girl and spoke things that he shouldn't he could get a whipping for that. If you fooled a girl up and got her with a arm full you had to take care of her. Now a boy can beat a girl up nearly to death and don't tell their mother nothing. I heard one slap a girl out here the other night and her jaw was all swelled up the next morning like she had a egg in it. And she made out like she had the toothache. I ain't no married man. I don't see nobody I want. I'm 'fraid to marry anybody for I reckon all the good ones been taken. Guess I'll have to order one from Sears and Roebuck.

Whenever mistress have a baby she would send for the slaves to come in and see the little mistress or little marster. For thrash they would grind up ivy, sheep bones and put camphor in it.

We would comb our head with cotton cards, some heads would be as lousy as a pet possum. Them with long hair would be wrapped with white cotton strings. We bathed nearly every night. They used to say if a cow moaned you would hear of somebody dying before another night. I can remember of two white men beating two niggers to death just for a little of nothing and the bad part was they didn't belong to either one of them.

The first nigger preacher I heard was old Bob Cooper. He used to preach down in the woods to the niggers. They put him up to get all the niggers together and they was planning to gather them all up and carry them to the army but the niggers got in the wind of it somehow and all of them broke and run and nothing was left but women and boys. I always said old Bob Cooper oughta been killed for that. After niggers all got free he was crossing the Ohio River and the white people made him, mule and all drop off in the river. I heard it said that "nothing never went over the devil's back, what it didn't come back and buckle under you."

They have college preachers now. They don't have religion like they used to. I saw old man George Jones do a thing one day that I never seen before or since. Right down here in the Methodist church one Sunday he got happy and actually flew around the altar, not a foot nor a hand was touching the floor. I believe he was really a Christian.

Free Negro

No, in those days, when my mother was coming up, white folks kept their ages, and the colored folks didn't even know. You know, even when they got ready to marry, it was the white folks that give them permission. Mother often said "I don't remember nothing 'bout my parents." I came from Virginia, they called it old Virginny, then you know, in her day. When white folks got a notion to move to Tennessee or anywhere, they just taken the colored folks up, and 'course my grandmother had to go, too. They traveled in wagons in those days, but my grandmother don't remember nothing about her parents, either. The biggest thing I remember about my grandmother was that she was foolish about her hair; it was black as satin, and she was what they called cold-creek Indian.

Well, they brought her from old Virginny to Tennessee when she was but a child; they settled in Gallatin. It is a big flourishing town now. While she was there, there came another family named Alaskas; this was grandpap's family. Now, grandma's folks was named Perry. You see, grandma was their housegirl, and grandpap was Alaska's house boy. They kept her because she was young and supple and could have lots of children. Ain't that hard? She waited on the missus, and did the little nice things about the house, you know. You see, their object was to raise her and sell her so she would make a lot of money for them.

Well, grandpap was young and just as black as satin, and real handsome, and grandma was gitting to the age where she liked young men, you know, they begin courting. I asked grandma why she wanted to fool with him, and she say he was nice, and handsome, and a right likely young man, you know. Well, they kept on courting back and forth, and finally she married him; and you know when she married him, he didn't have on nothing but a shirt, that's all they give them to wear then. Grandma wore a long cotton dress, sometimes no stockings and shoes; that's all they had to wear, ain't that hard?

When they went to camp meetings or to church, grandma rode up behind her white folks and grandpap rode up behind his'n. They went to preaching every Sunday and grandma said the preacher would say: "Servants obey yo' master" every Sunday. And you know, they thought that he was talking about the earthly master, and the white folks didn't want them to know no better. Grandma said they would feed you well, but they didn't enlighten you none, nor let you have no books to learn from. Ain't that hard?

They spun our clothes, you see, they was thrifty. And the shoes was nothing but treated goathide all rough on the inside.

Well, as I said, grandma got attached to grandpap. She thought he was the prettiest man she ever saw. They kept courting, and finally the two families decided one to buy the other; that is, either the Alaskas was to buy grandpap, or the Perrys buy grandma. Grandpap's people was a little bit better off than grandma's, so they bought grandma. Guess what they charged for her? They charged $100 for every year that she was old, yessir, thats what they charged for her, ain't that awful? They called that marrying them. Well, after so long a time my mother was born. Grandpap's white folks claimed mother. But grandpap was

155

smart; he wanted to come out of the woods. If you was smart enough to buy yourself, you could become a free man, but then you had to mingle with the free folks; that is, you couldn't have nothing to do with slaves, 'cause you might fool them off, too, you see. So if the white folks would consent to let you buy yourself, you could become free. Well, grandpap decided to buy himself, and so he told the white folks. He come up to Nashville and hired out in a hotel, called the Nashville Inn. He was what they called a bedroom servant. You see, the white folks, that is, his white folks hired him to the Nashville Inn, so he would pay for himself, do you understand? They needed the money, so they told him, "Well, Hardy, we need money, so we'll let you pay for yourself and you can be free." Now, every Saturday, he would make about $5 or $10 that he would give to them; now, you see that was just like a hundred dollars now. He didn't have no expenses cause he had plenty to eat and somewhere to sleep. Well, he worked and worked, till I guess he paid them about $800 in all for himself. Then one day, they sent for him, and they said, "Well, Hardy, you are a free man; you can go anywhere you please, but you can't take Catherine." Well, he was just like any other man, he wanted Catherine with him, so he turned 'round and the white folks made him pay the same for grandma. He worked and worked some more, and he finally paid for her. Then they come to town, and they still worked in this Nashville Inn. Grandma, she washed the fine linens, and let that money go on her freedom.

Well, you see, they had bought themselves, but they had left my mother, three years old up in Gallatin. Grandma said she cried and worried over her all the time. She was crazy about her child, and it was pitiful to hear her tell about how she worried about her. Then they put after old missus to know what she would ask for my mother. Old missus said: "Catherine is a likely child, and we will take care of her till she gets older, and then we can sell her for a lot of money." Well, they kept after the white folks, till finally they charged them, now mind you, for his own child, they charged him $350, just think of that. You see, she was 'bout three and a half years old, and they charged him $100 a year, ain't that awful? Well, they bought her, and you see, there was the three of 'em. Well, the white folks gave them a paper signed by them, and they could go anywhere in Tennessee they wanted to, but they wouldn't be free out of the state, you see. They was already here in Nashville, you know; well, has you ever been on the Square, up here at the market place? Right on this side of the Square is where I was born—in that brick house where they is an old paint factory right now. They named me Susanna; I was born in 1858 along in May.

Miss Lizzie Elliott, you oughta know her, well, anyway, she remembers that I was born about that time. I was awful smart, used to run and take messages, and do errands for folks; I liked to do errands for folks. Mr. Napier know all our people.

My grandmother had another boy and another girl, but my mother was the oldest child and she married a man, named Martin Howard. He was a candle maker; you know, they used to have these old candle makers; made good money in them days. Well, after I was born, my mother and father decided they was going to git something for themselves. They said: "Now, we been working for the white folks all the time, and we got a little saved up, so we going to make something for our children." So they got to work, and he opened up a carriage place. He run that place for forty years, right up there on the Square. Him 'n grandpap had four hacks, three express wagons, carryalls, they called them then, two drays, and about eight horses; that's what grandpap left her when he died. The old brick building is there today. He run that trade for years. Everybody knew him.

Well, my mother, she married by consent just like her mother and father did. But mother was free, but the white folks had to get permission from old man Howard to marry her. He's the same Howard that gave the Congregational Church over here on 12th Avenue to the colored folks. He was pap's master, you know. Old Howard was James D. Porter's brother-in-law. You know Governor Porter; he served three terms 'cause he was such a good white man. I used to have an old trunk with all the announcements and everything in them, but you know how things like that git away.

Way back in dem days people would have no doctors like they do now. They would go out and get wild sage; yes'm they used that for stomach ache, and they would get some dog fennel and make a real splendid tea. 'Nother thing they used to have was slippery elm tea, and they would put it in a little crock pitcher and jest set it aside and drink out of it when they got ready.

Most of the times they would give tansy tea to little babies and children for the colic. Then, sometimes, girls your size, you know, took this tansy tea. We used to use the old-fashioned quinine and asphidity for colds and such like ailments. You know tumors wasn't common like they is now. It was a rare thing to hear of the T.B., too. I was just studying the other day, you know, people ought to go back to the old land mark. I know you going to laugh when you hear this. You sho' won't believe this, but you know they used to wear pettiskirts, they called them then, and my mother used to quilt my skirts from way up here 'round the thigh down to the bottom. Yes siree, I know it's funny now, but one thing, you never could take no cold with that nice warm quilted skirt on, and long underwear and an old fashioned lined dress skirt.

The white folks here a little while back had a dinner and had all the folks 'round 'bout my age, and older 'n me, and they said they wanted to know all about the old times. You know, the white people is really considering going back to the land mark. They see the destruction of these days and times. You wouldn't never believe it, but it's so.

Now, they used to have us making rag carpets at night like this here one. Way they do, we would tear up the old calicos and things and tack 'em together in great long strings. Then they had a thing they called the warp and filling. Since you belonged to the white folks, they would task you like that every night after you got through with the field work and et your supper, yes sir every night, that's what you had to do; you sho' had them carpet things to tack. They had a shuttle and the thread warp and filling, and you wound it back and forth like this; that is, you pulled it this way, then the other way, and throw it through this a way, see? I don't have them kind of warps now, nor no rug made just like that; this was sewed by hand; yes sir, every stitch was put together by hand, after we had done twisted and plaited the rags by hand 'n everything. It was beautiful, though, and if you made 'em right pretty, the white people would let you have a Saturday night supper, and invite your girl friend and made light bread in an old fashioned oven, and have roast potatoes, you know. Way you would do, you would wrap them up in paper and bake 'em in the ashes, and then just take 'em up and wipe 'em off and put them on the table. Everybody had a tin plate and knife and fork, and maybe a spoon, and they was good eatings, too. Better'n they have now. After you did your work well, that was your party. They didn't come 'long with no ice cream and cakes, like they do now. They had one great big old cake, and they would cut each of us a well, twarn't no slice, it was a hunk, 'cause when you got through, you was good and full. Yes mam, I've went to many sech a party; they always said that my aunt Liza was a great hand for parties. My mother had sixteen children, and the way she would punish us would be to tell us she warn't going to let us go to aunt Liza's party.

Putting a colored person in jail? Well, you seldom had that in those days. They didn't 'low it. The po' white folks couldn't even come on our place. They tried to get the best white man among the po' trash for overseer. Most of the refined white folks wouldn't want the overseer to whip the niggers. They rather for them to be properly fed, and then they could work best, jest like cattle. My father's white folks would not have a poor white man on the place. That's de trouble with our folks, they is still jealous of the po' white man. Since colored people have got free, they is taking the white folk's jobs, and de white folks don' like it, they the one what ought to be jealous, and they is 'fraid if the colored girl come out in her straight hair and high heeled shoes, and neat dress, they will get their jobs.

I know 'bout a place downtown, where they wanted somebody, a kinda particular person to hand up the clothes, and Miss Buckner, what used to teach school, you know substitute, went down and ask for the job. Well, she got it, and them old clerks, the white girls, they just nagged her, and bothered after her and talked about her being a school teacher until she had to quit. I tell you, it's awful. She is got a job now, substituting again. The poor white folks has been the terror of the colored all their days. And you know, some colored folks is just as envious as the white folks, ain't that the truth? Yes sirree.

Now you take the census that they is going 'round taking every year or two. I think we oughter have colored folks to take our census and let the white folks take their own census, but colored folks jest won't hang together long enough to do 'em a bit of good.

When you hear the cow lowing, sho' sign of death! If the rooster come 'round the door crowing, you can just be sure a stranger you ain't seen in a long time is coming, yes siree, I knows that to be a fact. Jest as sho' as the cow lows, look out, somebody in the neighborhood is going away from here; why she will almost turn her head in the direction of the death, yes sir.

When the dog goes 'round the house howling, they is sho' going to be sickness or trouble in that house; sho' as you born. Down in this neighborhood, Roy Hid, he was a man doing well 'round here and then he commence to droop and begin to cough and his feet swelled. The dogs kept howling, and it warn't long 'fore that man went away from here. They tried all the hospitals but the dogs jest kept howling. 'Course, people don't like to say it, but it's so. He kept going back and forth out to Meharry and he been gone on to the jedgment now for over a month.

Down there, across the street from Zema Hill's section, a dog kept howling. I met a little lady on the street, and we was talking and Lillian—I don't know jest what kin she air to Zema Hill—well anyhow, the lady I was talkin' to, say, oh, Miss Lillian, you look so bad. I saw she looked bad, too, but I didn't want to say so. The lady I was with was Rev. Lee's wife, and would you believe, she left Lillian here by 'bout three months. That wasn't but 'bout six or eight months ago, and when I saw 'em that day, both of them was walking around as spry as you please, but Mrs. Lee sho' died fust and left Lillian here. 'Course she died, too, I knowed she was, cause she looked so awful bad. I'm just trying to show you about signs 'n things. The old folks say that if they stump their foot they going to be disappointed. Well, some folks says if you stump you right foot, but it's either foot.

When your hand itch, you going to git some money. My mother was good at that. Some folks say you going to shake hands with a stranger, but with me it meant money. You sho' going to git some money, if it warn't no more'n a dime. The reason these signs is going away is because people don't pay them no attention. They is too busy rushing around ain't dey? My grandmother could tell just as well when it was going to rain. She would say, "Going rain such 'n such a day." She'd be gitting ready to put up the ashes for making soap some time and she'd say: "I won't put up the ashes today, 'cause rain will put the fire out 'fore tomorrow night." Yes, that would be when she was going to make lye soap.

Well, she would jest look up at the sun and feel the air. People made their own soap in dem days. They would put up a barrel filled and then put wood ashes and six or seven buckets of water in it. Then they would open a hole underneath, and by seven or eight o'clock the bucket would be full of lye.

Yes, she would say, "Don't start the fire, 'cause we going to have rain." Well, way we did, we took two eggs and dropped them in the kettle to tell whether the lye was strong enough or not. If the egg come up on top it warn't strong enough—had to get some more ashes. Yes, I still make soap. Sometimes I sell two or three dollars worth of soap 'round here in the neighborhood. I can make it so the top will be real light and the bottom real brown. I calls it white folks on top and colored folks on the bottom. We used to have this old fashioned indigo that we used for bluing then. Make your clothes so nice and white, jest tied it up in a rag and ran it through the water.

Then we didn't use no baking powders. They had what they called saloratus, and we used it like we did any other leavening. Some folks called it sal soda. We used to put a little vinegar in a cup and then stir in the sal soda. You can't get no real hog lard now. I kin tell it apart from this here manufactured stuff. The hog lard is grainy and dark, and the compound lard is white and smooth. Lamb is like that, too. Some folks can't tell lamb from old fashioned mutton. Yes, plenty folks can't tell the difference. You see old mutton is bluish looking. It's bruised and old, and lamb is as red as can be and has great flakes of fat called mutton tallow in it. Mutton suet used to be all the grease that they used in them days. It is good for medicine, too. Just put some mutton suet in a jar, honey, and rock candy, and you got a good rub for any kind a grip of neuralgia. It will stop any cough or cold in the world. This is the pure goose grease. Now, this much here would cost about $5 in the drug store any time now. I made this myself.

Yes, folks do need to get back to the old land mark. I was jest reading in the paper the other day where there is a lady out here near Inglewood inviting people to come and see her old fashioned garden. She said they wouldn't see any of the new style flowers, nothing but hollyhocks, bachelor buttons, old maid roses, and sech like. I don't 'spect ya'll ever saw any of them kind, did 'ja?

My mother wasn't much on dreams, and things like that, but my grandma, sho' did believe in them. I never paid much 'tention to dreams myself, 'cause I was so busy working you know. Grandma say don't never tell yo' dream before breakfast, if you do, it won't come true. I don't member much of none of de dreams that grandma used to talk about, 'cause I was so young, you know.

We used to sing some real nice cute songs when I was a child—none of your jazz and jumpy tunes, nice and breezy though. Sometimes ma and me would be washing, and we would sing this together:

> Sister Mary in that day
> She took wings and fly away
> For to hear the trumpet sound
> In that morning, my Lord
> In that morning, in that morning
> Oh, how I long to go there
> In that morning.

When I is by myself at night, and feel lonely, I hums that to myself. Then, when I was little, and I would git up and be gitting ready for school in the morning, I used to sing this: Let's see, how did it go? (hums), then

> I'll away to the Sunday School
> I'll away to the Sunday School
> My mother calls me and I must go
> to meet her in the promised land
>
> I'll meet my father in the promised land
> My father calls me and I must go,
> To meet him in the promised land.

That was one of our Sunday school songs, and another one that went like this:

> I hope to meet you in the promised land
> My father calls me and I must go
> To meet you in the promised land.

You see, it's got the same tune, but the words is different. There would be about a hundred children singing that in Sunday school of mornings. We was all dressed up, least we thought we was. We had on cotton dresses, nice and clean and ironed, and was just as happy as could be. The teacher would pray, then start off one of the songs, and I would always help her to start the other children to singing 'cause I knew the songs, you know. Ma and me had done sung them all week. We used to sing "On Jordan's Stormy Banks I Stand"—you probably knows that one, don't you?

We lived right on the public square, I believe I told you, didn't I? And we, ma and me would be singing sometime while we was washing, and all the white folks what was working in the offices and things, would stop their work and come to the windows listening. It sounded good, too. That's one thing the colored folks is blessed. They certainly got the harp in their mouths. We used to have Sunday evening school. The Methodists had their meetings and things in the evening, and the Baptist had theirs in the day. And they would be uplifting in spirituals and preaching. Nowadays, they don't do nothin' in the church but jazz up all the songs; they is all right I guess, but they don't do nothin' but jazz—even the preacher got to prance all over the platform.

No, I ain't never had but one real vision, and it come to me one day. You know I always was religious inclined from a child. I was going down the main street in Zenia, Ohio one day, and something came over me—something like a light and it jest seemed to lift me up and then it got down at my feet, and it just seem to stay there, and I felt so different, and that light kept worrying me. I never heard a word said, it was just that light. Well, I told my mother, but she just turned me off kinda unconcerned; but that light jest kept on worrying me and then I told my grandma, and she say that the spirit of the Lord was touching me. Lord, I was so happy; I kept on talking 'bout that light. Ain't never seen it since. It has done been 'splained to me since. You know the Lord said, "Seek me and ye shall find me" and that's what I did. He said, "I am the light and you walk in that light," and he sho' meant for me to do it, too. That light went with me for years, 'cause the Lord say "After ye have found me, walk in my light." Sometimes the light get so bright in me, that I jest have to let it out, and let the whole world know 'bout it.

I am Baptist. If the spirit strike me I sho' will let you know it. No sirree, I ain't a-tall 'shamed. You know, I went to Bethlehem Center some time ago, and there was a white lady there, and they had testimonials; Miss Lettie Jackson carried me. And they ask somebody to sing an old fashioned hymn. They kept asking, and nobody didn't do nothin', then Miss Lettie asked me, and I thought awhile, and then I started singing:

> I'm going down to the river of Jurdan
> I'm going down to the river of Jurdan, etc.

I jest kept singing. Well, child, them white people nearly had a fit.

The Baptists have their testimonial meetings the first Sunday in every month. They all git together, all them old deacons, and they talks of their religious experience, and then they gits to really feeling good. The head deacon will git up and say something, and then they all fall in line. They all git to shouting and talkin' so, and they git so hot that they almost fergit to have communion. (Pilgrim Emanual, Peabody, Thursday night 7:30)

I went to St. Paul's Church down here the other night, and they had a testimonial meeting, and there was a woman preacher up there. There was some girls there from Pearl High that I know, the Compt girls, and you know that woman got so good, that I got good and happy, and them girls come home and tell their ma, "Sister Hall just took our church there last night." I told 'em they better quit talkin' 'bout me, be good if the gospel strike them, he, he.

That woman got up there, and she say, "Ain't they no witness for the Lord? " I said, "Yes, been a witness for forty long years." And then everybody praised God, and the woman said, "Thank God for a witness." Then she started singing: "When the Saints go Marching In", "Good Lord, I want to be in that Number," etc. You know the Baptists is terrible on the spirit. The voice of the Lord jest draw them.